Dancer's Resource

Dancer's Resource

The Watson-Guptill Guide to

- Academic Programs
- Internships and Apprentice Programs
- Residential and Artist-in-Residence Programs
- Studio Schools and Private Teachers
- Workshops and Festivals

Mark W. Jones

Getting Your Act Together™

Produced for Watson-Guptill Publications by
David Emblidge—Book Producer

Watson-Guptill Publications
New York

Getting Your Act Together™

Series Concept: David Emblidge

Series Editor: David Emblidge

Assistant Editor: Marcy Ross

Researcher: Jane Penn

Editorial Assistant: Robin Williams

Copy Editor: Rodalinde Albrecht

Database design: Chris Blair, David Emblidge

Book design & icons: Bill Cooke

Page makeup: Rose Tannenbaum

Illustrations: Roy Germon

Photographs: See credits with each image.

Indexer: Letitia Mutter

The text of this book was created in Microsoft Word and FilemakerPro for Windows, and pages were subsequently designed in QuarkXpress. Program descriptions were imported from the database using the X-Data extension. Display typefaces used include Frutiger and Officina Sans. Veljovic is used for the main text.

The Library of Congress Cataloging-in-Publication Data for this title is on file with the Library of Congress.

Contents

7 **Foreword**

9 **Introduction**
- How to Use This Book
- Definitions
- Acknowledgments

PART ONE

**Living to Dance,
Dancing to Live**

16 **On Becoming
a Dancer**
- A Career in Dance
- Modern Dance
- Ballet
- Musical Theater/Jazz
and Tap
- Ethnic Dance
- Other Traditions
- Choreography
- The Decision to Become a
Professional
- The Decision to Remain
an Amateur
- Getting Your Act Together

PART TWO

**Dance Programs in the U.S.
Today**

24 **Signing Up: Organizations
for Dancers**
- Membership Organizations
- Unions & Other Labor
Organizations

33 **Selecting a Program**
- Special Advice on
Summer Programs
- Special Advice on
Dance Schools
- Special Advice on
Academic Programs

37 **Dance Programs**
- State by State: Academic
Programs, Internships and
Apprentice Programs,
Residential and Artist-in-
Residence Programs,
Studio Schools and Private
Teachers, Workshops and
Festivals

PART THREE

The Business of Dance

180 **Finances**
- Financial Aid—The Inside
Scoop
- Getting Your Career
Started
- Special Advice for
Choreographers
- The Price Tag on Your
Work
- Running Your Business as
a Freelance Artist
- Taxes
- Investing for Your Future

PART FOUR

**Bibliography & Resources
Index**

189 **Bibliography & Resources**

193 **Index**

208 **About the Author**

208 **About Getting Your Act
Together**™

Foreword

DANCE HAS ALWAYS been thought of as a primary form of communication, yet we live in an era in which communication and the movement of ideas increasingly take place in the disembodied land of cyberspace.

So much has changed for dancers since my days as a dancer. There has been exponential growth in the opportunities to study dance, as well as a kaleidoscopic explosion of the kinds of dance that are offered, as the definition of dance continues to generously expand. And it is only recently that kinesthetic acuity has been recognized as a bona fide form of intelligence.

And much remains the same.

On the brink of a new century, dance is as it has always been—a primary and necessary form of communication. When we dance, our spirit and our thoughts find expression through our bodies on this earth. Perhaps that is why so many people are dancing, on and off the stage.

Most dancers I know will tell you they *have* to dance: It's not a choice, they are compelled. My need to dance has taken me on a remarkable journey from dancer, to choreographer, to producer and arts executive.

Dancing is as delicious as it is demanding, and dance training is remarkable preparation for any journey. To dance is to understand the big picture, as well as the details—for the discipline of dance teaches patience and attention to detail, only to have the steps transform themselves into dance that is transcendent.

This book serves as a very intelligent guide to the study of dance as an inescapable career path while offering insight, encouragement, and valuable information for anyone interested in dancing.

Liz Thompson
Executive Director,
Lower Manhattan Cultural Council
and former Director, Jacob's Pillow Dance Festival

Introduction

For nearly 30 years, I have been involved in dance. Over these 3 decades, I have known hundreds of dancers—modern dancers, ballet dancers, tap dancers, jazz dancers, performance artists, ballroom dancers and break dancers. In addition, there were the New Vaudevillians, mimes and performance artists with whom I have been privileged to work. While their styles varied radically, most had a common passion—a need to move.

This book, while intended primarily for those who dance, can be useful to anyone who loves dance. It is intended for readers across a wide range of ages, experience levels and stylistic interests. If you are a young dancer on a professional track, it will get you thinking about the substantial array of college and university programs available. If you are a professional dancer thinking about a career transition, it will give you some ideas about related areas of employment. If you love dance and are thinking about adult classes or have children whom you would like to introduce to dance, you may search about here for open classes for yourself and your kids.

Dancer's Resource looks at traditional and alternative paths to train and work in the dance field. The "gazetteer" section of the book, a state-by-state sampling of dance programs in the U.S., is not an exhaustive directory. Instead, it is a user-friendly orientation to varied opportunities available in academic settings, studio schools, workshops and festivals. We have included all the best programs that our research uncovered.

Before you settle down to the serious work of choosing a university for your undergraduate or graduate degrees in dance, take some time to browse through these pages. Imagine yourself in programs in different states. Dream about various paths, journeys you might take and great teachers with whom you might study.

How to Use This Book

Although I have written this book with performing artists in mind, I am aware of the allure of dance for those who might never become a performer or support themselves solely through their dancing. Part One, "Living to Dance, Dancing to Live," looks at what happens when your love of dance leads you to consider turning dance into a career. People dance for lots of different reasons, many of which have nothing to do with making a living. Yet, the art form exists within a complex marketplace that makes it possible for dancers' performing skills and choreography to have commercial value. This section respects your decision should you choose not to pursue a career as a dancer, but also gives you some handy advice should you be drawn ineluctably toward a dance-related career.

Part Two, "Dance Programs in the U. S. Today," is the fruit of Research Assistant Jane Penn's and my investigation into different kinds of places to study the art, the technical aspects and the business of dance. Programs profiled in this gazetteer represent only a portion of all the programs we researched. Our goal was to provide information on representative faculty, a snapshot of the curriculum and the subjective "feel" of the place. We have included some colorful, off-the-beaten-path possibilities. In sum, we selected programs because of their general excellence or their uniqueness, and we came up with some interesting alternatives to what one usually considers dance education.

The gazetteer uses icons to help you identify at a glance those that are *Academic Programs, Internships and Apprentice Programs, Residential and Artist-in-Residence Programs, Studio Schools and Private Teachers, Workshops and Festivals.*

Definitions

Academic Programs

Many, many schools today offer courses in dance, and you might even find beginning classes at your local community college. In order to rein in the huge universe of Academic Programs available nationwide, we kept our focus on those that offer graduate degrees. The terminal degree in dance is usually an MFA or MA. While some doctoral programs are offered and are listed here, professional performance experience, not a PhD., is inestimably valuable if you are seeking an academic position teaching dance as performance. Those interested in dance history or movement theory might want to pursue the PhD.

Internships and Apprentice Programs

These programs are important to the preprofessional and often provide the first performing experience with either a professional company or a student ensemble presenting community outreach and school programs.

Residential and Artist-in-Residence Programs

A Residential Program, which includes high schools that emphasize study of the arts, is typically devoted to housing artists for periods of days, weeks or even months. Also included under this heading are Artist-in-Residence Programs in which artists are invited to live and work at an institution where they are given access to its studios, staff and other resources in order to develop new work.

Studio Schools and Private Teachers

Many of these schools are affiliated with a professional dance company.

Some are headed by a noted former performing professional running the studio as proprietor. But generally these schools do not grant academic credit.

Workshops and Festivals

Two kinds of workshops are common. The first is an intensive program of study offered by a studio school as a supplement to its regular program. The second is a seasonal workshop or training program offered by a dance festival or arts center. Dance Festivals, or arts festivals that feature dance as an essential ingredient, provide not only instruction, but also valuable opportunities to work alongside or to encounter important professionals in the dance field in a casual, often idyllic, environment.

How the Information Is Displayed

As you read through the program profiles, think "Upstairs" and "Downstairs." Upstairs is the information block that looks like this:

Downstairs you will find our write-up of the program.

In the Upstairs section, most items are self-explanatory, but a few categories bear explanation.

Icons

 = Academic Programs

 = Internships and Apprentice Programs

 = Residential/Artist-in-Residence Programs

 = Studio Schools and Private Teachers

 = Workshops and Festivals

Arizona State University

 For ballet, jazz, modern dancers, choreographers S of Phoenix — Dept. of Dance, Main Campus, P.O. Box 870304, Tempe, AZ 85287 **Voice:** 480-965-6807 **Fax:** 480-965-2247 **Web Site:** www.asu.edu/cfa/dance **Contact:** Rose Welsh, Acad. Advisor **Founded:** 1885 **Open:** Year-round **Admission:** Audition (only for modern, ballet technique courses) **Deadlines:** Rolling **Cost:** $1,094 per semester for state residents, $4,670 per semester for nonresidents, plus $5,000 for housing **Financial Aid:** Loans; Scholarship; Work/Study **Size-Class:** 10-60 **Degree or Certification:** BFAs in Dance Studies, Performance and Choreography, Dance Education, MFA **Job Placement:** Yes

Contact Person: The one to ask for if you want well-informed, up-to-date information. The bigger the program, the harder it will be for would-be applicants to get through to the director, but go ahead and ask. Many programs have coordinators, secretaries or administrative assistants who are helpful and informative.

Address: The on-site mailing address where, usually, the program takes place. If you are contacting an organization by mail, remember to put the program name first so your inquiry will land on the right desk.

E-mail Address and **Web Site:** Until on-line usage has stabilized a bit more, expect a high rate of turnover with these two pieces of contact information. Some of the programs we contacted had Web sites under construction, multiple e-mail addresses and daily fluctuations in their on-line accessibility. If no Web site address is listed or the one provided is no longer in service, try searching for it, using the program's name as your keyword. That said, when a Web site is up and running, it's a remarkably efficient way to get current information, as well as a sense of the program's character and temperament, before deciding whether it's worth your while to make further inquiries.

Open: Most program dates shift a bit annually, so be prepared for minor variances here.

Admission: Almost all programs have an application form to complete, but after that, requirements vary widely. The rule of thumb is that programs requiring extensive sample work, a statement of purpose, a resume and references are more selective and more rigorous. The converse is generally true, too.

Deadlines: Some programs are sticklers for deadlines; others are open until the room fills. Financial-aid applicants often must apply earlier than others. When a program specifies an application or financial-aid deadline, respect it: get in the habit now of acting professionally.

Cost: Different programs reflect their costs in different ways. We have tried to harness the disparate information into a summary that will enable you to draw rough comparisons among the programs. The costs are based on information that was available during our year of research in 1998, and usually reflects 1998 fee schedules. Since the cost of any program generally increases over time, you will want to check for current figures.

Financial Aid: Because definitions and eligibility requirements for loans, scholarships and other financial aid vary widely, we simply pass on the financial-aid information as it was provided to us. Be sure to request a financial-aid application at the outset if you're in need, and as noted above, watch out for early deadlines for requesting financial aid.

Size—Attendees and **Size—Class:** Some programs told us their total number of attendees and others responded with a typical enrollment for a single class or workshop. Either or both can be meaningful, so we have reported these figures as received.

How the Information Was Gathered
My research assistant and I would love to have visited every program in person. However, that would have added easily a year to our research. Over the course of a long career in dance, I have, in fact, visited many

of the schools and dance companies listed here, and I have seen scores of dance companies in performance. We called program directors and talked with them about the history and direction of their programs; studied brochures, catalogues and application forms; visited Web sites; and spoke to participants in various programs. We were not skeptical in our questioning, but asked for—and accepted at face value—each program's story as given to us. We weighed the general and "niche" value of each program and then, through interviews and a review of supplementary materials, dug more deeply into those that caught and held our interest. The upshot is that this book makes a serious effort to be objective and accurate about facts and information while also in-dulging itself, and you, in personalized descriptions of the programs. Some programs in each of our categories are better than others, and no one "size" fits all. The worlds of professional dance and dance training are always in flux, so contact the programs that interest you to obtain the most current information.

How You Can Help with the Next Edition

Readers are invited to respond. Please correct our mistakes, offer your perspectives and tell us what else you would like to see in the next edition. Also, let us know where you bought or borrowed this book. Write to: Editors, Getting Your Act Together™, c/o Watson-Guptill Publications, 1515 Broadway, New York, NY 10036.

Acknowledgments

INFORMATION AND HELP ON this project came from all quarters, and I am indebted to the many program directors and administrative assistants who sent us information and answered our questions. I would like to thank Barbara Weisberger, the inspired and inspiring founding artistic director of the Pennsylvania Ballet, for giving me my first job in dance, and my friend and former college professor Richard E. LeBlond, Jr,. for urging me to get into the then-unknown field of arts administration. Jane Penn deserves a gigantic amount of credit for her untiring work as research assistant. I also thank Emma Beyn, who worked diligently to gather materials and information, and Marcy Ross for her work in photo research and handling editorial revisions. Finally, I want to thank Leslie Hansen Kopp of Preserve, Inc., for her assistance in developing the "Only Connect" section; Keith F. Spencer, for his support and encourage-ment, and all the wonderful, generous dancers who have inspired and informed my life's work.

PART ONE

Living to Dance, Dancing to Live

On Becoming a Dancer

'M SURE EVERYONE WHO has been drawn to dance as a career remembers a transforming moment when they just "knew" dance was for them. For me it was seeing a performance of George Balanchine's *Serenade* when I was 22 years old. Too old and too klutzy to consider dancing, I had to be content with helping to create those magical moments on stage by being an arts administrator. For some of the dancers I know, the moment came when they studied dance with a gifted teacher. In any case, the dance changed us, irrevocably.

In the 1970s and early 1980s America experienced a dance "boom." The number of dance performances skyrocketed and attendance set new records. Most colleges had a dance series and more people began to study dance. Even the President's son (Ron Reagan) was a dancer! In the academic world dance began to be separated from physical-education departments, where it had been tucked away for years, and was integrated into the liberal-arts curriculum. However, the dance boom soon went bust. By the early 1990s, subsidies from the National Endowment for the Arts in support of touring, individual artists and dance companies had withered; colleges were going through a demographically induced belt tightening; and dance was increasingly eclipsed by opera and jazz as the "hot" art forms.

As we approach the new millennium, interest in dance seems to be on the rise. Perhaps a heightened awareness about our bodies or the fitness craze has fed this, or maybe it is just the compelling nature of dance itself.

But what is dance? In *The Language of Dance*, the great German expressionist Mary Wigman said, "The dance is a form of expression given to man just as speech, philosophy, painting or music. Like music, the dance is a language which all human beings understand without use of speech." While I certainly agree with Wigman, I think it goes even deeper. I think the compelling thing about dance, especially contemporary dance, is its ability to communicate emotional experiences. The influential dance critic John Martin termed this "metakinesis," in his book *Introduction to the Dance*. He defined metakinesis as the transference of an aesthetic and emotional concept from the consciousness of one individual to that of another. Martin's view was that the movements of a dancer's muscles are transferred by kinesthetic sympathy to the muscles of the spectator. This theory is open to the objections that not all dance is, in fact, an expression of emotion and that even when dances are expressions of emotion they do not communicate these emotions by directly arousing them in the spectator. Dance might instead communicate something more abstract or rational—think of the choreography in many of the works of George Balanchine and Merce Cunningham. These are nearly devoid of emotion.

While all this is a means of explaining what dance is, I prefer the broader definition that dance is a rhythmic, patterned movement in time and space and that it is art as imitation, expression or form. This seems to cover all the bases without getting into difficult and often flawed aesthetic theories. In defining what dance is, I must also mention the views of Connecticut College's Susanne K. Langer, who is closely associated with the development of modern dance. As Langer expressed in her book *Feeling and Form*, the physical materials of rhythmic motions or patterns in space are transformed by the choreographer into an illusion. In her view dance creates the illusion of "interacting forces" or dynamic "powers" that seem "to move the dance itself." In *The Classic Ballet*, Lincoln Kirstein said that ballet was "aerial" and modern dance, "terrestrial."

Regardless of what theory one ascribes to dance, there is no question that performing is a potent means of self-expression. Even if you don't pursue choreography, as a performer you have the means to move an audience to tears, laughter or joy through the power of your performance skills. Dance is also a very glamorous profession. Dancers, and only dancers, can bring a palpable exaltation to an audience just as powerful as a performance by a great musician or the best actors. In my view, dance is one of the great gifts of our cultural life.

A Career in Dance

In his book *How to Dance Forever,* Daniel Nagrin contends, "To choose to be a dancer is a lonely act of defiance." He goes on to explain that many people view a dance career as absurd or impractical because of the early age at which most dancers retire. While this is true in some cases, it is by no means a hard-and-fast rule.

Alicia Alonso, Margot Fonteyn, Martha Graham, Erick Hawkins, Merce Cunningham and many other performers danced in their 60s, 70s and even 80s. While you might not find Maya Pliesetskaya's *Dying Swan* the most compelling performance you have ever seen, the fact of the matter is that she is still performing at 70-something.

The myth of early retirement also ignores the fact that most dancers make a career transition at some point. They become college professors, independent teachers, arts administrators, dance therapists, artistic directors, or even lawyers, accountants and videographers.

What follows is a partial list of avenues or areas of specialization that you might choose to pursue. Today's dancers are generally trained in a variety of techniques. It is also harder these days to pigeonhole styles or techniques. For example, many ballet companies have modern-dance works in the repertoire. Conversely, contemporary choreographers are reaching to classical dance for materials and new work. The acclaimed choreographer Twyla Tharp has moved more and more toward ballet, while at the same time drawing on popular culture for music and themes. That being said, here are some comments on different styles and genres that can give your career a sense of direction or focus.

Modern Dance

There used to be a myth among some people in the dance world, especially among those who have not studied a lot of dance, that modern dance was a "natural" way of moving and that anyone could do it. While there is some truth in the natural part, this should not be taken to mean that little or no technique is required. As any dance major at a college knows, modern dance requires just as much training and discipline as ballet.

It is true that early proponents of modern dance, Isadora Duncan in particular, felt that they had rediscovered the natural way to dance. Duncan waxed poetic about this in *The Art of the Dance*: "If we seek the real source of the dance, if we go to nature, we find that the dance of the future is the dance of the past, the dance of eternity... the movement of waves, of winds, of the earth...." Duncan, as you can imagine, had nothing good to say about ballet. She attacked ballet for vainly striving against the natural laws of gravitation, producing sterile movement, which does not give birth to future movement and dies as it is made. Obviously, modern dance has its passionate proponents.

Modern dance is one of the most vibrant fields in the performing arts in the United States. There are many companies and opportunities in the commercial arena and many fine training programs in the academic world. We suggest that you try to focus on one or more choreographers whose work you find appealing as you choose a place to study. If you are a ballet dancer and modern dance also appeals to you, it is possible to change or broaden your focus. Just remember to release your torso, and you'll be on your way.

Ballet

Lincoln Kirstein, the great chronicler of contemporary ballet, maintained that it was all in the feet. That is to say, he believed the root of ballet training was in the five academic foot positions. Fortunately, since the time of Isadora Duncan, modern-dance people have lost some of their antagonism toward ballet, and stylistic lines have blurred and fused, making for interesting new work, challenging to dancers and audiences alike.

When one speaks of ballet today, one generally refers to the classical vocabulary of movement developed in Western Europe based on the five positions of the feet, which are the basis for teaching the Vaganova method and all other major ballet techniques. This movement vocabulary embraces the performance of works ranging from the classical ballets of Petipa, such as *Swan Lake* and *The Sleeping Beauty,* to the romantic ballets, such as *La Sylphide* and *Giselle.*

The terms "classical" and "romantic" are often at opposite ends of the spectrum. However, in reality, the same technique and training are required for the performances of classical and romantic ballets so often different in mood. Moreover, classical technique and training are needed for the performance of the great ballets by Balanchine and other contemporary choreographers.

One last important point on the ballet field should be made. There used to be a lot of talk in the ballet world of an American ballet style based on "athleticism" as opposed, for example, to the British "reserve" or Russian "flamboyance." This is hogwash. The real difference in style, observed by *New York Times* dance critic Anna Kisselgoff, is determined by one who shapes the artistic identity of a particular company or school. The New York City Ballet dances the way it does, not because it is an American company, but because George Balanchine trained it for so many years.

As you seek training or look toward joining a ballet company, consider the repertoire that you are most drawn to and plan accordingly. We give some guidance in this area in the gazetteer, but as you make connections and seek information, you should ask questions of teachers and administrators. The good news is that the best academic programs, such as the one at Juilliard, prepare the well-rounded dancer, ballet or modern. Such programs will increase, not limit, your options.

Musical Theater/Jazz and Tap

Yes, you can make a good living performing in shows. If you have good dance technique, reasonably good looks and a decent voice, you can probably make more money than modern or ballet dancers.

In the 1940s and 1950s Jerome Robbins revolutionized American musical theater by seamlessly integrating dance into the book and musical score. This effort reached its pinnacle in *West Side Story*. Following in his footsteps were Bob Fosse, Michael Bennett and other masters who rejuvenated the American musical theater. To me there is nothing more entertaining and thrilling than a great work of musical theater.

Good dancing is a requirement of any musical, whether it is produced in New York or in one of the fine regional theaters in the United States. Recently, standards in this genre have risen for two reasons: dance training is generally better, and choreographers and directors are more skilled and demanding. The result is more work and better work, in which choreography plays a central role.

Currently, many successful dance-driven shows are on Broadway, and this trend will probably continue well into the future. The life of a Broadway gypsy or regional-theater gypsy can be very exciting and pays well. While there is no set rule, you will probably earn two or three times what a dancer in a not-for-profit modern or ballet company makes.

Ethnic Dance

While there aren't as many ethnic-dance companies as there are modern and ballet companies, you can find employment here, particularly if you are seeking part-time work. As I write this book, the hottest dance form is Irish step dancing, as realized by Riverdance and a number of other companies. This is BIG business!

Be mindful of names. For example, Ballet Hispanico, a professional company in New York City, is neither a ballet company nor a Spanish dance company, as one might suspect. It is really a modern-dance company with a Hispanic flavor. The United States has a respectable number of Hispanic dance companies based on flamenco or folkloric traditions, companies based on African or Asian traditions and even groups based on Native American dance traditions.

Other Traditions

Baroque Dance, Folk Dance and Children's Dance Theater are but three of the other areas in which you might want to specialize. A number of professional companies working in these areas offer satisfactory, professional-level compensation and other rewards for those interested in working with children, for example.

Choreography

Many dancers decide to choreograph at some point. After dancing for a number of years as a professional, you begin to understand the art form and can then work with choreographers. This, in turn, leads naturally to the possibility of creating your own dances, for either yourself or an ensemble. Many companies offer their artists opportunities to choreograph. To be sure, choreography is not for everyone, but it can lead to an entirely new dance career if it is your passion. For someone who is truly gifted in this area, opportunities are abundant in both the not-for-profit and the commercial realms.

The Decision to Become a Professional

At some point in your study of dance, you must ask the question: Do I have a passion to perform? You must have a burning desire to perform or you'll never make it: dancing professionally requires a lot of discipline, hard work and usually considerable economic sacrifice.

In choosing to become a professional dancer, you elevate your commitment to the medium. It is no longer an infatuation, but more like a marriage, complete with responsibilities and sacrifices. It begins to shape the way your life unfolds. In exchange for a heightened commitment, you expect to reap rewards in terms of financial gain and personal satisfaction. However, in dancing, as in many professions and all marriages, the good stuff does not always come easily.

Dancing is competitive. For many of the same reasons you might want to make a career as a dancer, plenty of other people do, too. In addition, while the interest in dance and the number of dance companies might be increasing, there will always be more people who want to make a living at dancing than there will be organizations to support them. In time, the less talented, less passionate and/or less highly motivated dancers will eventually drop away and take up other work. The desire of every new professional is to be one of those who can weather the competition and build a successful career.

The demands on a professional dancer are quite different than those on even the most gifted amateur. Professionals must produce top-quality work on every assignment, no matter how they feel or what logistical limitations they face. It does not matter if a company's artistic director or choreographer breathes fire, or if the stage is too hard or if the choreography is difficult to remember. Professional dancers produce professional work, no matter what the circumstances. A noted choreographer's reputation is based not on a few fabulous pieces, but on a consistent string of excellent compositions. The same holds true for a professional dancer.

Dancing is one of those fields that calls so strongly to some people that they never actually work through the process of making the decision to become a professional. They know right from the beginning that they are and always will be dancers. They have a love affair with movement that leaves them no other choice. Establishing a career, then, is a manifestation of the inevitable.

For most of us, though, the decision to become a professional needs to be carefully considered.

Do not become a dancer by accident or default. Do not take up professional dancing just because you find dancing enjoyable and cannot think of anything else to do. It is too challenging a career and requires too much sacrifice. If the well-documented, minimal income of most freelance dancers isn't enough to scare you off, then the cattle calls of auditions might be. Before Desmond Richardson hit the big time as a dancer with both Alvin Ailey and the American Ballet Theatre, as wel as on Broadway, he worked tirelessly for years, building his technique and career. You simply have to want it with everything you've got, and then you have to build your career in dance as carefully, and strategically, as you would in any other field. The decisions you make deliberately and carefully, rather than just fall into, will ultimately yield greater satisfaction.

The Decision to Remain an Amateur

The root of the word "amateur" is "lover." The amateur gets to do what he or she loves, without having to answer to anyone else. Many individuals who are most passionate about dance prefer to remain amateurs all their lives, rather than sacrifice their deep personal relationship with the art form to the exigencies of earning a living. Many of us know the example of the composer Charles Ives, a successful insurance executive, who composed primarily for his own pleasure and personal needs. Ives achieved serious recognition only long after he was gone

Many talented people have a career in another field, an occupation elsewhere, and spend their evenings, weekends and vacations pursing their interest in dance. Amateur dancers can be as skilled as professionals. They remain amateurs to preserve the harmonious relationship they have with their own work and their family. Anyone who loves dancing and dance should think carefully about what will be lost by becoming a professional, as well as what will be gained. It would be a shame to have one's love affair with dance ground down by the need to earn some cash.

Getting Your Act Together

Whether dancing is a career or an avocation for you, your desire to use this book shows that you take it seriously. You recognize the need to hone your skills and to learn new ways of developing your work. You see how shifting market forces and the newly important game of networking have changed the way in which one pursues an artist's career. In picking up this book, you seek to expand your knowledge about dance, to acquire specific skills or to advance your vision.

This book has been created to help you. It catalogs hundreds of different ways in which to advance your life in dance, whether you choose to make dance your profession or to pursue it as an amateur. You will find descriptions of programs and training facilities for all types of dance, plus organizations of and for dance and dancers, festivals and specialized schools and academic institutions that have strong dance programs.

All dancers thrive on the satisfaction of delivering a spectacular, flawless performance that moves an audience to enthusiastic applause. It is our wish that the information offered here will help you to become the dancer you want to be.

PART TWO

Dance Programs in the U.S. Today

Signing Up: Organizations for Dancers

IMMEDIATELY BELOW, YOU WILL find a listing of national and regional associations, organizations and unions that you might want to join or contact for information. In a number of cases, regional organizations are listed because they provide unique programs or resources. Many additional state, regional and local organizations are not listed here because of space limitations. We suggest that you contact your state arts council for additional sources. In the gazetteer of program descriptions that follows, you will see certain programs that are sponsored by, or produced in association with, some of the organizations listed here. If noteworthy, we give some information about the association in this section.

Dance is seldom a solitary act. Even if you are a solo artist, you will not want to work in a vacuum. By associating with colleagues you can exchange information and ideas, make important contacts and benefit from the resources.

There is much to be said for joining appropriate professional or amateur dancers' organizations. We all learn from one another, both on the artistic side and the business side of dance. Especially for people who live in far-flung places, away from the hub of dance and other artistic activity in major cities like New York, Boston, Chicago and San Francisco, an organization's newsletter and annual meeting might be the best and only place to hear what peers and colleagues are doing about the same opportunities and problems you might be facing. The better organizations emphasize service: insurance plans, job networking, how-to skills, workshops, etc. We advise spending your membership dollars only for these real benefits.

We often see resumes listing memberships in shell organizations that provide no real services or benefits and offer no warmth, camaraderie or collegial networking to their members. Dancers are no more immune than other workers to the American penchant for "joining up," what Garrison Keillor pokes fun at when he says his *Prairie Home Companion* radio show is brought to you by the "American Federation of Associations."

Unfortunately, no one organization specifically serves all the needs of dancers. In the list that follows, however, you will find a number of excellent organizations to meet your specific needs and interests.

Membership Organizations

Adventures In Movement for the Handicapped
Who: 250 handicapped child and adult dancers, friends and supporters.
What: Service organization offers free movement programs for handicapped individuals, training, workshops, seminars for teachers and students; also provides special classes for friends and family members of handicapped dancers. Founded 1958. **Contact:** AMH, 945 Danbury Rd., Dayton, OH 45420; 937-294-4611; fax: 937-294-3783; email aimkids@aol.com **Membership:** Open to all.

African Heritage Center for African Dance
Who: More than 60 dancers interested in learning African dance and music techniques. **What:** Founded in 1959, organization preserves African dance and music by providing workshops, seminars, classes and events; also offers scholarships and archival information. **Contact:** AHCAD, 4018 Minnesota Ave. NE, Washington, DC 20019; 202-399-5252; fax: 202-399-5252; Web site: www.indiansinc.com **Membership:** Open to all. Annual dues.

American College Dance Festival Association
Who: 250 dance institutions and individuals. **What:** ACDFA sponsors college dance festivals regionally and nationally. Founded 1973. **Contact:** ACDFA, 4431 Lehigh Rd., Box 399, College Park, MD 20740; 301-405-8552; fax: 301-405-8551; email: acdfs@bellatlantic.net; Web site: www.fsu.~svad/dance_pages/acdfa/acdfhm.html **Membership:** Open to all. Annual dues.

American Dance Guild
Who: 300 dance educators and students. **What:** Teaches and provides information for teachers in dance; provides lecture demonstrations and support services. **Contact:** ADG, 31 W. 21st St., 3rd Fl., New York, NY 10010; 212-627-3790; fax: 212-675-9657 **Membership:** Eligibility requirements. Annual dues.

American Dance Legacy Institute
Who: More than 200 dancers, teachers, students, individuals and organizations supporting dance. **What:** Established to provide all Americans with the opportunity to practice, enjoy and participate in the art of dance. Provides workshops, publications, support services, performances, distance learning workshops, residencies, talent searches, funds for student dancers and stipends for mentorships. **Contact:** ADLI, Box 1897, Providence, RI 02912; 401-863-7596; fax: 401-863-7529; email: Dance_Leg@Brown.edu; Web site: www.brown.edu/Departments/Theatre_Speech_Dance/Amer._Dance_Legacy_Inst..html **Membership:** Open to all. Annual dues.

American Dance Therapy Association
Who: 1,300 dance/movement therapists and supporters **What:** ADTA works to establish and maintain high standards of professional education and competence in the field of dance/movement therapy. Established in 1966; provides ADTA newsletter, monographs, bibliographies; holds annual conference and

supports formation of regional groups, seminars and workshops. **Contact:** ADTA, 2000 Century Plaza, Suite 108, 10632 Little Patuxent Pkwy., Columbia, MD 21044; 410-997-4040; fax: 410-997-4048; email: info@adta.org; Web site: www.ADTA.org **Membership:** Open to all. Annual dues. Discounts for students.

American Society of Russian Style Ballet

Who: 150 ballet dancers, companies and individuals. **What:** Lecture demonstrations, seminars, newsletter and consultations on the Russian style. **Contact:** ASRSB, P.O. Box 990003, Boston, MA 02199; 617-437-9401; fax: 617-783-5605; email: ddrummond2@juno.com **Membership:** Open to all. Annual dues.

Career Transitions for Dancers

Who: 1,250 professional dancers. **What:** Provides vocational assessment and career counseling free of charge to professional dancers who seek a second creatively satisfying vocation; offer scholarships to eligible applicants. Founded 1985. **Contact:** CTD, 200 West 57th St., Suite 808, New York, NY 10019; 212-581-7043; fax: 212-581-0474; email: ctfd@aol.com **Membership:** Eligibility requirements.

Chicago Dance Coalition

Who: More than 300 dancers, choreographers, companies and organizations. **What:** Provides monthly newsletter with information on workshops, auditions, performances and employment opportunities in the Chicago area and related articles. **Contact:** CDC, 200 North Michigan Ave., Suite 404, Chicago, IL 60601; 312-419-8384; hotline: 312-412-8383; fax: 312-419-0602; email: cdcstaff@ameritech.net **Membership:** Open to all. Annual dues.

Congress on Research in Dance

Who: Dancers, choreographers, companies and organizations. **What:** Encourages research in all aspects of dance and related fields; fosters exchange of ideas, resources and research methods in dance through publications, conferences, symposia, institutes and other media; publishes biannual research journals; sponsors an annual international conference and regional conferences. **Contact:** CORD, SUNY Brockport, Dept. of Dance, 350 New Campus Dr., Brockport, NY 14420; 716-395-2590; fax 716-395-5413; email: pennycat@asuvm.inre.asu.edu. **Membership:** Open to all. Annual dues.

Dallas Dance Council

Who: More than 300 individual dance supporters in the Dallas metropolitan area. **What:** Founded in 1970, the council promotes and supports dance by presenting performances, seminars, lecture demonstrations, master classes and a quarterly calendar and newsletter. **Contact:** DDC, Sammons Center for the Arts, 3630 Harry Hines Blvd., Dallas, TX 75219; 214-348-4116. **Membership:** Open to all. Annual dues. Discounts for students.

Dance Heritage Coalition
Who: Dancers, librarians, dance organizations and other dance-related individuals and supporters. **What:** National alliance of institutions mobilized in 1984 to protect the legacy of dance and address the need to improve the state of dance documentation and preservation. **Contact:** DHC, P.O. Box 15130, Washington, DC 20003; 202-707-2149; fax: 202-707-0621; email: mfor@loc.gov; Web site: http://marvel.loc.gov:70/00/research/dance/about.dhc **Membership:** Open to all.

Dance Notation Bureau
Who: Approximately 175 dancers, choreographers, students, organizations and other individuals interested in preserving dance. **What:** Records dances using Labanotation (a written language of movement), allowing continued performance. DNB Archive houses scores of almost 600 dances by more than 160 choreographers. Membership provides circulating materials in DNB library. Founded 1940. **Contact:** DNB, 33 W. 21st St., 3rd Fl., New York, NY 10010; 212-807-7899; fax 212-675-9657; email: notation@mindspring.com; Web site: www.dance.ohio-state.edu **Membership:** Open to all. Annual dues. Discounts for students.

Dance Professionals Associates, Ltd.
Who: 150 dance companies, organizations, individuals, associates, juniors and students. **What:** Supports the needs of current and future dance professionals by providing access to affordable and practical information and resources needed for career development and personal security. Members receive access to health insurance, employment opportunities, newsletter, income-tax service and listing in DPA Internet Directory. Founded 1997. **Contact:** DPA, 440 East 81st St., Suite 6G, New York, NY 10028; 212-535-3757; fax: 212-535-3757-x51; email: DanceProfessionals@worldnet.att.net; Web site: www.dancepro.com. **Membership:** Open to all. Annual dues. Discounts for students.

Dance Theatre Workshop
Who: More than 600 independent artists, companies and institutions in New York and across the country. **What:** Not-for-profit, community-based organization that provides artist sponsorship programs and production facilities, as well as a broad spectrum of administrative, promotional and technical services to the New York artistic community. Also manages a national performance network linking presenters and artists across the country. Founded 1965. **Contact:** DTW, 219 W. 19th St., New York, NY 10011; 212-691-6500; fax: 212-633-1974; email: dtw@dtw.org; Web site: www.dtw.org **Membership:** Open to all.

Dance/USA
Who: 300 professional dance companies, individual dancers and choreographers. **What:** National service organization for not-for-profit professional dance. Sponsors conferences and workshops, and publishes quarterly newsletter. Awards grants to individual choreographers in California. Founded 1982.

Contact: Dance/USA, 1156 15th St., NW, Suite 820, Washington, DC 20005; 202-833-1717; fax: 202-833-2686; email: danceusa@artswire.org; Web site: www.danceusa.org **Membership:** Open to all. Annual dues.

Dancers Responding to AIDS

Who: 125 companies, dancers, artists, volunteers and other organizations. **What:** Founded in 1991, this fundraising program of Broadway Cares/Equity Fights AIDS offers financial assistance to individuals with HIV or AIDS. **Contact:** DRA, 165 W. 46th St., Suite 1300, New York, NY 10036; 212-840-0770; fax: 212-840-0551; email: DRADANCE@aol.com; Web site: www.bcefa.org **Membership:** Open to all.

Danspace

Who: Independent dance artists and supporters. **What:** Offers innovative dance artists opportunities for growth and development through the support and presentation of their work. **Contact:** Danspace, 131 East 10th St., New York, NY 10003; 212-674-8112; fax: 212-529-2318; email: danspaceny@aol.com **Membership:** Open to all.

Emergency Fund for Student Dancers

Who: Student dancers. **What:** Provides financial assistance for emergencies to professional students enrolled in full-time programs at one of the seven member schools in New York City: Alvin Ailey American Dance Center, Merce Cunningham Studio, the School of Dance Theatre of Harlem, Martha Graham School of Contemporary Dance, Erick Hawkins School of Dance, Laban/Bartenieff Institute of Movement Studies and the Limón Institute; also provides loans, assistance and information on medical care, movement therapy, nutrition, social services, counseling and temporary housing. **Contact:** Any of the seven member schools. **Membership:** Open to all.

Florida Dance Association

Who: 400 dance companies, organizations, choreographers, individual dancers, students and dance patrons. **What:** Founded in 1972, FDA provides members with Florida Dance Directory, newsletter, technical assistance, seminars and consultations regarding non-profit incorporation, financial management and budgeting. Presents Florida Dance Festival. **Contact:** FDA, 300 NE 2nd Ave., Miami, FL 33132; 305-237-3413; fax: 305-237-7609; email: fldance@flaphil.com **Membership:** Open to all. Annual dues.

Harlem Dance Foundation

Who: 150 dancers, choreographers and dance companies. **What:** Supports dance in Harlem. Provides publications, information, and financial assistance. **Contact:** HDF, 144 W. 121st St., New York, NY 10027; 212-662-2057; fax: 212-662-2762 **Membership:** Open to all.

Laban/Bartenieff Institute for Movement Studies

Who: Dance educators, dancers, dance organizations and supporters. **What:** Dedicated to education and research in the field of movement studies; major center for the development and study of the principles of movement analysis formulated by Rudolf Laban and further developed by his student and colleague Irmgard Bartenieff; offers Certificate Program in Laban Movement Studies, bi-annual conference, publications and other resources. **Contact:** LIMS, 234 Fifth Ave., New York, NY 10001; 212-477-4299; fax: 212-477-3702; email: limsinfo@erols.com **Membership:** Open to all. Annual dues.

Middle Eastern Culture and Dance Association
Who: 100 Middle Eastern dancers and supporters. **What:** Provides close communication within the Middle Eastern dance community. Sponsors events and workshops, and publishes biannual newsletter. **Contact:** MECDA, P.O. Box 946, Rosemead, CA 91770; 626-285-4776; fax: 626-285-1827; Web site: www.mecda.org **Membership:** Open to all. Annual dues.

Minnesota Dance Alliance
Who: 360 choreographers, dancers, dance professionals, companies and members of the artistic community. **What:** Supports and fosters dance arts in Minnesota. Founded in 1979, MDA offers newsletter, discounts to Alliance-sponsored classes, seminars, workshops and performances. Members also have access to studio space and eligibility to apply for grants and fellowships. **Contact:** MDA, 528 Hennepin Ave., Suite 600, Minneapolis, MN 55403; 612-340-1900; Web site: tcfreenet.org/ip/arts/mndalliance **Membership:** Open to all. Annual dues. Discounts for students.

National Association of Schools of Dance
Who: 47 dance schools and studios. **What:** Founded in 1981, national service organization and accrediting institution, provides quarterly newsletter, an annual conference and educational advice to degree-granting and non-degree-granting dance institutions. **Contact:** NASD, 11250 Roger Bacon Dr., No. 21, Reston, VA 22090; 703-437-0700; fax: 703-437-6312; email: kpm-nasd@aol.com; Web site: www.arts-accredit.org **Membership:** Eligibility requirements. Annual dues.

National Dance Association
Who: 25,000 dance educators, administrators, choreographers, companies, dance science and medicine specialists and other dance-related individuals. **What:** Founded in 1932, this is the largest alliance supporting dance education in America. Provides members with materials on dance and dance education, national dance-education standards and guidelines, a national convention, workshops and publications, plus access to group health insurance and to NDA's choreography evaluation project. NDA members receive enrollment in American Alliance for Health, Physical Education, Recreation and Dance (AAPERD). **Contact:** NDA, 1900 Association Dr., Reston, VA 20191; 703-476-3436; fax: 703-476-9527; email: nda@aahperd.org **Membership:** Open to all. Annual dues. Discounts for students.

National Dance Council of America
Who: Competing professional dancers, adjudicators, and professional and amateur dance teachers. **What:** Founded in 1962, national governing organization representing the dance profession. Sponsors dance competitions,

professional certification and quarterly newsletter. **Contact:** NDCA, P.O. Box 22018, Provo, UT 84602; 801-378-8381; email: Lee_Wakefield@ byu.edu; Web site: www.ndca.org **Membership:** Eligibility requirements. Annual dues.

National Museum of Dance

Who: Individuals interested in dance and dance history. **What:** The only museum in the country devoted exclusively to professional American dance. Houses galleries, rotating dance exhibits and Hall of Fame. Also houses the Swyer School for the Performing Arts. Members have access to master classes, lecture demonstrations, studio performances, panels and lectures. Founded 1986. **Contact:** NMD, South Broadway, Saratoga Springs, NY 12866; 518-584-2225; fax 518-584-4515; Web site: www.dancemuseum.org **Membership:** Open to all. Dues.

Pentacle

Who: More than 100 dancers and dance companies. **What:** Handles fiscal and administrative aspects of dance companies, including bookings. Provides dancers with a studio and video resources. An umbrella group for the National Dance Repertory Enrichment Program, the Foundation of Independent Artists, the National Performing Arts Mailing List, Arts in Education and Unique Projects, Inc. Founded 1976. **Contact:** Pentacle, 104 Franklin St., New York, NY 10013; 212-226-2000; fax: 212-925-0369; email: pentacleus@aol.com **Membership:** Open to all.

Philadelphia Dance Alliance

Who: More than 350 dance-related individuals, dancers, choreographers and dance department heads at universities and colleges, companies and students. **What:** Service organization founded in 1971. Provides educational programs, discount tickets, seminars and a monthly newsletter. **Contact:** PDA, 1429 Walnut St., 16th Fl., Philadelphia, PA 10102; 215-564-5270; fax: 215-564-5270; email: dance@libertynet.org; Web site: www.libertynet.org/dance/ **Membership:** Open to all. Annual dues. Discounts for students.

Pittsburgh Dance Council

Who: 1,000 individual and organizational dance supporters. **What:** Organization committed to expanding the visibility, appreciation and presentation of dance in the Pittsburgh area while nurturing the field of dance on local, national and international levels; presents dance companies and individual dancers at local venues; sponsors educational events, lecture demonstrations and outreach programs. Founded 1969. **Contact:** PDC, 719 Liberty Ave., Pittsburgh, PA 15222; 412-355-0330; fax: 412-355-0413; Web site: www.dancecouncil.org **Membership:** Open to all. Annual dues.

Preserve, Inc.

Who: Individual dancers, choreographers, librarians, archivists, national repositories and local networks of the dance and art world. **What:** National center for archival documentation and preservation of the performing arts.

Established in 1987; offers publications, workshops and seminars on organizing and collecting archival materials, conservation techniques, access to Internet services, professional archivists and dance specialists for on-site assistance in evaluation and organization of historical materials, and videotaping and viewing facilities for performance documentation and oral and video histories. **Contact:** Preserve, Inc., P.O. Box 28, Old Chelsea Station, New York, NY 10011-0028; 212-741-7163; fax: 212-741-6452; email: info@preserve-inc.org **Membership:** Open to all.

Professional Dance Teachers Association

Who: 250 professional dance teachers. **What:** Sponsors dance workshops, competitions and events. **Contact:** PDTA, P.O. Box 91, Waldwick, NJ 07463; 201-447-0355; fax: 201-652-2599; email: hoctordance@earthlink.net; Web site: www.dancecaravan.com/98pdta.html **Membership:** Eligibility requirements. Annual dues.

Society of Dance History Scholars

Who: Individuals and institutions committed to the academic discipline of dance studies. **What:** Promotes study, research, discussion, performance and publication in dance history and related fields. Members receive twice-yearly newsletter, members directory, voting rights and a copy of Studies in Dance history. Founded 1978. **Contact:** SDHS, Dance Program, University of Minnesota, 106 Norris Hall, 172 Pillsbury Dr., SE, Minneapolis, MN 55455; 206-523-6553; Web site: www.public.asu.edu **Membership:** Open to all. Annual dues.

Texas Clogging Council

Who: Cloggers and clog supporters. **What:** Created in 1982 to provide avid cloggers with a channel of communication. Sponsors annual Texas Clogging Rally, workshops and competitions; also provides members with two quarterly newsletters, access to educational library and various publications. **Contact:** TCC, 8222 Bent Tree #256, Austin, TX 78759; email: TCC@Texas-Clogging.com; Web site: www.texas-clogging.com. **Membership:** Open to all. Annual dues.

United States Amateur Ballroom Dancers Association

Who: Competitive, college and social amateur ballroom dancers. **What:** Organizes local, regional and national competitions and charitable events. USABDA hosts the annual Dancesport Festival and provides members with newsletter, contact lists and invitations to local and national events. Founded 1965. **Contact:** USABDA, 1472 Buckridge Circle, Southampton, PA 18966; 800-447-9047; fax: 717-235-4183; email: usabdacent@aol.com; Web site: www.asabda.org. **Membership:** Open to all. Annual dues.

Unions & Other Labor Organizations

Actor's Equity Association
Who: Actors, singers and dancers in live theater. **What:** Protects the employment rights of its members and enforces equity (labor) rules in live theater. Provides access to health care, pension plan, newsletter, hotline, national and local publications and bulletins. **Contact:** AEA, 165 West 46th St., New York, NY 10016; 212-869-8530; hotline: 213-462-0955; fax: 212-719-9815. **Membership:** Eligibility requirements. Annual dues.

American Federation of Television and Radio Artists
Who: 80,000 artists, broadcasters, actors, dancers, announcers, singers and other talent. **What:** National labor union affiliated with the AFL-CIO; provides members with contracts, health and retirement benefits, scholarships and other services. Publishes quarterly AFTRA magazine. Founded 1937. **Contact:** AFTRA, 260 Madison Ave., 7th Fl., New York, NY 10016; 212-532-0800; email: aftra@aftra.com; Web site: www.aftra.com **Membership:** Open to anyone who performs or intends to perform in AFTRA's jurisdiction.

American Federation of Musicians
Who: International umbrella organization in the U.S. and Canada with more than 115,000 individual musician members. **What:** World's largest performing artists' union; founded in 1896. Directs musicians to their local unions; serves members with publications such as the *International Musician* newspaper; and provides emergency union protection to traveling musicians. **Contact:** AFM, 1501 Broadway, Suite 600, New York, NY 10036; 800-762-3444; fax: 212-764-6134; email: info@afm.org; Web site: www.afm.org **Membership:** Available through local affiliates. Annual dues.

American Guild of Musical Artists
Who: More than 150,000 musicians, singers and dancers. **What:** Founded in 1936, this national organization provides its members with sample contracts, access to health insurance and credit unions and newsletter. **Contact:** AGMA, 1727 Broadway, New York, NY 10019; 212-265-3687; fax: 212-262-9088 **Membership:** Eligibility requirements. Annual dues.

American Guild of Variety Artists
Who: Actors, dancers, singers and announcers performing in live variety-entertainment atmosphere. **What:** Provides members with sample contracts, newsletter, national and regional publications, access to health insurance, pension plans and membership directory. **Contact:** AGVA, 184 Fifth Ave., 6th Fl., New York, NY 10010; 212-675-1003. **Membership:** Eligibility requirements. Annual dues.

Screen Actors Guild
Who: 88,000 members in 20 local groups. **What:** AFL-CIO affiliate. Publishes quarterly magazine covering union activities, topics of general interest, book reviews and obituaries. Organizational structure includes committees on affirmative action, agent relations, film society, government review, legislation,

performers with disabilities, senior performers, stuntpersons, wages and working conditions, women and young performers. Founded 1933. **Contact:** SAG, 1515 Broadway, New York, NY 10036; 212-944-1030; Web site: www.sag.org **Membership:** Eligibility requirements. Annual dues.

Society of Stage Directors and Choreographers

Who: 1,400 professional choreographers and directors. **What:** Provides individuals with sample contracts, benefits, bimonthly newsletter and career-development support. Founded 1959. **Contact:** SSDC, 1501 Broadway, Suite 1701, New York, NY 10036; 212-391-1070; fax: 212-302-6195 **Membership:** Eligibility requirements. Annual dues.

United Scenic Artists

Who: 2,200 scenic, costume, lighting and other designers and artists. **What:** Labor union providing contracts and benefits for professional scenic designers and other artists employed by television, theater and motion-picture studios; and producers of commercials. Affiliated with International Brotherhood of Painters and Allied Trades. Founded 1918. **Contact:** USA, 16 W. 61st St., 11th Fl., New York, NY 10023; 212-581-0300 **Membership:** Eligibility requirements. Annual dues.

Selecting a Program

YOU'RE SHOPPING FOR YOUR first personal computer. You envision all the uses you will have for your computer and how it will enable you to really get your life in order. In the computer store and the mail order catalogs you browse, there is an overwhelming array of possibilities. Dells, Microns, Hewlett Packards, Gateways, IBM, Apples. What you need is a computer-shopping consultant!

In the dancing department, the array of possibilities can also be dizzying. Until, that is, you take inventory of what you really want or need and the physical gifts you bring to the task. If you have the drive to be a professional, to you dance will be like food and drink is to someone who is hungry and thirsty. It will be totally absorbing for you. Next you need to take stock of the body God has given you and your musicality, sense of rhythm and coordination. You don't need a perfect body, but it helps, particularly if you are going to be a ballet dancer, where good turn out and good feet are the norm.

In selecting a place to study, imagine yourself in various environments. Are they rural or urban? Are you taking classes with lots of people or only a few? Is it competitive or laid-back? If you are studying with a famous teacher, does this inspire you or intimidate you? The more questions you ask yourself before you begin your search, the better choice of program you will eventually make.

Special Advice on Summer Programs

There is a huge array of summer programs in dance. Practically every ballet and modern-dance company and school has a program. There are festivals and many academic institutions running summer programs. If you are serious about pursuing professional status, summer programs can provide an opportunity to stretch yourself by exploring for a short time in a new, uncharted area. If all you have studied is ballet, take a modern dance intensive, or tap or jazz dance to see how you like it. Spend a summer at one of the major summer dance festivals to soak up the environment and determine if this really is the world you want to inhabit in the future. Just being there is a lesson in itself.

If you are an aspiring young professional and if one summer you visit a place like the American Dance Festival or Jacob's Pillow Dance Festival, you will be about as close to paradise as possible. The mix of a rural setting with top-notch professionals and colleagues who love dance will undoubtedly become a memorable experience for you. In May of every year, *Dance Magazine* publishes a list of summer study programs. With this annual guide and the information in our book, you will be able to choose programs for requesting additional materials or to plan auditions, if necessary.

Special Advice on Dance Schools

The caliber of instruction at dance schools can vary widely. However, there are some indicators to help you judge the quality of a school or studio. Age and reputation are important factors. Longevity usually means a certain degree of quality. Also, many schools are affiliated with professional dance companies. Often because of their substantial budget and prestige, these schools are able to afford excellent instructors. Company-affiliated schools also have the advantage of offering direct access to performing opportunities and training that is performance-oriented.

You can also tell a great deal by looking at the size of the faculty and by reviewing their biographical information. If a school has a lot of different kinds of classes and a small faculty, chances are that the teachers will not be particularly expert in all categories: jazz, tap, ballet and modern dance. If you plan to be a professional in one of these areas, you should seek a place to study with individuals who have danced professionally. Moreover, there is a vast difference between studio work and stage work. As Doris Humphrey notes in *The Art of Making Dances,* "Dance training, with its years and years of technique in a studio, is very incomplete and unrealistic indeed. The stage differs radically from the physical and psychological space of the studio...."

Finally, if you can make a visit, you should assess the environment in which you plan to study. What are the studios like? Are they clean and well maintained? How is the floor? Forgiving or punishing? How large are the classes? Do you think you would function better in a smaller school that is less competitive and where you receive more individual attention, or in a larger school where the competition with other dancers gives you another kind of energy? Are the classes accompanied by live music? The renowned choreographer José Limón once said, "Dancers are musicians," and music performed live is an important part of high-quality dance instruction.

Special Advice on Academic Programs

One often sees statistics that demonstrate that a college degree raises your anticipated lifetime earnings by a substantial amount over what a high-school graduate would expect to make. In dance, this would probably hold true for someone seeking an academic position; but for performing artists, a degree has almost no impact on earnings. For ballet dancers, it is particularly difficult to take time out of prime dancing years to earn a degree. Understanding this, some enlightened institutions, such as the Boston Conservatory and University of Utah, provide academic credit for professional dance experience, thereby helping professional dancers earn a college degree.

Interestingly, since the end of the dance boom in the mid-1980s, many colleges have developed first-rate programs in dance. These programs, long since liberated from the physical-education depart-ments, have excellent programs to develop both the technique and intellect of the emerging dance professional. Some are linked to theater and music departments, but some stand on their own. They are often sanctuaries for former performers, and many of the programs provide training for future dance employment in nonperformance areas.

Nevertheless, because there is a great deal of uncertainty related to a performing career in dance, a college degree might prove invaluable later in life. It might also provide the basis for a second career after your dancing days are over, or serve as a source of part-time employment while you are dancing. Every dancer needs to make a long-term plan, considering various options.

Recently, numerous college dance programs have hired faculty with professional performing experience. Gone are the days when a dance faculty consists only of academics. It is now more important to have experienced professionals on the university staff, plus visiting artists who are working in the field and professional dance companies coming to the campus to perform. All this benefits the emerging dance profes-sional by providing access to the information and connections one needs to lay the basis for a career.

In selecting an undergraduate dance program, you should first consider the type of program and the kind of degree offered. Generally, a BFA (Bachelor of Fine Arts) degree offers the highest proportion of classes in dance, a BA degree offers fewer dance classes and a BS degree probably offers the least of all.

Next you should consider the curriculum and determine what course work is most relevant to your interests. For example, if your passion is performing and to a lesser degree choreography, you will want to make sure that courses are offered in these areas and that there is adequate opportunity for you to perform with or compose for a college ensemble.

You should take the same approach you used for finding a dance school in your teens. That is to say, you should visit and critique the place, observe a class and check the biographies of the teachers or faculty for professional experience. One of the most important bell-wethers in assessing a school is the number of graduates who have gone on to major performing careers.

In the dance world, the MFA (Master of Fine Arts) is the terminal degree for a performing artist. In the gazetteer section, we have included nearly every dance program in America that offers graduate degrees in dance. This degree, plus a decade of performing experience with a major company, would make you a qualified candidate for a college or university position, should you choose to take up teaching when your performing career is over. There are also some interesting doctoral programs (devoted mostly to dance history) listed in this book.

One final suggestion based on personal experience and prejudice: The best dancers I know have gone after a well-rounded dance education. That is to say, they have concentrated on ballet, modern dance, jazz or tap, but they have also learned about other dance forms, such as ethnic and folk dance, studied music, anatomy and other subjects perhaps not directly related to their career. My friend Carolyn Adams, a former principal dancer with the Paul Taylor Company, attended college not because she was the least bit uncertain about wanting to pursue a performing career, but because she thought of herself as a person as well, and she wanted the "rounding out" that a college experience can provide.

Dance Programs

Academic Programs

Internships and
Apprentice Programs

Residential and
Artist-in-Residence Programs

Studio Schools and
Private Teachers

Workshops and Festivals

Alabama

Alabama School of Fine Arts

For ballet, jazz dancers Central Alabama — 1800 8th Ave. N., Birmingham, AL 35203 **Voice:** 205-252-9241; 800-473-ASFA (AL only) **Fax:** 205-251-9541 **E-mail:** admissions@asfa.k12.al.us **Web Site:** www.asfa.k12.al.us **Contact:** Therese Laeger, Chair **Founded:** 1971 **Open:** Sept.-June **Admission:** Audition, interview **Deadlines:** Feb. **Cost:** Free tuition for state residents, $1,265 per semester for nonresidents, plus $730-$1,060 for housing **Financial Aid:** Scholarship **Size-Attendees:** 40 **Size-Class:** 10-15 **Degree or Certification:** High-school diploma **Job Placement:** Yes

T HE REPUTATION OF the Alabama School of Fine Arts (ASFA) has grown steadily since its founding in 1971. No longer led by master teacher Dame Sonia Arova, the dance department still follows in her footsteps with the present director, Theresa Laeger, a former student and colleague. After graduating from ASFA in 1974, Laeger danced with the Birmingham Ballet and the Cleveland Ballet before returning to Ballet South as ballet mistress and as a teacher at ASFA. Wes Chapman, former ABT star and technical whiz kid, is AFSA's most famous alumnus, and now operates his own dance company, Ballet South, in conjunction with the school.

ASFA is for students in grades 7 to 12. With 5 other concentrations besides dance, enrollment numbers around 350 full-time students. Alabama residents pay no tuition, since the school is funded by the state legislature, and scholarships are available to defray the cost of room and board. Most of the students are housed on campus.

The curriculum is thorough and intensive, with classes ranging from pointe to jazz, along with music appreciation, dance history and piano lessons. As with any conservatory of this rank,

students graduate into top dance companies from New York City Ballet to Frankfurt Ballet, as well as into top academic conservatories about the country.

The school moved into a beautiful new facility 1993. Easily accessible from the interstates, it is around the corner from the Birmingham Museum of Art and Public Library, the McWane Science Center, the Birmingham Civil Rights Institute and Jefferson Civic Center.

University of Alabama

For ballet, jazz, modern dancers, choreographers 1 hr. SW of Birmingham — College of Arts and Sciences, Dept. of Theatre and Dance, P.O. Box 870239, Tuscaloosa, AL 35487 **Voice:** 205-348-5283 **Fax:** 205-348-9048 **E-mail:** pmccray@woodsquad.as.ua.edu **Web Site:** www.as.ua.edu/theatre **Contact:** Edie Barnes, Dir. of the Dance Program **Founded:** 1831 **Open:** Year-round **Admission:** Written application, ACT and SAT tests, transcripts, audition for summer program **Cost:** $1,297-$3,404 tuition, $1,650-$3,300 room and board **Financial Aid:** Loans; Scholarship; Fellowship; Stipend; Work/Study **Size-Attendees:** 200 **Degree or Certification:** BA in Dance **Job Placement:** Yes

W HAT SETS THIS academic program apart is its recent partnership with American Ballet Theatre. The University of Alabama program also provides dance majors with training that is above average.

Students have the opportunity to focus on ballet, modern and jazz, and can audition for not just 1 but the 2 resident dance companies, Dance Alabama! and The Alabama Repertory Dance Theatre. However, during the summer time is when the UA program shines as it plays host to The American Ballet Theatre Summer Intensive. The 3-week intensive with guest faculty, such as Alabama native Wes Chapman, the ballerina Cynthia Harvey, Shawn Black (now dancing with Twyla Tharp) and John Summers, is open to the advanced dance majors in the program with scholarship opportunities offered through the dance department.

The university is not far from the beaches along the Gulf of Mexico, New Orleans, Atlanta and the Great Smoky Mountains.

Alaska

Alaska Dance Theatre

👣 🔄 🌟 *For ballet, jazz, modern dancers* On the Gulf of Alaska — 2602 Gambell St., Anchorage, AK 99503 **Voice:** 907-277-9591 **Fax:** 907-274-3078 **E-mail:** adt@alaska.net **Web Site:** www.alaska.net/~adt/adt.htm **Contact:** Alice Bassler Sullivan, Dir. **Founded:** 1981 **Open:** Year-round **Admission:** Open classes and/or seasonal auditions for the company **Deadlines:** June for summer, late Aug. for fall, Dec. for spring **Cost:** $223-$719 per semester; class card $70 plus registration fee **Financial Aid:** Scholarship **Size-Attendees:** 500

NOT TO BE OUTDONE by the "lower 48," Alaska Dance Theatre (ADT) possesses a dance company and school of significant repute with a comprehensive list of classes and events to keep professionally minded youth on their toes. With 5 faculty members dividing their time between classes in ballet technique, jazz, creative dance, modern and sports conditioning, the school runs from 10 A.M. to 9 P.M. Monday to Saturday. In collaboration with Alberta Ballet of Canada, ADT presents a production of *The Nutcracker,* for which students can audition and professionals from around the country are hired. Performances and special events abound throughout the year, including the Fairbanks Summer Arts Festival and the Anchorage Symphony Halloween Concert, along with the more creative events, such as the Whale Fat Follies fundraiser in August.

Juneau Dance Unlimited

👣 🌟 *For ballet, jazz, modern, tap dancers, choreographers* Capital city in the Alaskan panhandle — P.O. Box 21545, Juneau, AK 99802 **Voice:** 907-463-5327 **Fax:** 907-463-3601 **E-mail:** nashdance@worldnet.att.net **Contact:** Matthew Nash, Artistic Dir. **Founded:** 1975 **Open:** Year-round **Admission:** Open **Deadlines:** Rolling **Financial Aid:** Scholarship; Work/Study **Size-Attendees:** 200 **Size-Class:** 10

FORMED IN 1975 to promote dance educational and performance opportunities for youth and adults, Juneau Dance Unlimited has recently engaged Matthew Nash, a seasoned choreographer, as its new artistic director. Nash's New York-based contemporary ballet company, Splinters & Shards, is often in residence in Juneau. This company's artists have danced with well-known ballet and modern companies, and they teach and present performances when in residence. In addition to an annual *Nutcracker,* there are two other annual performances, both of which include students from the school.

Juneau Dance offers a full schedule of ballet, modern, tap and jazz classes and a graded syllabus for all ages and interests. Six faculty members present special workshops in specific forms like hip-hop and African dance. The school also recently brought native dancers from Atka Island in the Aleutians for a residency in cooperation with the public-school system.

Juneau Dance is exploring international exchanges with the professional company and ballet academy in Vladivostok, and plans to continue Nash's work in Mongolia. Its long-term goal is to provide dance education and performances throughout the Alaskan panhandle.

North Star Ballet School

For ballet dancers Alaskan interior — P.O. Box 73486, 1800 College Rd., Fairbanks, AK 99707 **Voice:** 907-451-8800 **Fax:** 907-451-8809 **E-mail:** nsdf@polarnet.com **Web Site:** www.nsdf.com **Contact:** Norman Shelburne, Dir. **Founded:** 1987 **Open:** Year-round **Admission:** Registration, audition (for scholarships and company) **Deadlines:** Aug. for first semester, Dec. for second semester, May for summer **Cost:** $10 per class; $140-$635 per semester; $280-$1,270 per year **Financial Aid:** Scholarship; Work/Study **Size-Attendees:** 120 **Size-Class:** 15-25

A COMBINATION OF company, school and service organization, North Star Ballet School gets high marks for providing Alaska's Great Interior with a well-thought-out, professional training ground for young aspirants and avocational dancers. The company also branches out to serve artists in the field by hiring professionals from around the country to perform in classic repertory, such as that obligatory "cash cow," *The Nutcracker*. Under the direction of Norman Shelburne, North Star presents not only holiday classics but also a mix of classical and contemporary dance during the spring season. Trainees have 3 opportunities to perform on stage: the main company, the apprentice company and the junior company.

The curriculum offers 8 levels of ballet, along with separate levels for boys, pointe for girls, pas de deux, modern and adult ballet classes. The faculty is led by Norman Shelburne, who also runs the main company. A graduate of the University of Utah and former member of Ballet West, Shelburne served as artistic director of the Lexington Ballet in Kentucky before arriving in Anchorage. Other faculty includes Sue Perry, who danced professionally with Pittsburgh Ballet Theater and with Ruth Page's Chicago Ballet and was the principal dancer with BalletMet in Ohio. Another plus for this progressive studio is the fact that over the last 10 years, the North Star Dance Foundation has awarded more than $45,000 in scholarships to students in need.

University of Alaska–Anchorage

For modern, ballet, jazz, tap dancers On a wooded campus near town — 3211 Providence Dr., Anchorage, AK 99508 **Voice:** 907-786-1707 **Fax:** 907-786-4630 **E-mail:** aycas@uaa.alaska.edu **Web Site:** www.uaa.alaska.edu/cas **Contact:** Jill Flanders Crosby, Prog. Coord. **Founded:** 1917 **Open:** Year-round **Admission:** Application, audition, transcripts, writing sample **Deadlines:** Mid-Sept. **Cost:** $75 per credit for state residents, $234 per credit for nonresidents **Financial Aid:** Loans; Scholarship; Fellowship; Stipend; Work/Study **Size-Class:** 10 **Degree or Certification:** BA

A LTHOUGH THIS PROGRAM lacks an independent degree track for dance majors, the offerings are standard fare for a smaller academic program. Courses include the requisite ballet, jazz and modern-dance courses. Colorful additions, such as African/Haitian and "Borealis Dancers," flesh out the program. Borealis provides students with an opportunity to learn to perform various dance routines including Russian, folk, Swedish folk, German-inspired character dance, Charleston, gold miners character dance and can-can. Jill Flanders Crosby, the coordinator of the program, brings to the department her studies in dance forms from Ghana and American jazz dance and music.

The university's campus is picturesquely located against a backdrop of breathtaking beauty, including Mt. McKinley, 133 air miles to the north. Anchorage prides itself on being a great place to live and a great place to visit.

Arizona

Arizona State University

🏠 ⌂ ✸ *For ballet, jazz, modern dancers, choreographers* S of Phoenix — Dept. of Dance, Main Campus, P.O. Box 870304, Tempe, AZ 85287 **Voice:** 480-965-6807 **Fax:** 480-965-2247 **Web Site:** www.asu.edu/cfa/dance **Contact:** Rose Welsh, Acad. Advisor **Founded:** 1885 **Open:** Year-round **Admission:** Audition (only for modern, ballet technique courses) **Deadlines:** Rolling **Cost:** $1,094 per semester for state residents, $4,670 per semester for non-residents, plus $5,000 for housing **Financial Aid:** Loans; Scholarship; Work/Study **Size-Class:** 10-60 **Degree or Certification:** BFAs in Dance Studies, Performance and Choreography, Dance Education, MFA **Job Placement:** Yes

ACADEMIC AND performance programs at Arizona State University (ASU) provide professional training in the areas of traditional and nontraditional dance. The curriculum centers on the study of modern dance, with additional courses in ballet and ethnic dance. On the undergraduate level, the BFA program has 4 concentrations: dance studies, performance, choreography and dance education. The graduate program leading to an MFA, dedicated to much of the same, also encourages exploration of unconventional areas of study.

Recent artists visiting ASU include Kevin O'Day, Bebe Miller, Ralph Lemon and Liz Lerman. Masterclasses and residencies have attracted a long list of companies and performers, among them Pina Bausch, Dance Theatre of Harlem, Agnes de Mille, Louis Falco, Twyla Tharp, the Royal Winnipeg Ballet, David Rousseve and Paul Taylor. The department's resources include 7 dance studios, 2 performance labs/theaters, costume shop, multimedia learning center, sound lab and movement rehab lab. The multimedia learning center is a student-based learning and instructional-media-design facility specializing in creating learning tools for ASU dance curricula. A place where students can view videotapes, use the Internet for dance research, and work with digital audio and video, the center complements all aspects of the dance curriculum. Nearby Gammage Center for the Arts and Scottsdale Center for the Arts bring in dance companies from around the country, exposing students to professionals of the highest caliber. Unusual here is the fact that no auditions are held for students who want to enter the dance-degree program. On the other hand, all students accepted into

Nelson Fine Arts Center, Arizona State University, Tempe (Antoine Predock, architect).

the dance preprofessional program must then petition for acceptance into one of the BFA programs. Tempe is a college town near a sprawling desert city, Phoenix. Surrounding territory is beautiful but austere, arid but colorful.

School of Ballet Arizona

For ballet dancers 3645 E. Indian School Rd., Phoenix, AZ 85018 **Voice:** 602-381-0184 **Fax:** 602-381-0189 **Contact:** Kee-Juan Han, Dir. **Founded:** 1986 **Open:** Year-round **Admission:** Registration, audition for trainee program **Deadlines:** Mid-Aug. for first quarter, Oct. for second quarter, Jan. for third quarter, June for summer intensive **Cost:** $10 per class, $178-$198 per semester, $89-$509 per quarter **Financial Aid:** Scholarship; Work/Study **Size-Attendees:** 150-200 **Size-Class:** 15-25

T HIS SCHOOL SERVES as Arizona's professional training ground for aspirants to the world of professional ballet, as well as to Ballet Arizona, whose artistic director, Michael Uthoff, won a great reputation for training young professionals at the Hartford Ballet. A well-respected company, Ballet Arizona provides the Southwest region of this country with all the trappings of a nationally recognized dance company, complete with school, apprentice program and company. The faculty has been imported from around the country and the globe, providing the school with a first-class, diverse training regimen. For those seeking professional advancement in the world of ballet the opportunity exists; so does the chance to take dance class for the sheer enjoyment of it.

The school offers all the requisite classes for the young trainee, including ballet, pointe, character, creative movement, modern and Pilates instruction. Vaganova and the English system of instruction are the preferred methods of teaching at the school. This is thanks to Kee-Juan Han, who studied both techniques as a professional dancer. A former soloist with the Boston Ballet, Han also has a long list of teaching credits, from Hubbard Street Dance Company, to Vail International Dance Festival. He now serves both as director of the school and as the company's principal teacher. The staff consists of 9 faculty members whose credits range from the Zurich Ballet to the Children's School for the Arts in Moscow. The facility has 3 large studios and boasts live accompaniment in all classes.

University of Arizona–Tucson

For ballet, jazz, modern dancers, choreographers Southern Arizona — Division of Dance, Gittings Building, #121, P.O. Box 210093, Tucson, AZ 85721 **Voice:** 520-621-4698 **Fax:** 520-621-6981 **E-mail:** UADANCE@CCIT.ARIZONA.EDU **Web Site:** www.arizona.edu **Contact:** Jory Hancock, Div. Head **Open:** Spring, fall **Admission:** Written application, audition **Deadlines:** Apr. 1 (undergrad.), Feb. 1 (international grad.), June 1 (transfer, grad.) **Cost:** $1,132 per semester for state residents, $4,708 per semester for nonresidents **Financial Aid:** Loans; Scholarship; Fellowship; Stipend; Work/Study **Size-Attendees:** 170 **Size-Class:** 30 **Degree or Certification:** BFA in Dance, MFA in Dance **Job Placement:** Yes

T HE DANCE DIVISION at University of Arizona–Tucson, offering a BFA and MFA option, is considered one of the top programs in the United States. The program is one of the few programs nationally offering a triple-track concentration in which ballet, modern and jazz dance are equal areas of study. The department defends this broad-based education by asserting that its graduates are "more than ever before securing professional jobs as performers after graduation."

Since 1992 the university has produced such special events as the Jazz Dance Festival, attracting students from throughout the United States, and Europe. Each year a renowned guest artist is in residence during the festival, and students have an opportunity to work with a variety of jazz dance masters. An impressive number of dance concerts—about 6—are presented each year, including the Spring Centennial Hall Concert, presented in the 2,400-seat performance venue on the university's campus. The resident dance ensemble tours nationally and internationally to such locations as Mexico, Japan, Holland, Chicago and the Kennedy Center in Washington, DC. Both the BFA and MFA programs emphasize studio work and performance. The masters program, however, is designed for mature dance artists, as well as for teachers and scholars. Visiting artists are also in abundance with recent guests, including the Murray Louis and Nikolais Dance Company, the Miami City Ballet, Gus Giordano Jazz Dance Chicago, Hubbard Street Dance, Pilobolus and David Parsons. The university also hosted a 6-week residency with Bill T. Jones, during which he mounted his now classic work, *Uncle Tom's Cabin/ The Last Supper.*

Yuma Ballet Academy

For ballet dancers, choreographers SW Arizona, on the California border — 2341 E. 16th St., Yuma, AZ 85365 **Voice:** 520-329-4762 **Contact:** Jon Cristofori, Dir. **Open:** Year-round **Admission:** Open (audition to determine level) **Deadlines:** Rolling **Cost:** $10 per class **Financial Aid:** Scholarship; Work/Study **Size-Attendees:** 50-150 **Size-Class:** 10-20

A SMALL OPERATION that makes up for its size by offering its students the full resources of a school and company, the Yuma Ballet Academy also offers a preprofessional program for young dancers eager to train intensively. For students in the advanced division, instruction in pointe work and variations is included, along with performance opportunities in the affiliated company, Ballet Yuma, Arizona's "only honor company recognized nationally by Regional Dance America."

Arkansas

University of Arkansas–Fayetteville

For ballet, jazz, modern dancers, choreographers NW Arkansas — Dept. of Drama, 619 Kimpel Hall, Fayetteville, AR 72701 **Voice:** 501-575-2953; 800-377-8632 **Fax:** 501-575-7602 **E-mail:** info@uark.edu **Web Site:** www.uark.edu **Contact:** Andrew Gibbs, Dept. Chair **Founded:** 1957 **Open:** Year-round **Admission:** Written application, audition, transcripts **Deadlines:** As early as possible for fall, Jan. 15 for scholarship **Cost:** $93 per credit for state residents, $253 per credit for nonresidents **Financial Aid:** Loans; Scholarship; Fellowship; Stipend; Work/Study **Size-Attendees:** 50-100 **Size-Class:** 10-25 **Degree or Certification:** BA **Job Placement:** Yes

THE DANCE DEPARTMENT at this university is admittedly small, and is integrated into the drama department. But if your interest in dance leans more toward the theatrical side of the field, you might find what you are looking for at this rather well-respected department. No formal major is offered for dancers; the courses given are general technique classes in ballet and modern.

Specialized classes include dance for the theater, jazz, tap and choreography. Those with Broadway aspirations will find their niche here. The facilities are also quite good: 4 theaters ranging from a 75-seat black-box space to a state-of-the art 1,200-seat proscenium theater. Class sizes are limited to allow for individualized attention.

Located near the gorgeous Buffalo River and Beaver Lake recreational areas, Fayetteville is definitely a university town, with plenty of hangouts to keep students occupied between exams.

California

Ballet Pacifica

 For ballet dancers, choreographers
Midway between Los Angeles and San Diego
— 1824 Kaiser Ave., Irvine, CA 92614 **Voice:**
949-851-9930 **Fax:** 949-851-9974 **Web
Site:** www.ocartsnet.org/ballet_pacifica
Contact: Molly Lynch, Dir. **Founded:** 1995
Open: Year-round **Admission:** Audition
Deadlines: Rolling **Cost:** 8-class card $64
Financial Aid: Scholarship; Work/Study
Size-Attendees: 100 **Size-Class:** 20

B ALLET PACIFICA is a program on the move. Under the watchful direction of Molly Lynch, who has set her sights on transforming a familiar name in the dance community into a professional, midsize operation, both the school and the company are slated in the next several years to acquire professional status. As the name of the school suggests, Lynch is striving to adopt a curriculum fashioned more in the tradition of a conservatory, geared to students who are interested in launching a professional career. The school is young, in operation only since 1995, but already it has the stature of a preprofessional operation.

The conservatory offers a full-time program, complete with classes in ballet technique, pointe, men's class, variations, repertory, pas de deux, nutrition, music, character, modern and cross-training conditioning. A rather illustrious advisory committee has been assembled to assist Lynch in the evaluation of the entire program, including faculty, students and curriculum. The committee includes such names as Janice Plastino, chair of the dance department at UC Irvine; Robert Sund, former dancer with the San Francisco Ballet; and David Allan, international choreographer and former dancer with the National Ballet of Canada. The conservatory recently moved into new headquarters featuring 3 spacious studios, as well as a conditioning workout room. The faculty is assembled from around the globe and includes such guests as David Allen and Janek Schergen.

California Ballet School

 For ballet dancers, choreographers 8276 Ronson Rd., San Diego, CA 92111 **Voice:** 619-560-5676 **Fax:** 619-560-0072 **Contact:** Clarissa Palhegyi, School Mgr. **Founded:** 1968 **Open:** Year-round **Admission:** Written application, registration fee, placement class **Deadlines:** Rolling **Cost:** $28 per month **Financial Aid:** Scholarship; Work/Study **Size-Attendees:** 300 **Size-Class:** 15-25

O NE OF THE LARGER West Coast company/schools, the California Ballet School boasts a total of 28 faculty members at 5 locations throughout the San Diego area. The facility has been providing the local community with a dance center for the last 30 years. Many faculty members have enjoyed performing careers with the major dance institutions of this country, such as the New York City Ballet, the San Francisco Ballet and the Joffrey Ballet.

In addition to classical ballet training, the school offers classes in jazz, tap, body mechanics and Spanish dance. A Saturday-afternoon workshop program provides lessons in makeup, mime and production. The junior company provides performing opportunities for advanced members of the preprofessional division.

California Institute of the Arts

For ballet, modern dancers, choreographers N of Los Angeles, overlooking the city of Santa Clarita — School of Dance, 24700 McBean Pkwy., Valencia, CA 91355 **Voice:** 805-255-1050; 800-545-2787 **Fax:** 805-253-1562 **Web Site:** www.calarts.edu **Contact:** Cristyne Lawson, Dir. **Founded:** 1961 **Open:** Year-round **Admission:** Written application, audition **Deadlines:** Feb. 1 for fall, Nov. 15 for spring **Cost:** $16,350 tuition (full-time enrollment) **Financial Aid:** Loans; Scholarship; Fellowship; Stipend; Work/Study **Size-Class:** 15-25 **Degree or Certification:** BFAs in Dance, Performance, Production; MFAs in Dance, Choreography **Job Placement:** Yes

I F THE CALIFORNIA lifestyle combined with a cutting-edge curriculum appeal to you, perhaps you should consider the California Institute of the Arts, affectionately known as Cal Arts. The emphasis here is on tutorial mentoring, which allows students to design their course of study with the help of practicing artists. The graduate and undergraduate fine-arts degrees have an emphasis on performance, composition or production.

Interestingly, admission is based on talent alone, with no consideration given to class standing, grade-point average and test scores. The school was founded by Walt Disney in 1961, when he brought about the merger of the Los Angeles Conservatory of Music and the Chouinard Art Institute. The School of Dance was added when the facility moved to its present location in 1971. The emphasis on choreography and performance is underscored by the weekly showings, which must be attended by every dance student. The Dance Ensemble, founded in 1980, enables the members of the faculty to continue performing and choreographing by using each other, alumni, guest artists and the most advanced students. The school stresses individual artistic development and the nurturing of personal aesthetics. Notable faculty include Dean Cristyne Lawson, who danced with Martha Graham and was a founding member of the Alvin Ailey Company; Tina Yuan, who teaches composition, also a product of the Graham and Ailey companies; and Liz Maxwell, a former member of Donald Byrd/The Group. In its catalog, Cal Arts is refreshingly honest about its facilities and their occasional shortcomings, noting, for instance, a "sprung floor covered with ancient Marley flooring." But the beautifully landscaped 60-acre campus is blessed with magnificent views: the Santa Clarita Valley is surrounded by the Tehachapi Mountains to the north, the San Gabriels to the east and the Santa Susannas to the west.

MFA student in motion, California Institute of the Arts, Valencia.

California State University–Long Beach

🏠 🌼 *For modern dancers, choreographers* On the Pacific, part of metro Los Angeles — 1250 Bellflower Blvd., Long Beach, CA 90840 **Voice:** 562-985-4747 **Fax:** 562-985-7896 **Web Site:** www.csulb.edu/~dance **Contact:** Judith Allen, Dept. Chair **Founded:** 1970 **Open:** Spring, fall **Admission:** Written application, audition, resume **Deadlines:** Mar. 15 **Cost:** $940 per semester for state residents, $240 extra per credit for nonresidents **Financial Aid:** Loans; Scholarship; Fellowship; Stipend; Work/Study **Size-Attendees:** 120 **Degree or Certification:** BFA in Dance, MFA in Dance **Job Placement:** Yes

ONE OF THE LARGEST academic dance programs in the country, and certainly in California, CSU–Long Beach currently offers BA, BFA and MFA degrees. The school has grown steadily since its inception in 1970. The program has an enrollment of approximately 90 undergraduates and 30 graduate students. The BFA program is for those interested in professional careers as dancers and/or choreographers, and the BA program is for those interested in teaching, dance/movement therapy, notation and journalism. The MFA degree was introduced in 1993 with an emphasis on performance and/or choreography.

The degree programs emphasize modern-dance technique, choreography and performance. The Dance Center houses 7 large dance studios, classrooms, clinic, costume shop, media center, recording studio, computer lab, video/film editing room and the Martha Knoebel Dance Theatre. Guest choreographers set works on students for the two major concerts each year, and masterclasses by guest artists are regularly offered. The affiliated touring company, Dance Machine, conducts community outreach presentations in local schools. Dances set on students at CSU–LB include works by José Limón, Gerald Arpino, Merce Cunningham, Bella Lewitzky, Donald McKayle, Lar Lubovitch and Martha Graham. Master teachers, such as Rebecca Wright, George de la Pena and Risa Steinberg have served on the faculty. The credentials of the permanent faculty span classical and modern dance, based on work in companies, such as American Ballet Theatre, Bill T. Jones/Arnie Zane, Martha Graham Dance Company and Merce Cunningham Dance Company.

Contra Costa Ballet Centre

👣 🌼 *For ballet dancers* 30 mi. E of San Francisco — 2040 N. Bway., Walnut Creek, CA 94596 **Voice:** 925-935-7984 **Fax:** 925-932-3221 **Contact:** Richard Cammack, Zola Dishong Cammack, Dirs. **Open:** Year-round **Admission:** Registration (year-round program), audition (summer program) **Deadlines:** Summer program: Mar. (auditions), Apr. (financial aid, registration) **Cost:** $36-$112 for class card, $795 summer-program tuition **Financial Aid:** Scholarship **Size-Attendees:** 90-100 **Size-Class:** 15-20

ONE OF THE WEST'S best-kept secrets, this regional school and its affiliated company near San Francisco serve as an excellent training ground for those interested in a professional career in ballet. Credit goes primarily to the school's directors, Richard and Zola Dishong Cammack, both formerly affiliated with the San Francisco Ballet School as performers and administrators. He served as the director of the school for 11 years and she served on the faculty. In 1987, they

DELL DAVIS

Dancers in line at the Contra Costa Ballet Centre, Walnut Creek.

47

took over the reins at the Contra Costa Ballet Centre (CCBC), bringing not only their wealth of knowledge in teaching and school management but also the cream of the crop in guest artists and teachers.

Charles Anderson, former New York City Ballet member and son of Zola Dishong, is a regular fixture at the school both as a guest artist during the company's biannual performances and as a guest choreographer. Other artists who have graced the stage at the Dean Lesher Regional Center for the Arts include Yan Chen (soloist with the American Ballet Theatre), Jian Wang (of the New York City Ballet), Christopher Anderson (soloist with the San Francisco Ballet) and Heather Dowell (with the Atlanta Ballet). Advanced students not only benefit from exposure to and the opportunity to perform alongside such artists, but also receive equally impressive contact in the classroom.

Guest teachers and choreographers during the intensive summer program have included the likes of Michael Smuin, former Director of the San Francisco Ballet; Evelyn Cisneros and Pascale Leroy from the San Francisco Ballet; and Violette Verdy and Suki Schorer, two outstanding former ballerinas with the New York City Ballet and now equally respected for their achievements as teachers and directors. In consequence, CCBC students have gone on to perform in major American and European ballet companies. Performance opportunities are available for intermediate- and advanced-level students who perform with the Contra Costa Ballet during *Nutcracker* season in December and in the summer, in conjunction with the Summer Intensive. The facility boasts 3 large studios with state-of-the-art sprung floors. According to Michael Smuin, "The best way to judge a teacher is by his pupils and Richard and Zola's pupils populate the finest companies throughout the world. Individually, they are trained, schooled, experienced; together they are unbeatable."

Dance Center

For jazz, ballet, hip-hop, tap dancers, choreographers *Greater Los Angeles — 11491 Chandler Blvd., North Hollywood, CA 91601* **Voice:** 818-980-3336 **Fax:** 818-980-8687 **E-mail:** ladance@leonardo.net **Web Site:** www.recruitex.com/dancex/tremdanc.htm **Contact:** Karen Willes, Dir. **Founded:** 1972 **Open:** Year-round **Admission:** Written application **Deadlines:** Rolling **Cost:** $70 for 10 classes **Financial Aid:** Scholarship; Work/Study **Size-Attendees:** 100 **Size-Class:** 5-25

ALTHOUGH IT HAS recently changed its name to the Dance Center, this studio still carries the cachet of Joe Tremaine's reputation. It is a mecca for those interested in jazz dance, and no wonder, since Tremaine is arguably Hollywood's king of popular dance forms, from jazz to hip-hop. The program specializes in the kind of jazz—not to be confused with the jazz dance taught at schools like the Ailey—that makes it to revues and television, what some would affectionately term "jazz for hoofers." The curriculum ranges from jazz technique to hip-hop and funk/stomp, with tap and ballet thrown in for good measure. Most of the teachers are professional choreographers. Tremaine's new Dance Center is just the ticket if your ambition leans toward Hollywood or Broadway.

Marin Ballet Center for Dance

For ballet dancers, choreographers Marin County, outside of San Francisco — 100 Elm St., San Rafael, CA 94901 **Voice:** 415-453-6705 **Fax:** 415-453-5894 **E-mail:** MBallet@pacbell.net **Web Site:** www.marinballet.org **Contact:** Cynthia Lucas, School Dir. **Founded:** 1957 **Open:** Year-round **Admission:** Written application **Deadlines:** Rolling **Cost:** $12 per class, $850 for 4-week program **Financial Aid:** Scholarship; Work/Study **Size-Attendees:** 500 **Size-Class:** 10-25

FOUNDED IN 1957 by Leona Norman, who danced professionally in Europe and South America, the Marin Ballet Center features a curriculum geared toward the emerging professional. With the recent departure of its artistic director, Mikko Nissenen, to the Alberta Ballet, the center is run by a directorate of 3 former professional dancers, 2 of whom have ties to the Marin Center.

The director of the school, Cynthia Lucas, was with the National Ballet of Canada for more than 20 years, most recently as ballet mistress in charge of the classical repertoire. Performance director Leslie Crockett oversees the substantial number of performances given by the young performance ensemble and by adults. Crockett has deep roots in the California dance scene. She trained with her mother, Barbara Crockett, founder of the Sacramento Ballet. Later she danced with the San Francisco Ballet and was a teacher in the San Francisco Ballet School for a number of years. Cynthia Pepper, the director of outreach services, danced with Bella Lewitsky and the Donald Byrd Company; she is both a choreographer and a filmmaker.

The facility has 6 studios and a 150-seat studio theater and a library. A unique and distinctive feature of this school is the wealth of performance opportunities it provides. The students themselves constitute the performing company; in addition to *Nutcracker,* there are 3 other major offerings, as well as dozens of less formal studio programs, outreach programs and community events. The adult performing unit offers special performances in the studio theater. The center's enrollment has grown to 500 students, with 100 adults and 400 preprofessionals. The list of distinguished alumni includes San Francisco Ballet principal Joanna Berman and American Ballet Theatre principal Cynthia Harvey, together with scores of other professionals—always a good indicator of quality training.

Mills College

For ballet, modern dancers, choreographers Across the bay from San Francisco — Dance Dept., 5000 MacArthur Blvd., Oakland, CA 94613 **Voice:** 510-430-2175 **Fax:** 510-430-3272 **Contact:** Kathleen McClintock, Assoc. Prof. **Founded:** 1941 **Open:** Sept.-June **Admission:** Application **Deadlines:** Mar. 1 for BA; Feb. 1 for MA, MFA (fall admission only) **Cost:** $17,250 for BA; $11,130 for MA, MFA **Financial Aid:** Loans; Scholarship; Work/Study **Size-Attendees:** 30 **Degree or Certification:** BA, MA, MFA in Dance **Job Placement:** Yes

THIS PREDOMINANTLY women's college in Oakland has a lot going for it. First, it is small—20 graduate students and 10 undergraduate students in dance—which means plenty of attention. Second, it's close to San Francisco, one of the country's top cultural centers with professional and semiprofessional dance groups in modern, ballet, jazz and ethnic dance. And third, the program has an impressive roster of faculty and guest faculty, as well as artists in residence and guest choreographers.

The graduate department is coeducational and offers both MA and MFA degrees. There is also the college major, which allows a student to construct an undergraduate program of study combining disciplines. The Mills dance curriculum encompasses 3 areas of study: history and theory, choreography and technique. Each senior choreographs and prepares her own group and solo dances for concert presentation and completes an individual research project. Graduate students may elect a research or performance thesis as the culmination of their 2-year program. Guest choreographers for the Mills Repertory Dance Company have included Lori Bellilove, Bill Evans, Joe Goode, Lucas Hoving, Margaret Jenkins, Bebe Miller, Donald McKayle and Marlies Yearby. Molissa Fenley is in residence 2 weeks each year until the year 2000. Choreographer June Watanabe has been a part-time associate professor at Mills since 1986, and most recently dance critic Mary Cochran was an assistant professor for the 1997–1998 school year.

Oakland Ballet Academy

For ballet dancers, choreographers 2968 MacArthur Blvd., Oakland, CA 94602 **Voice:** 510-530-7516 **Fax:** 510-452-9557 **Contact:** Ronn Guidi, Dir. **Open:** Year-round **Admission:** Written application **Deadlines:** Rolling **Cost:** $100 for 10 classes **Financial Aid:** Scholarship; Work/Study **Size-Attendees:** 100-200 **Size-Class:** 10-20

WHILE THERE IS NO official connection between the Oakland Ballet Academy and the Oakland Ballet, both have the same artistic director. Ronn Guidi is the proprietor and director of both the academy and the ballet company. The academy offers classes at very reasonable rates.

ODC Performance Gallery School

For ballet, ethnic, modern dancers, choreographers 3153 17th St., San Francisco, CA 94110 **Voice:** 415-863-9830 **Fax:** 415-863-9833 **E-mail:** school@ odcdance.org **Web Site:** www.odcdance.org **Contact:** Kimi Okada, Dir. **Founded:** 1971 **Open:** Year-round **Admission:** Open, audition (summer intensive, some workshops), registration fee **Deadlines:** Rolling **Cost:** $9 per class **Financial Aid:** Scholarship; Work/Study **Size-Attendees:** 150 **Size-Class:** 5-25

THIS IS A FULL-SERVICE dance space offering a 200-seat performance venue, a producing program for Bay Area independent and emerging artists, and a year-round training curriculum, along with the nationally recognized attached company, ODC San Francisco. It is the California version of New York's downtown dance scene.

Classes offered at the school range from ballet (although it is not usually offered during the month of July) to yoga. The faculty represents a cross-section of artists making up the prolific Bay-area dance scene. Kimi Okada is the director of the school and associate choreographer for ODC San Francisco. Her background covers both theater and dance; she has collaborated with the likes of Bill Irwin and Robin Williams. Other faculty include Stuart Gold, a former member of the Limón Company, and Ellie Klopp, associate artistic director of the Margaret Jenkins Dance Company. The school produces such worthwhile programs as its audition series, which formally goes about linking choreographers and artistic directors looking for dancers with dancers seeking employment. This is done within the structure of a workshop series, which is not in itself new or unusual. What is special is that the audition series enables dancers to get a feel for a particular artist's technical style, and to be considered for future work with that choreographer. Classes are open for observation by other artistic directors. The participants are almost exclusively independent choreographers from the Bay area, including ODC San Francisco. The school also offers a pilot program for emerging choreographers, providing affordable performance space and rehearsal facilities, as well as seminars in marketing/PR, technical production and aspects of self-production.

San Diego School of Ballet

For ballet dancers, choreographers
5304 Metro St., San Diego, CA 92110 **Voice:** 619-294-7374 **Fax:** 619-294-7378 **E-mail:** SDBallet@aol.com **Contact:** Robin Sherertz Morgan, Dir. **Founded:** 1988 **Open:** Year-round **Admission:** Written application, audition, processing fee, resume **Deadlines:** Rolling **Cost:** $11 per class, $1,680 for summer program **Financial Aid:** Scholarship; Work/Study **Size-Class:** 24

HAVING CELEBRATED its tenth anniversary in 1998, the San Diego School of Ballet and its affiliated company may make its mark as a regional company of note in the coming millennium. In recent years, the school has acquired some heavy hitters by way of faculty, and contact with such teachers is a building block in any successful dance career. First on the list is director Robin Sherertz Morgan, who began her dancing career with the original San Diego Ballet Company. Following her stint with San Diego, she went east to train at the School of American Ballet and later joined the New York City Ballet. After turning down an offer to join Pacific Northwest Ballet in 1986, Sherertz Morgan decided her talents would be best used in her hometown where she once again settled, making her name in the dance community there. She founded the San Diego School of Ballet in 1989 and has steadily built the school's and the company's reputations in the area.

Other notable faculty members include Dame Sonia Arova, who is responsible for putting the Alabama School of Fine Arts on the map. Not coincidentally, she codirected the original San Diego Ballet in 1971 with her husband, Thor Sutowski, who has also returned to San Diego School of Ballet as a faculty member. Arova, a principal dancer with Ballet Rambert, the Metropolitan Ballet and American Ballet Theatre, as well as one of Rudolf Nureyev's frequent partners, has earned a reputation for excellence in the field of ballet both as teacher and as artistic director. Class offerings (Monday through Saturday) include preballet, ballet technique, pointe, variations, partnering and Pilates.

San Francisco Ballet School

For ballet dancers, choreographers Downtown — *455 Franklin St., San Francisco, CA 94102* **Voice:** 415-553-4667 **Fax:** 415-861-2684 **Contact:** Pam Lord, Dir. **Founded:** 1933 **Open:** Year-round **Admission:** Written application, audition, registration fee, video of choreography **Deadlines:** Late June for fall/spring semesters, May 1 for summer session **Cost:** $1,540-$3,600 for fall/spring semester, $750-$825 for summer session **Financial Aid:** Scholarship; Work/Study **Size-Attendees:** 100-200 **Size-Class:** 10-25

ARGUABLY THIRD ONLY to the American Ballet Theatre and the New York City Ballet in terms of recognition and prestige, the San Francisco Ballet has an affiliated school that offers young hopefuls the training necessary to gain employment in any one of the 3 companies. The school is patterned after NYCB's School of American Ballet (and no wonder: SFBS director Helgi Tomasson was an NYCB star for over a decade). It demands all the nailbiting and single-minded ambition required of students in a school of this caliber. So proceed with caution. Tender souls with no turnout need not apply.

Approximately 60 percent of the dancers in the San Francisco Ballet company received at least part of their training at the school. Other students have gained employment with such companies as ABT, NYCB, Pacific Northwest Ballet, Stuttgart Ballet and

Frankfurt Ballet. Classes included technique, pointe work, pas de deux, men's technique and music theory.

The staff hails from around the world, with cosmopolitan credentials to match, including professional careers with such companies as the Kirov, the National Ballet of Cuba, the National Ballet of Spain, Roland Petit's National Ballet of Marseilles and the American Ballet Theatre. Students have the benefit of working closely with the dancers from the company, since the school and the company are housed in the same facility. Also, the company has an apprentice program open to select students from the school for a 1-year period. The San Francisco Ballet building is spectacularly beautiful, and a work of architectural art. The studios are light and airy, and the facility includes weight-training equipment and a physical-therapy room.

San Francisco Dance Center

For ballet, ethnic, jazz, modern, tap dancers, choreographers In the heart of San Francisco — 50 Oak St., 12th Fl., San Francisco, CA 94102 **Voice:** 415-863-3229 **Fax:** 415-863-1180 **E-mail:** linesbal@pacbell.net **Web Site:** www.citysearch7.com/E/V/SFOCA/0000/99/51/ **Contact:** Pam Hagen, Gen. Mgr. **Open:** Year-round **Admission:** Open **Deadlines:** Rolling **Cost:** $90 for 12-class card **Financial Aid:** Scholarship; Work/Study **Size-Class:** 5-40

SAN FRANCISCO DANCE Center claims to be the largest dance studio on the West Coast. And it very well might be. The faculty alone numbers 37, and the classes offered range from ballet, to African dance and drum. Not

An Ounce of Prevention

Ask any group of dancers what their favorite cure-all is, and you're bound to receive as many answers as there are dancers. For amateurs and professionals alike, the quest for the perfect physical therapy, the ideal liniment, the miracle painkiller, is as much a part of the dancer's daily regimen as the *plié* and *tendu*. Whether you're trying to combat a structural flaw in your physique, such as scoliosis, or you're coming back from a specific injury, the options available for lengthening, strengthening, opening, lifting and general fussing are numerous, ranging from acupuncture to Alexander. Unfortunately, most dancers wait until they are injured before they consider some form of physical therapy. And then the therapy is rehabilitative rather than preventive. Almost without exception dancers sustain at least one injury during their careers, so choosing a treatment is inevitable. And once you start, the choices are endless.

A few words of warning, however. Most dancers will probably have at least one less-than-positive story to relate about either a misdiagnosis or a treatment in which little was done to alleviate the problem. Often the success of therapy is only as good as the relationship between the therapist and patient. If you don't feel comfortable with your practitioner, you probably will not be asking the right questions or communicating your problems, which will inevitably hinder getting the best treatment. Also, just because a doctor or therapist has a lot of degrees following his or her name or has been recommended as the Second Coming, this person might not be right for you. Sometimes it is best to be wary and not to take a diagnosis as the gospel. Get a second opinion, do your own research, experiment with different methods, talk to as many people as you can. The more information you have, the better prepared you are

surprisingly, the center has 5 studios, which are also home to many local companies. The most famous of these is Lines Contemporary Ballet, directed by Alonzo King. Aficionados of King take note: he is also on the ballet faculty here. The availability of private coaching is another plus for this studio.

While the center leans most heavily toward ballet instruction, the diversity of styles is quite extensive. Classes are available in 6 categories: ballet, modern, flamenco, jazz, bodywork (including floor, barre, Feldenkrais, Bartenieff, Pilates, yoga and body alignment), and traditional (including Brazilian, East Indian and African dance). Training in physical comedy is also available, although not always.

San Jose Dance Theatre

For ballet dancers, choreographers *1 hr. S of San Francisco — 1717 Technology Dr., San Jose, CA 95110* **Voice:** 408-345-4373 **E-mail:** Ballettsj@aol.com **Web Site:** www.balletbtsj.org **Contact:** Pamela Stevens, Exec. Dir. **Founded:** 1954 **Open:** Year-round **Admission:** Written application, audition, registration fee **Deadlines:** Rolling **Cost:** $12 per class **Financial Aid:** Scholarship; Work/Study **Size-Attendees:** 100 **Size-Class:** 10-25

THE SAN JOSE DANCE Theatre has enjoyed several incarnations, beginning as Paul E. Curtis Jr.'s Los Gatos Academy of Dance and the West Valley Ballet Foundation back in 1954. SJDT reinvented itself within the last few years by consolidating with the

to combat whatever ails you.

And if the pain is persistent and the injury is not getting better, listen to your body and the specialist. Unfortunately, most dancers have a high threshold of tolerance for pain, and this often leads them to trouble. Some of the best doctors in the field are those who know how to get a dancer on stage, even one with a break or fracture. However, because pain is a part of the business, make it your business to know your limits and when you're doing more harm than good. Taking time off can be the hardest remedy for a dancer to accept. However, as the adage goes, "An ounce of prevention is worth a pound of cure." Remember to respect your body: it's your most important tool.

Thankfully, conditioning therapies, alignment techniques and holistic remedies abound. Floor barre and Pilates are two of the most commonly used methods to align and strengthen the torso, and increase flexibility. But following a close second are

Yoga, Alexander Technique and White Cloud. Most dancers have patronized a chiropractor's office, along with sampling Shiatsu, rolfing, trager, acupuncture and the good old-fashioned sports massage. The names that accompany many of the apparati used in these techniques can be likened to a medieval torture chest, such as "The Reformer" or "The Rack," or they resemble something out of a romper room for toddlers, including balloon-shaped rubber balls, multicolored Therabands, foam rollers, and wooden toys—along with a host of other gadgets, thingamajigs and gizmos. It's all legit. Remember, the cures for ailments and injuries often entail years of trial and error. There are no quick fixes to body problems, and just as with dancing, it can be a never-ending process to get your body where you want it to be. But that can be part of the challenge and fun of dance—if you're willing to persevere.

—Jane Penn

Gary Palmer Dance Company. As a result the new SJDT comprises an affiliated professional dance company, an academy of ballet, a preprofessional student company (SJDT II), annual community events (including that holiday standby, *Nutcracker*) and numerous educational programs that serve special populations.

The academy offers a full curriculum including creative movement, ballet technique, pointe technique and, when available, jazz, character and Spanish dance. The facility has 3 spacious studios and a faculty of 6.

Students from the academy are chosen by audition to become members of San Jose Dance Theatre II.

San Jose State University

🏠 *For ballet, ethnic, jazz, modern dancers, choreographers* 1 hr. S of San Francisco — College of the Humanities and Arts, 1 Washington Sq., San Jose, CA 95125 **Voice:** 408-924-4673 **Fax:** 408-924-5046 **Web Site:** info.sjsu.edu/web-dbgen/catalog/departments/MUDA.html **Contact:** Fred Mathews, Dept. Chair **Open:** Year-round **Admission:** Written application, audition, transcripts, writing sample **Deadlines:** Jan. for fall, Sept. for spring **Cost:** Free tuition for state residents, $246 per semester unit for nonresidents **Financial Aid:** Loans; Scholarship; Fellowship; Stipend; Work/Study **Degree or Certification:** BA in Dance **Job Placement:** Yes

D ANCE IS ONE OF the fastest-growing majors at this large urban university in the heart of Silicon Valley. Formerly part of the theater department, the dance program has recently come into its own as an equal partner in the School of Music and Dance. Fred Mathews, former member of the Limón Dance Company and codirector of his own company, Mathews-Masters, chairs the dance program. Other notable faculty members include Janet Van Swoll in ballet and Annette MacDonald in tap and jazz.

The School of Music and Dance has ties to important professional arts organizations. Music professor Irene Dalis is the general director of Opera San Jose and Mathews is a master teacher and advisor to the Limón Dance Company, resident in San Jose. These affiliations offer abundant opportunities for additional preprofessional training and a bridge to the professional world. Although San Jose now exceeds San Francisco in population, it is a livable city with small-town friendliness and a safe feeling. The campus has the usual combination of state-university buildings with good-sized studio and performance spaces. The University Dance Theater is a well-respected group at the American College Dance Festivals and has been performing recently with members of the Limón Dance Company.

Stanford University

🏠 *For ballet, jazz, modern dancers, choreographers* 30 min. S of San Francisco — Dance Division, Roble Dance Studios, 375 Santa Teresa, Palo Alto, CA 94305 **Voice:** 650-725-0735 **Fax:** 650-725-7242 **E-mail:** jross@Leland.stanford.edu **Contact:** Janice Ross, Prof. **Founded:** 1920 **Open:** Year-round **Admission:** Application, resume, audition, GRE, BA (for graduate study) **Deadlines:** Feb. 1 (grad program), Jan. 1 (undergrad program) **Cost:** $22,110 tuition **Financial Aid:** Loans; Scholarship; Fellowship; Stipend; Work/Study **Size-Attendees:** 300 **Degree or Certification:** MA in Education with Dance Specialization **Job Placement:** Yes

I F YOU WANT THE IVY League experience out west, coupled with graduate work in dance, Stanford is arguably *the* place to go. As in the rest of the university, the MA program is quite selective, and requirements for earning the degree are intensive. No more than 4-6 Master's candidates are accepted into the program each year, allowing for a high level of individualized attention. The program looks for candidates interested in developing their teaching, intellectual and, most important, creative or choreographic methods and skills. The dance department has 7 permanent faculty members recognized in modern, ballet, Afro-American and Latino dance, as well as a dance historian/critic, and a dance ethnographer. All highly successful in their respective careers, the faculty reflects the university's standards of excellence and selectivity. Stanford's undergraduate dance course offerings include a wide range of technique classes, which graduate students are also encouraged to take.

Sunny, upscale Palo Alto is an attractive, sophisticated academic cum high-tech-company community.

University of California–Irvine

For ballet, ethnic, jazz, modern dancers, choreographers Midway between Los Angeles and San Diego — Dance Dept., MAB 300, School of the Arts, Irvine, CA 92697 **Voice:** 714-824-7284 **Fax:** 714-824-4563 **E-mail:** oars@uci.edu **Web Site:** www.uci.edu/academic/ **Contact:** Alan Terricciano, Chair **Founded:** 1965 **Open:** Year-round **Admission:** Written application, audition, GRE, transcripts **Deadlines:** Jan. 15 **Cost:** $8,394 for state residents, $13,238 for non-residents **Financial Aid:** Loans; Scholarship; Fellowship; Stipend; Work/Study **Size-Attendees:** 160 **Size-Class:** 3-10 (studio) **Degree or Certification:** BA in Dance; BFAs in Choreography, Performance; MFA in Dance **Job Placement:** Yes

ONE OF THE LARGER dance programs in California, UCI boasts an impressive faculty who seem to be the driving force behind the program's success. Of course, the teaching artists who gravitate towards the program do so largely because of the openness of its department heads and the high caliber of its students. Donald McKayle, David Allan and Alan Terricciano are 3 stellar faculty members.

McKayle is a 5-time Tony Award nominee whose classic choreographic works include *Rainbow 'round My Shoulder, Games,* and *Songs of the Disin-*

herited. He is busy penning a biography, *I Will Dance With You.* Allan is a renowned ballet choreographer and from 1997 to 1988 was soloist dancer for the National Ballet of Canada. Terricciano is an award-winning composer whose most recent work, *The Seven Deadly Sins,* featured original scores for 7 different choreographers, including McKayle. Other noteworthy events in dance at UCI include McKayle's 14-member Etude ensemble being selected to perform at the prestigious Black Dance Conference in Durham, North Carolina. Adding to the school's resources, philanthropist John Herklotz pledged $100,000 to establish the Dorathi Bock Pierre Program for Ballet Studies.

The dance department is also composed of 12 part-time faculty members, including former dancers with the Joffrey, Eliot Feld and Frankfurt ballet companies. Multiple levels of ballet, modern, jazz, tap and Spanish dance are offered. Additional courses, such as ballroom dance and a selection of world dance forms, vary from year to year depending on faculty. In the past, hula, African and Aztec dance have been available. The MFA program welcomes former professional dancers who are looking for a career transition. Former company members of Martha Graham, Les Grands Ballets Canadiens, Joyce Trisler, Philadanco and Ballet Theatre of Boston have enrolled in the graduate program. The program formally states that it does not impose a "UCI" style on its dancers but rather supports individuality. (Not such an obvious comment, since many academic programs do tend to promote one particular style, to the detriment of dancers who don't fit the mold.) Other advantages include the facility's proximity to the Orange County Performing Arts Center and the Irvine Barclay Theatre (on campus), which present such companies as the Kirov Ballet, the Royal Danish Ballet, Merce Cunningham, Alvin Ailey and David Parsons. The campus is 5 miles from beautiful Newport Beach.

University of California– Los Angeles

For ballet, ethnic, jazz, modern, tap dancers, choreographers Dept. of World Arts and Cultures, 124 Dance Building, Box 951608, Los Angeles, CA 90095 **Voice:** 310-825-8537 **Fax:** 310-825-7507 **E-mail:** wtemple@arts.ucla.edu **Web Site:** www.arts.ucla.edu **Contact:** Christopher Waterman, Dept. Chair **Founded:** 1907 **Open:** Year-round **Admission:** Written application, audition, transcripts **Deadlines:** Nov. 30 **Cost:** $5,000 per year for residents, $15,000 per year for nonresidents **Financial Aid:** Loans; Scholarship; Fellowship; Stipend; Work/Study **Size-Attendees:** 100-300 **Size-Class:** 10-30 **Degree or Certification:** BA in Dance; MA in Dance, Dance Movement Therapy; MFA in Dance **Job Placement:** Yes

THE MOTTO OF UCLA's School of Arts and Architecture declares that "Here you will be challenged to create, recreate, and research the artwork that will lead us into the 21st century: 'to push into a forest where there is no guide. To risk. To stand right out on the edge'." Whether or not one is inclined toward such an ambitious accomplishment, the university's department of World Arts and Cultures is definitely worth a look. The program is designed to meet the needs of anyone interested in dance from an ethnographic or global standpoint. Because it is also supported by one of the country's largest institutions, the resources of the program are vast. For example, the dance building houses 4 studios, a costume shop, a computer laboratory, classrooms and 2 studio-theaters. Performances are presented in 1 of 3 professional theaters ranging in size from 250 to 1,800 seats. The University Research Library houses the largest collection of dance literature on the West Coast; the Powell Library houses a dance videotape collection; and the Music Library houses 45,000 disc and tape recordings, 60,000 books and 75,000 volumes of scores.

The curriculum for the program ranges from traditional academia to the exploration of nontraditional dance styles from around the globe (Africa, Latin America, Asia and Europe). Special emphasis is placed upon body-conditioning techniques and movement analysis, such as Laban, anatomy, kinesiology, Feldenkrais, Bartenieff and Pilates. Innovative courses in multimedia, performance art, music, lighting and costume design complete the coursework. The obligatory guest-artist residencies also figure prominently in the department's schedule of activities.

Innovative dancemakers and scholars constitute the faculty list. Victoria Marks, formerly of London Contemporary Dance School and celebrated in her own right as a cutting-edge choreographer, is an assistant professor. David Rousseve, who heads his own successful dance company, was a visiting professor in 1998. Permanent members Judy Mitoma, whose specialty is Asian and Pacific Island cultures, and Colin Quigley, who specializes in interdisciplinary studies among dance ethnology, ethnomusicology and folklore, are among the 13 faculty members. The Department of World Arts and Cultures is relatively new, founded in the fall of 1995. Before its establishment, the department ran a well-respected traditional dance program, which was integrated into the current program. Opportunities are abundant for study abroad, either to complete fieldwork associated with a Master's thesis, or on scholarship, which is widely available. The UCLA Dance Company, composed of faculty and students, presents professional productions on campus and at venues in the community.

University of California–Riverside

For dance history scholars, choreographers *E of greater Los Angeles — Dept. of Dance, 1124 Sproul Hall, Riverside, CA 92521* **Voice:** 909-787-5424 **Fax:** 909-787-5461 **E-mail:** fred.strickler@ucr.edu **Web Site:** www.ucr.edu/CHSS/depts/dance/Dancehome.html **Contact:** Fred Strickler, Chair **Open:** Year-round **Admission:** Written application, GRE, essays, interview **Deadlines:** Jan. 14 for fall term **Cost:** $9,500 for residents, $18,800 for nonresidents **Financial Aid:** Loans; Scholarship; Fellowship; Stipend; Work/Study **Size-Attendees:** 25-27 **Size-Class:** 8-20 **Degree or Certification:** BA in Dance, PhD in Dance History and Theory **Job Placement:** Yes

OFFERING ONE OF THE few PhD programs in dance in the United States, this specialized program provides students with the opportunity to engage in original research at an advanced level in the emerging fields of cultural and historical studies of dance. Prerequisites for the program include a working knowledge of movement, an acquaintance with some system of movement observation and analysis, and preparation in general historical and cultural studies. For those who want to approach dance from the scholarly angle, Riverside provides all the resources you could desire, plus a few more probably not even imagined by the incoming student.

The sky is really the limit at UCR. The range of courses and research projects can incorporate dance aesthetics, body politics, gender, ethnic and class considerations, bodily learning and composition, and relationships between dance and contemporary culture. The UCR dance faculty draws from a variety of academic and creative backgrounds, including choreography, history, media studies, comparative literature, anthropology, political science, dramaturgy, architecture and cultural studies. Examples themselves of the diverse choices one has as a dance scholar here, faculty interests range from the obvious to the bizarre, such as "postcolonial identity formations" and "critical reappropriation of Marxist, feminist and postculturalist theories for the study of representation and performances of subaltern moving bodies"! Riverside is part of the ever-growing metro Los Angeles with its own big-city look and feel.

Colorado

Academy of Colorado Ballet

For ballet, modern dancers, choreographers *Central Colorado, facing the front wall of the Rockies — 1278 Lincoln St., Denver, CO 80203* **Voice:** 303-837-8888 **Fax:** 303-861-7174 **Web Site:** www.coloradoballet.org **Contact:** Martin Fredmann, Artistic Dir. **Founded:** 1951 **Open:** Year-round **Admission:** Audition **Deadlines:** August 14 **Cost:** From $166 per semester or $35 per month, $950 for 4-week summer program or $300 per week **Financial Aid:** Scholarship; Work/Study **Size-Attendees:** 195 **Size-Class:** 15-18

AFTER DANCEASPEN went belly-up, the Colorado Ballet in Denver assumed the leading role as the mountain state's best training ground for students of ballet. Offering a rigorous schedule of classes, the academy provides all the necessary fundamentals of a proper ballet education.

The 46-year-old academy is the official school of the Colorado Ballet. The headquarters in Denver has 6 studios, with an additional space in Littleton. The staff are graduates from Russian, other European and U.S. ballet programs, and are well versed in teaching, performing and choreography. All students who wish to enroll in the preprofessional program must audition. The academy offers complete ballet training in the Russian tradition through a curriculum including technique, variations, historic dance, character, pointe, pas de deux and modern dance.

Mikhail Baryshnikov: Extending a Career

I was fortunate enough to be working at American Ballet Theatre (ABT) in the mid-1970s when Baryshnikov made his debut in *Giselle.* A quarter of a century later he electrified the press and audiences by presenting a brilliant program of modern dance solos in New York City and around the world. In the years since he first thrilled audiences with his superb ballet training and line in the old ballet masterpieces at ABT, Baryshnikov has come miles stylistically. He has danced at New York City Ballet, excelling in the Balanchine technique, and has performed the work of Twyla Tharp, some would say better than anyone else. In recent years he has fearlessly delved into the works of choreographers as diverse as Mark Morris and José Limón. His White Oak Dance Project has commissioned many of these works for "Misha" and his small ensemble. While Rudolf Nureyev late in his career danced in works of Martha Graham and José Limón, Misha has surpassed his predecessor as "world's greatest dancer" by reaching even further outward from his ballet roots. Baryshnikov continues to bring the same energy and joy to his dancing I saw so long ago, and I hope he will continue his artistic journey for many years to come.

—*Mark Jones*

Legendary Baryshnikov in José Limón's *Chaconne.*

Aspen Ballet

For ballet, ethnic, jazz, modern, tap dancers West-central Colorado skiing country — 110 E. Hallam St., Suite. 107, Aspen, CO 81611 **Voice:** 970-925-7175 **Fax:** 970-925-1127 **E-mail:** asebal@aol.com **Contact:** Eleanor Rouse, Gen. Mgr. **Founded:** 1990 **Open:** Year-round **Admission:** Open, with placement audition **Deadlines:** Rolling **Cost:** $10-$15 per class **Financial Aid:** Scholarship; Work/Study **Size-Attendees:** 240 **Size-Class:** 12

FORGET THE RIGORS of big-city centers, where the top companies and schools vie for domination. Aspen Ballet, a relative newcomer to the Colorado dance scene, combines the pastoral beauty of the Colorado landscape with the professionalism of any east- or west-coast center. The school is composed of transplanted professionals from around the country. Combining their talents, they have formed a rather unique institution that has instant clout.

The affiliated company is even younger than the school. It is the brainchild of former dancers Jean-Philippe Malaty and Tom Mossbrucker, both of whom have had successful careers, Mossbrucker as a principal dancer with the Joffrey Ballet for the last 17 years. The 2 have built a company of 10 dancers from around the country, including 2 from the school, performing outreach and light touring in the western region of the United States. The school is a year-round operation with a summer session that also attracts students from around the country. The permanent faculty of 5 is supplemented by another 2 during the summer, offering classes in body-conditioning using Pilates and Swiss Ball methods, ballet technique, variations, pointe, Spanish and jazz. During the fall and winter, the classes are pared down to include ballet, jazz and tap. The facility is located in 2 studios, one in the Red Brick Arts and Recreation Center in the west end of Aspen, easily reachable by bus, and the other at Colorado Mountain College, a little ways out of town but also on a bus line.

Cleo Parker Robinson Dance Ensemble

For ballet, ethnic, jazz, modern, tap dancers, choreographers Mountainous central Colorado — 119 Park Ave. W., Denver, CO 80205 **Voice:** 303-295-1759 **Fax:** 303-295-1328 **Contact:** Judy Lyons, School Admn. **Founded:** 1970 **Open:** Year-round **Admission:** Registration **Deadlines:** Rolling **Cost:** From $15 for 4 classes, one-time $5 registration fee **Financial Aid:** Scholarship; Work/Study **Size-Attendees:** 100-150 **Size-Class:** 5-25

ONE OF THIS COUNTRY'S premier black dance ensembles, the Cleo Parker Robinson Dance Ensemble began as a grassroots company. Now, almost 3 decades later, the ensemble exists as a multicultural, performing-arts institution with educational outreach as its cornerstone activity. The entire operation comprises a year-round school, an international summer dance institute, an arts-in-education project, an intervention program and a 300-seat theater.

Both the company and the school are housed in the Cleo Parker Robinson Dance Theatre, a renovated 24,000-square-foot, 3-level historic Shorter AME Church located in Denver's Five Points area. The school offers residencies, masterclasses and a full school curriculum. The classes are mostly taught by members of the professional company; guest teachers are brought in to teach masterclasses. The school offers 3 programs: ballet, modern, and jazz and tap. Also available are specialty classes, such as house dancing, performance improvisation, movement meditations, West African dance, Egyptian dance and collective rhythms of the drum. Classes are offered from 10 A.M. to 8 P.M., Monday through Saturday.

David Taylor Dance Theatre

 For ballet, jazz, modern dancers, choreographers About 20 min. S of central downtown Denver — 2539 W. Main St., Littleton, CO 80120 **Voice:** 303-797-6944 **Fax:** 303-794-5855 **Web Site:** www.artstozoo.org/dtdt **Contact:** David Taylor, Dir. **Founded:** 1979 **Open:** Year-round **Admission:** Written application, audition for summer intensive **Deadlines:** Rolling **Cost:** $10 per class **Financial Aid:** Scholarship; Work/Study **Size-Attendees:** 75-100 **Size-Class:** 10-20

W HAT KIM ROBARDS does for Colorado's modern dance community, David Taylor does for ballet. However, Taylor has a bit more competition, with such companies as the Colorado Ballet and Aspen Ballet filling Colorado's ballet niche. However, he is still a force to be reckoned with, as his tenure in the state, like that of Robards, dates back to the 1970s. He is without question a permanent fixture in the ballet community.

Although Taylor offers classes year-round, he really shines during the summer. A 4-week summer intensive is offered for intermediate/advanced dancers, although the option does exist to take single or weekly classes. The range of classes is quite impressive, running the gamut from ballet technique to jazz, variations and modern. Supplemental courses are available in dance history, repertory, choreography, musicality, foot care for pointe, stage makeup, nutrition and injury prevention. The faculty is impressive: guests such as Milton Myers, a master teacher in the Horton vocabulary, and James Clouser, a former dancer with the American Ballet Theatre, and the Royal Winnipeg Ballet, offer their expertise in their respective disciplines.

Kim Robards Dance

For ballet, jazz, modern, tap dancers, choreographers Mountainous central Colorado — 821 Acoma St., Suite. A-1, Denver, CO 80204 **Voice:** 303-825-4847 **Fax:** 303-825-4846 **E-mail:** kimrobards-dance@msn.com **Web Site:** www.kimro-bardsdance.org **Contact:** LaRana Skalicky, Asst. to Dir. **Founded:** 1990 **Open:** Year-round **Admission:** Written application, audition, registration fee **Deadlines:** Rolling **Cost:** $10 per class **Financial Aid:** Scholarship; Work/Study **Size-Attendees:** 100 **Size-Class:** 5-20

A FAMILIAR NAME IN the Colorado dance scene, Kim Robards operates one of the state's largest dance studios geared more towards the modern dancer than the ballet dancer. Robards has been Colorado-based for almost two decades, and is quickly becoming the state's strongest proponent for dance, dance education and performance. Earning a Master's degree in dance from the University of Colorado at Boulder, she had her early training in the Humphrey-Weidman technique, followed by Graham at the Graham School in NYC with Christine Dakin. In addition to her own school, Robards is also on the faculty at the Academy of Colorado Ballet.

Established in 1990, the school provides training in modern dance, ballet, tap and jazz for all ages, beginners through professionals. Workshops are also offered throughout the year, along with performance opportunities during year-end showings in conjunction with the Academy of Colorado Ballet and Robards's own affiliated dance company.

University of Colorado–Boulder

For modern, ballet dancers, choreographers 25 mi. north of Denver — Dance Div., Dept. of Theater and Dance, Box 261, Boulder, CO 80309 **Voice:** 303-492-7357 **E-mail:** thtrdnce@stripe.colorado.edu **Web Site:** www.colorado.edu **Contact:** Nada Diachenko, Dir. **Open:** Sept. to May **Admission:** Resume, critical writing sample, transcripts, audition, BA or BFA in Dance, GPA over 2.75 **Deadlines:** Feb. 1 for fall, no spring admission process **Financial Aid:** Loans; Scholarship; Fellowship; Stipend; Work/Study **Size-Attendees:** 12-50 **Size-Class:** 10-80 **Degree or Certification:** MFA in Dance, Certification in Pilar and Alexander techniques **Job Placement:** Yes

H ERE'S A STRONG DANCE program that over the years has attracted a steady stream of modern-dance luminaries to guest teach, work in residence and develop new works. The names include Jane Comfort, Liz Lerman, Mark Dendy, Ann Carlson, Meredith Monk and Chuck Davis. The program's MFA degree offers 2 areas of concentration: choreography/performance and body therapies. The body-therapies concentration is a unique aspect of this program, developed as a result of the 2 Boulder-based learning institutes: the Pilates Center and the Alexander Institute.

For those students who are interested in acquiring certification in either of the above therapies, a specially designed joint dance MFA and physical-therapy certification program is offered. However, before pursuing a body-therapies emphasis the student must be officially accepted into one of the 2 training programs. Also, because of the intensive nature of the joint program, students generally need to tack on an additional year or 2 to the standard 2-year MFA degree. Thankfully, since the joint program has been in the works for a while, advisors are able to guide and forewarn students interested in pursuing such a concentration. The school is located in the beautiful, cosmopolitan town of Boulder, north of Denver on the front range

of the Rockies. About 23,000 of the town's total population of 85,000 are students at the University of Colorado–Boulder.

Vail International Dance Festival

For ballet dancers, choreographers West of Denver, deep and high in the Rockies — P.O. Box 309, Vail, CO 81658 **Voice:** 970-949-1999 **Fax:** 970-949-9265 **Contact:** Katherine Kersten, Producing Dir. **Founded:** 1989 **Open:** Summer **Admission:** Written application, audition, photo **Cost:** $15 audition fee, $1,875 tuition **Financial Aid:** Scholarship; Work/Study **Size-Attendees:** 90 **Job Placement:** Yes

I N EXISTENCE SINCE 1989, the Vail International Dance Festival is a summer affair that has risen to the top of the heap. It is heavily sponsored by local money and illustrious figureheads, such as former president Gerald Ford, who serves as honorary director. The festival offers both the intermediate and advanced student a place to train and, most important, a place to network. How practical that can be for a dancer in the middle of Colorado is debatable, since most of the faculty members are predominantly of European and Russian stock. However, if you are looking to head east across the Atlantic, going west from New York to Vail might work in your favor.

The summer program, in partnership with the Bolshoi Ballet Academy, is an intensive and demanding course for the serious preprofessional student, trainee or company apprentice, ages 15-19. It is the only program of its kind on these shores that offers students the rigorous training of the famous Bloc Academy. A major emphasis of the program is on the challenges, both technical and artistic, that male dancers in particular face. For this reason, male and female dancers study in separate technique classes. Master teachers and artistic directors from dance companies are regularly featured guests, along with the Bolshoi faculty. In 1998, masterclasses with

Mme. Claude Bessy, director of the Paris Opera Ballet School, were offered along with guest artists Serge Golovine of the Paris Opera and Pytor Pestov of Stuttgart. At every opportunity students are brought in contact with mentors who can advise about professional aspirations. Conferences between the young dancers and artistic directors who are interested in discussing trainee or apprentice positions with their respective companies are a standard feature.

Courses cover classical technique (including pointe), men's class, repertoire, variations, partnering, Russian culture and history lectures and nutrition workshops. Faculty includes such dancers as Michael Ho, soloist with the London Festival Ballet, and Denise Schultze, ballet mistress for Ballet West, faculty member for the National Ballet School of Canada and director of the Royal Ballet School in London. A special teacher's-training course is also offered over a 5-day period during the workshop. The conference attracts ballet teachers and administrators from the United States and abroad who are interested in networking, discussing dance-related topics and attending seminars on the field.

Connecticut

Connecticut Ballet Center

For ballet, ethnic, jazz, tap dancers
Coastal Connecticut, convenient to New York City — 20 Acosta St., Stamford, CT 06902
Voice: 203-978-0771 **Fax:** 203-961-1928
Contact: Brett Raphael, Artistic Dir.
Founded: 1994 **Open:** Year-round **Admission:** Open **Deadlines:** Rolling **Cost:** $100 for 10 classes **Financial Aid:** Scholarship; Work/Study **Size-Attendees:** 150 **Size-Class:** 15-25

AN OFFSHOOT OF the Connecticut Ballet Company rather than an independent entity, the Connecticut Ballet Center offers a light schedule, with artistic director Brett Raphael leading most of the ballet classes. Although offerings might be slim, the program includes all the necessary training for a versatile dancer: pointe, jazz, creative movement, tap, character and flamenco.

Students perform at the Vail International Dance Festival, Vail.

Connecticut College

For ballet, ethnic, jazz, modern dancers, choreographers *E coastal Connecticut — 270 Mohegan Ave., New London, CT 06320* **Voice:** 860-439-2830 **Fax:** 860-439-5365 **E-mail:** lhwan@ conncoll.edu **Web Site:** www.camel. conncoll.edu **Contact:** Lan-Lan Wang, Dept. Chair **Founded:** 1948 **Open:** Year-round **Admission:** Written application, audition, transcripts, interview **Deadlines:** June 15 for summer festival, deadlines for each semester vary **Cost:** $1,500 for summer festival **Financial Aid:** Loans; Scholarship; Fellowship; Stipend; Work/Study **Size-Attendees:** 100-150 **Size-Class:** 10-25 **Degree or Certification:** BA in Dance **Job Placement:** Yes

BENEFITING FROM ITS close proximity to Manhattan, Connecticut College offers its students a program that is made up of working professionals from the city, who come in either to teach masterclasses, to lecture or to choreograph on the students. While the college might no longer be a leader in modern-dance activity, it does retain the cachet of having been a guiding force in the development of the art form when the American Dance Festival moved from Bennington, Vermont, to the Connecticut College campus in 1948. Martha Myers, dean of the American Dance Festival, designed the dance major in 1971 to enable young people interested in performance, choreography and teaching to develop a foundation of knowledge in dance within a liberal-arts environment. The college still embodies the same visionary spirit that put it on the map 5 decades ago.

Today the college hosts an international dance festival that attracts not only performers from around the globe, but also audiences and participants from across the United States. The festival is an eclectic mix of ballet, modern and ethnic, including styles like Tibetan/Mongolian dance, West African dance, ballet and tai chi. Artists, such as Joy Kellman and Liz Lerman, teach week-long workshops, and students can participate in choreographic residencies with artists from around the world. For 1998, Ying Hou from China, Natalya Lewtchenko from Russia and Alden Lugnasin from the Philippines created works on the students in their native styles. The dance department actively encourages its students to participate in international dance festivals and workshops, and to study at dance institutions abroad. The dance major consists of 4 full-time faculty and includes choreographer Dan Wagoner, dancer George de la Pena and a host of guest artists, part-time faculty and visiting lecturers, including such names as Sara Rudner, Mark Dendy, Ron Brown and David Dorfman. Guest speakers in recent years have included Trisha Brown, Jennifer Tipton (lighting), Yvonne Rainer and Bebe Miller. The program emphasizes 2 areas of study: performance and choreography, and dance studies.

Hartford Conservatory

For ballet, ethnic, jazz, modern, tap dancers, choreographers *Central Connecticut, midway between Boston and New York City — 834 Asylum Ave., Hartford, CT 06105* **Voice:** 860-246-2588 **Fax:** 860-249-6330 **E-mail:** hartfordconservatory@ snetnet.com **Web Site:** www.hartford conservatory.org **Contact:** Brenda Dranoff-Lopez, School Dir. **Founded:** 1890 **Open:** Year-round **Admission:** Written application, audition **Deadlines:** Rolling **Cost:** $20 registration fee, $150 for 10 classes **Financial Aid:** Scholarship; Work/Study **Size-Attendees:** 100-200 **Size-Class:** 10-25

THIS WELL-KNOWN community arts school offers dance and music in the heart of Hartford, convenient to public transportation and parking. In existence since 1890, the school has a well-defined program that for many dancers was their first taste of the dance studio. Besides weekly classes, a summer dance-intensive program is offered for teens and young adults along with a teacher-training program for dance professionals. Classes include introduction to dance technique, ballet, modern/jazz, tap and hip-hop. Students also have an opportunity to perform for parents and friends during the formal, end-of-term recital.

Nutmeg Conservatory for the Arts

For ballet dancers, choreographers NW Connecticut, 30 min. W of Hartford — 21 Water St., Torrington, CT 06700 **Voice:** 860-482-4413 **Fax:** 860-482-7614 **E-mail:** info@nutmegballet.org **Web Site:** www.nutmegballet.org **Contact:** Sharon Dante, Exec. Dir. **Founded:** 1970 **Open:** Year-round **Admission:** Written application, audition (video acceptable) **Deadlines:** Rolling **Cost:** $25 application fee **Financial Aid:** Scholarship; Work/Study **Size-Attendees:** 65-100 **Size-Class:** 10-30 **Job Placement:** Yes

A SUPERIOR, PREPROFESSIONAL training program offering extensive educational and performance opportunities is the Nutmeg Conservatory for the Arts, named for its home state's nickname. Following in the tradition of some of the larger New York conservatories, Nutmeg has already established an impressive track record, with many of its alums graduating into the top ballet companies both here and abroad. Lest you think this school is out of the loop as far as location is concerned, it does have the advantage of being close to such well-known cultural hot spots as Tanglewood, Jacob's Pillow, Yale Summer School of Music and Art (at Norfolk) and the Saratoga Performing Arts Center.

Nutmeg Ballet was founded in 1970 by Sharon Dante, a young ballet student who studied in Torrington, Connecticut, and later danced professionally with the nearby Hartford Ballet. Dante returned to her hometown determined to provide the community with its own school of ballet. In 1984 the school was put on the map when Nutmeg principal dancer Victoria Mazzarelli won the only gold medal at the first New York International Ballet Competition at City Center. Today both the school and the company continue to ride the momentum built over the last 15 years. The company maintains a year-round performance schedule at its 1,700-seat art-deco-style Warner Theater in Torrington, and at the Centennial Theater at Westminster School in Simsbury.

Students have the opportunity to appear in full-length productions, such as *Nutcracker, Coppelia, Cinderella, Sleeping Beauty* and other classics. The curriculum is based on the Vaganova syllabus. Serious dance students can audition each year for entrance into the preprofessional training programs. Talented high-school juniors and seniors can complete their secondary education by taking up residence in Torrington while pursuing this intensive dance apprenticeship. Cooperative educational liaisons are fostered with the University of Connecticut, Northwestern Connecticut Community College, area high schools and the local YMCA. Dance-related subjects, such as drama, mime, character dance, stage combat, stage makeup, nutrition and music theory are offered in workshops throughout the academic semester. Private lessons with the Nutmeg Conservatory music department are also encouraged, with instruction in piano, ballet accompaniment, voice, woodwind and string instruments available for a separate fee.

The conservatory also runs an intensive summer training program from early July to mid-August, with a specialized coaching week (by invitation only), immediately following the summer program. Former Nutmeg students now work with such companies as the Zurich Ballet, the Hartford Ballet, Ballet West, Joffrey Ballet and American Ballet Theatre.

School of Dance Connecticut

 For ballet dancers, choreographers Central Connecticut, midway between Boston and New York City — 226 Farmington Ave., Hartford, CT 06105 **Voice:** 860-525-9396 **Fax:** 860-249-8116 **Web Site:** www. arts-online.com/hfballet.htm **Contact:** Enid Lynn, Dir. **Open:** Year-round **Admission:** Written application, audition, interview, transcripts **Deadlines:** Early Sept. for fall semester **Financial Aid:** Loans; Scholarship; Fellowship; Stipend; Work/Study **Size-Attendees:** 800 **Degree or Certification:** BFAs in Dance Performance, Dance Education **Job Placement:** Yes

WITH MORE THAN 800 students and 110 classes per week together with a university-level BFA program, the School of Dance Connecticut (formerly the Hartford Ballet) ranks among the most respected institutions in classical ballet. The BFA program, produced in association with the Hartt School at the University of Hartford, was named one of the top 15 dance programs in the United States by the *College Guide of Performing Arts Majors* and one of the top 9 professional studio schools in the United States and Canada by *Dance Teacher Now*.

The BFA program offers emphases in either performance or teaching. The performance program is intended as preparation for a professional performing career and includes classical ballet, Martha Graham technique, repertory and production. The teaching program prepares professional educators to teach in universities and private studios and schools of dance. The program also supports professional dancers who wish to make the transition from a performing career to a teaching career.

The faculty includes many notable figures in the world of ballet and modern dance, among them Maria Youskevitch, former soloist with the American Ballet Theatre and former faculty member at the Alvin Ailey School and Interlochen Arts Academy; and Monica Levy, the award-winning choreographer who has created works for many of the major ballet companies in America.

The school's intensive summer program is offered in a pair of 3-week segments, in 12 locations across the country. Auditions are required.

JENNIFER W. LESTER

Melissa Wishinski, School of Dance Connecticut.

Trinity College

For modern, ballet dancers, choreographers Central Connecticut, midway between Boston and New York City — Theater and Dance Dept. 300 Summit St., Hartford, CT 06106 **Voice:** 860-297-2330 **Fax:** 860-297-5380 **E-mail:** dworin@trincoll.edu **Web Site:** www.trincoll.edu **Contact:** Judy Dworin, Dance Dept. Chair **Founded:** 1918 **Open:** Year-round **Admission:** Written application, audition **Cost:** $28,970, includes room, board, other fees **Financial Aid:** Loans; Scholarship; Fellowship; Stipend; Work/Study **Size-Attendees:** 50-100 **Size-Class:** 5-25 **Degree or Certification:** BA in Dance **Job Placement:** Yes

TRINITY HAS EARNED A reputation for attracting a certain type of female student who would fit in at any one of the Seven Sister colleges but instead found herself on a beautiful, 100-acre campus in the equally blue-blood domain of Hartford, Connecticut. Ill-founded stereotypes aside, Trinity offers a fine curriculum that emphasizes individuality, exploration and serious thought. The program is a

The Princess Grace Foundation: A Legacy in Motion

During her lifetime, Princess Grace of Monaco—former American actress, Grace Kelly—was deeply committed to helping aspiring young artists. Following her death in 1982, the Princess Grace Foundation-USA was created to awards scholarships, apprenticeships and fellowships to young professionals. A national program, supporting U.S. residents, the focus is on emerging artists in theater, dance and film.

In a certain sense the Princess Grace Foundation is a counterpoint to flashy ballet competitions, such as the one in Jackson, Michigan, which tend to reward technical bravura. The foundation provides scholarships for dancers completing their academic training and fellowships for young professionals. Two recent Princess Grace fellows are Melissa Wishinski, now with the Royal Ballet, and Bradon McDonald, who joined the Limón Dance Company.

Wishinski, age 17, was born in Boston and joined the Hartford Ballet (now Dance Connecticut) in the 1997-98 season after a 2-year apprenticeship. She attended the Chautauqua Institute summer dance program and began attending the School of the Hartford Ballet in 1994. Among her other awards are the 1997 Prix de Lausanne Premier Prix Espèces and the bronze medal in the junior division of the USA International Ballet Competition — in Jackson, Michigan.

McDonald hails from Lowville, New York, a rural, upstate community where he received tap-dancing lessons beginning at the age of 5. From there, McDonald moved on to the Juilliard School, graduating in 1997, having performed brilliantly in both ballets and in modern-dance repertoire. McDonald has danced and choreographed for the Ballet Metropolitano de Caracas, the Brown University Dance Ensemble and the Juilliard Dance Ensemble. He was a scholarship student at the New York State Summer School of the Arts and the Alvin Ailey School. In his final year at Juilliard, McDonald received a Presidential Scholarship from the Art Recognition and Talent Search. Since joining Limón, McDonald has become a featured dancer in the company's masterworks and in new works commissioned by Limón.

By establishing the foundation and its focus on young artists, Princess Grace's executors are making an enduring contribution to the continued vitality of American dance.

combination of theater and dance in the truest sense: students have to divide their classes equally between the two disciplines.

The program focuses more on performance than on any one, specific discipline. As a result, projects arise out of student interest in exploring the connections between performance and other fields of study. For example, a student studying religion might investigate sacred forms of dance or a student interested in Irish history might write and direct his or her own play about contemporary Irish politics. For the dancer, the creative challenges are numerous and varied. Students exploring movement throughout the semester can develop a final group project involving the entire class in a performance piece that can speak to such issues as gender or the environment. Also in the spirit of collaboration, dancers can choreograph a project that includes spoken text or a narrative line, and actors can expand their performance skills by studying various movement techniques. While the dance program at Trinity emphasizes modern dance, opportunities exist for students to explore their interest in classical ballet both on and off the campus. Classes in intermediate and advanced ballet are offered at Trinity. And the nearby Dance Connecticut offers internships and classes in which Trinity students can also participate.

One of the strongest programs offered at the college is its internship program, especially the Trinity/La MaMa New York City Performing Arts Program. Based at La MaMa, world-famous center for interdisciplinary study and innovation, the program takes place during the fall semester, and includes professional training, internships with major theater and dance companies and seminars. Students also attend 2 to 3 concerts each week and meet a wide range of directors, choreographers and performance artists. La MaMa also sponsors a similar program abroad, in which students travel to selected sites throughout the world to research indigenous theater and dance forms. The dance/theater program boasts 17 faculty members and a student-to-teacher ratio of 10:1.

Delaware

Central Delaware Dance Academy

For ballet, jazz, tap dancers, choreographers, Central Delaware, just S of Dover — 177 Old Camden Rd., Camden, DE 19934 **Voice:** 302-697-2218 **Contact:** Daniel Kaiser, Dir. **Founded:** 1968 **Open:** Year-round **Admission:** Open, placement audition **Deadlines:** Rolling **Cost:** $15 registration fee, $12 per class, $97 unlimited classes per month **Financial Aid:** Scholarship; Work/Study **Size-Attendees:** 150

WHILE THIS ACADEMY has undergone many incarnations in the past 3 decades, its current position as the school affiliated with the Delaware Ballet renders it the premier training center in the state.

This is largely thanks to director Daniel Kaiser, who assumed control of the school in the early 1990s. Coming from a family of dance professionals, Kaiser himself enjoyed a career with the Pennsylvania Ballet. Members from the Delaware Ballet regularly attend the intermediate/advanced classes he teaches. Junior-level divisions are overseen by Diane Drulis, who also runs the tap department. The facility houses 3 studios, dedicated with equal emphasis to ballet, tap and jazz.

District of Columbia

American University

For ballet, ethnic, jazz, modern, tap dancers, choreographers Dept. of Performing Arts, 4400 Massachusetts Ave., NW, Washington, DC 20016 **Voice:** 202-885-3424 **Fax:** 202-885-1092 **E-mail:** afa@american.edu **Web Site:** www.american.edu **Contact:** Naima Prevots, Dir. of Dance **Founded:** 1973 **Open:** Year-round **Admission:** Written application, audition, resume, GPA over 3.00 **Deadlines:** Rolling **Cost:** $19,178 annually for tuition **Financial Aid:** Loans; Scholarship; Fellowship; Stipend; Work/Study **Size-Attendees:** 35 grad students, 15-20 undergrad dance minors **Size-Class:** 17-20 **Degree or Certification:** MAs in Dance, Arts Management; Graduation Certificate in Dance and Health Fitness Management **Job Placement:** Yes

THE DANCE DEPARTMENT at this noted university offers students with a more unconventional background a place to explore their interest in dance. The dance program differs from those at most other universities in that it is more flexible and encourages students with degrees in different disciplines to apply. The program is tailored to individual needs and strengths, enabling students to be exposed to new ideas while pursuing their specialization in depth. Students can take courses in arts management, music and theater, as well as in anthropology, literature, psychology and many other disciplines.

The department's reputable artist-in-residence program includes the likes of Doug Elkins, Laura Dean, Twyla Tharp and Meredith Monk. Graduate students are encouraged to choreograph and perform original pieces. The broad curriculum offers courses in history, criticism, principles of movement (including Feldenkrais, Alexander and Bartenieff), repertory, modern, jazz, tap, African and ballet. Students can obtain internships in the district with such leading arts organizations as the National Theater, the John F. Kennedy Center for the Performing Arts, the Corcoran Gallery and Wolf Trap. The facility is located in a residential area 10-20 minutes from some of the nation's great cultural institutions, including the Smithsonian, the National Endowment for the Arts and the Washington Ballet.

Washington School of Ballet

For ballet, ethnic, jazz, modern dancers, choreographers 3515 Wisconsin Ave. NW, Washington, DC 20016 **Voice:** 202-362-1683 **Fax:** 202-362-1311 **E-mail:** wballet@washingtonballet.org **Web Site:** www.washingtonballet.org **Contact:** Septima Weber, Dir. **Founded:** 1944 **Open:** Year-round **Admission:** Written application, audition **Deadlines:** Rolling **Cost:** From $1,050 for 5 weeks of 15 classes **Financial Aid:** Scholarship; Work/Study **Size-Attendees:** 400

COFOUNDED BY Mary Day, the powerhouse former director of the school and its affiliated company, the Washington School of Ballet has gained recognition as a first-rate training ground for young professionals. It also supports one of the better regional dance companies in this country. Septima Weber, the current director, continues the 50-year tradition of excellence, with the support of

associate director Rex Bickmore.

For serious young dancers the school offers a time-release program by arrangement with the students' respective high schools; auditions are required and classes run from September through mid-June. The school also runs an open-class program for adults and an intensive, 5-week summer program. The curriculum includes classes in ballet, pointe, modern, jazz, variations and repertory. Advanced students have performance opportunities through the Washington Ballet's outreach activities. The school now boasts 5 studios; 2 of them, recently constructed in a new wing, have wonderful natural light. The young dancers have the opportunity to perform ballets by Marius Petipa, Michel Fokine and Choo San Goh, as well as new works commissioned specifically for the troupe. Alums of the school, attesting to its superior training, include such luminaries as American Ballet Theatre's artistic director Kevin McKenzie, Dance Theater of Harlem's Virginia Johnson and ABT principal Amanda McKerrow.

Located in Washington's beautiful Cleveland Park area, the school is 5 blocks north of the National Cathedral and convenient to public transportation.

Florida

Academy of Ballet Florida

👣 *For ballet, jazz, modern, tap dancers, choreographers* Atlantic coastal Florida — 500 Fern St., West Palm Beach, FL 33401 **Voice:** 561-659-1212 **Fax:** 561-659-2222 **Web Site:** www.balletflorida.com **Contact:** Marie Hale, Artistic Dir. **Founded:** 1973 **Open:** Year-round **Admission:** Written application, placement audition **Deadlines:** Rolling **Cost:** $72 for 10 classes **Financial Aid:** Scholarship; Work/Study

THE ORIGINS OF THIS well-respected company and training facility date back to 1973, when it was co-founded by Marie Hale and Lynda Swiadon, now, respectively, its artistic director and its company manager. From fairly humble beginnings, the academy has expanded to offer classes throughout the year, Monday through Saturday, in a variety of techniques, including ballet, modern, jazz and tap. More than 100 of its students have gone on to professional careers in dance, with such companies as the American Ballet Theatre, the Stuttgart Ballet, the Houston Ballet and Paul Taylor.

The emphasis here is on classical training, with a strong preprofessional program for those seriously considering a career in dance. For those who are not, the academy has an open adult program offering not only the above techniques, but also conditioning classes, such as aerobics, step and exercise. The faculty, which consists of more than 15 instructors, includes Claudia Cravey, formerly of the Washington Ballet and the Harkness Ballet, as well as current members of the company. Students benefit from the close association and performance opportunities with a professional regional company.

Florida State University–Tallahassee

🏠 *For ballet, modern dancers, choreographers* Florida panhandle, 40 mi. N of the Gulf of Mexico — Graduate Admissions A2500 UCAMontgomery Jym, Tallahassee, FL 32306-2400 **Voice:** 850-644-3420; 850-644-3500 **Fax:** 850-644-0197 **E-mail:** gradasms@admin.fsu.edu **Web Site:** www.fsu.edu **Contact:** Elizabeth W. Patenaude, Dept. Chair **Founded:** 1960 **Open:** Year-round **Admission:** Written application, audition, GRE, transcripts **Deadlines:** Rolling, auditions in Jan., Apr., Nov.; to qualify for financial aid students must apply by early Jan. for fall term **Cost:** $3,145 per term for 12-hour graduate enrollment for state residents, $10,475 for nonresidents **Financial Aid:** Loans; Scholarship; Fellowship; Stipend; Work/Study **Size-Attendees:** 100-250 **Size-Class:** 10-15 **Degree or Certification:** BFA in Dance, MFA in Dance **Job Placement:** Yes

THIS UNIVERSITY can back up its claim of having "one of the country's outstanding professional dance programs." Offering both a BFA and an MFA degree program, the department—by its mere size—has just about everything a student could want or envision. With a faculty numbering 17, and additional artists in residence and guest teachers, the program is one of the largest in the country. Bigger alone is not necessarily better: the credentials are equally impressive. Faculty members have enjoyed careers spanning the classical to the modern idioms with companies the likes of Dance Theatre of Harlem, the San Francisco Ballet, Bella Lewitzky, the Royal Ballet and the Martha Graham Company. Choreographer Jawole Willa Jo Zollar, an alumna of the university, is artist in residence.

Part of the dance department's mission is to serve as a repertory center, focusing both on the reconstruction and production of established dance masterworks and on the development of new and original dance repertory. As a result, the list of repertory both commissioned and acquired reads like a "who's who" of dance: Doris Humphrey, Antony Tudor, Anna Sokolow, Donald McKayle,

George Balanchine, José Limón, Charles Weidman, Alwin Nikolais, Martha Graham, Ted Shawn, Violette Verdy, Lar Lubovitch, Hanya Holm and Shapiro and Smith. The companies and institutions that its students have gone on to dance with and teach at are equally extensive and impressive. The governing vision of the dance department—whose story spans 60 years—is one of a "conservatory within the university." The graduate program emphasizes individualized study, with an appraisal of students' undergraduate background and previous work, identifying and remedying any deficiencies in training. Graduate study comprises dance technique, a seminar in dance history and research and a written and oral dissertation. The program is rather rigorous, but it offers the MFA student a significant degree of mentoring, support and flexibility.

FSU is within an easy drive of some of the world's most beautiful beaches. The climate permits year-round outdoor activity.

Students in performance at the Harid Conservatory, Boca Raton.

Harid Conservatory

🏠 *For ballet dancers, choreographers* Florida's Gold Coast, midway between Fort Lauderdale and West Palm Beach — 2285 Potomac Rd., Boca Raton, FL 33431 **Voice:** 561-997-2677 **Fax:** 561-997-8920 **Contact:** Gordon Wright, Dir. **Founded:** 1987 **Open:** Year-round **Admission:** Written application, audition, academic excellence **Deadlines:** Rolling **Cost:** $7,650 for regular school year, $1,575 for summer program **Financial Aid:** Scholarship; Work/Study **Size-Attendees:** 250 **Size-Class:** 15-25 **Degree or Certification:** HS Diploma and Cert. of Completion **Job Placement:** Yes

O N A PAR WITH Interlochen and Walnut Hill, the Harid Conservatory offers serious preprofessionals the opportunity to train with the best while at the same time keeping up with an academic program. The 4-year program combines ballet training with high-school coursework. This enables students not only to graduate into the top companies in the country, but to do it with a high-school diploma,

a tricky maneuver for a young ballet dancer. In addition, students receive a full scholarship with their acceptance for the regular academic year. The scholarship covers the costs of academic, dance and other classes; selected cultural and educational field trips; and transportation related to those activities. Room, board, dance clothing and other supplies are charged to students, although limited financial scholarship aid is available for those costs also.

Established in 1987, the conservatory provides high-quality, professional training for gifted young dancers and musicians. An audition is required for admission to this international program. The curriculum includes ballet and related dance courses, the fundamentals of music, dance, music and art history; nutrition, physiology and conditioning, career-related seminars; and dance performance. Each year, Harid invites a number of internationally recognized guest teachers, choreographers and artistic directors to visit the conservatory and work with the students. Artists, such as Claude Bessy, Fernando Bujones, Lou Conte, Helgi Tomasson and Ben Stevenson, have taught masterclasses here. And the faculty has a long list of impressive credentials, including stints with the Paris Opera Ballet, the Kirov and the Royal Winnipeg Ballet.

The school has trained a Princess Grace Awardee, and can list several students now dancing with the Boston Ballet, the New York City Ballet, the American Ballet Theatre, Pacific Northwest, the Miami City Ballet, and the Pennsylvania Ballet. The transition to such companies is not surprising since students are well versed in both contemporary and classic ballets upon graduation. The dance division's repertoire has included choreography by such masters as Hans van Manen and George Balanchine, as well as such ballet standards as *Le Corsaire, Grand Pas de Deux, Giselle, Sleeping Beauty* and *Swan Lake.* The facilities are themselves are impressive, too: 3 large studios in a facility that is 12,300 square feet with 22-foot-high ceilings, natural light, 10-foot mirrors and a special dance surface.

Miami City Ballet School

For ballet dancers, choreographers *Just N of Miami, at the southeastern tip of Florida* — 905 Lincoln Rd., Miami Beach, FL 33139 **Voice:** 305-532-4880 **Fax:** 305-532-2726 **E-mail:** school@ miamicityballet.org **Web Site:** www.miamicityballet.org **Contact:** Edward Villella, Dir. **Founded:** 1993 **Open:** Year-round **Admission:** Written application, audition **Deadlines:** Rolling **Cost:** $300-$2,096 for Sept. to June program, $150-$750 for summer session (fees vary according to level) **Financial Aid:** Scholarship; Work/Study **Size-Attendees:** 350 **Size-Class:** 15

THE FACT THAT THIS young program is styled after Balanchine's School of American Ballet should come as no surprise since New York City Ballet star Edward Villella heads

the organization. An outgrowth of the Miami City Ballet—widely recognized as one of the country's most successful regional companies—the school owes much of its success to Villella and his ties to NYCB. Since this is one of the few regional ballet companies that has licensed an extensive number of Balanchine works, Villella has no problem filling his programs with first-rate repertoire. But the company has grown into more than merely a NYCB offshoot during its 2 decades of existence, acquiring a distinctly Miami-based flavor and reflecting the Latin culture of Miami. One can only assume the school will follow in its parent's footsteps.

The school was founded in January, 1993, in order to provide a professional program for the serious ballet student. Students have the opportunity to flex their performance muscles with a year-end showcase featuring Balanchine classics, such as *Raymonda Variations* and *Tarantella,* and new works by company members. Advanced students also have the opportunity to perform with company members in outreach programs in the tri-county area. Selected final-year students might be invited to learn some of the repertory for the season and participate in Miami City Ballet performances. This helps to facilitate the transition from student to professional. The student division accepts students by audition only, placing them in 1 of 7 divisions according to age, experience and ability. The program includes classes in technique, pointe, partnering and variations. For the serious student considering a career in ballet, the practical dictates of education are addressed by means of the school's affiliation with nearby Miami Beach High School, which gives credit for ballet as an elective course. For its part, Miami City Ballet School schedules many of its professional classes after academic-school class hours.

The ballet school is invitingly located 3 blocks from Miami City Ballet and close to spectacular beaches and exciting metropolitan Miami.

New World School of the Arts

For ballet, ethnic, jazz, modern, tap, dancers, choreographers 300 NE 2nd Ave., Miami, FL 33132 **Voice:** 305-237-3582 **Fax:** 305-237-3738 **E-mail:** dlewis@mdcc.edu **Contact:** Daniel Lewis, Dean of Dance **Founded:** 1987 **Open:** Year-round **Admission:** Written application, audition **Deadlines:** Rolling **Cost:** $1,200 per year for residents, $3,000 per year for nonresidents **Financial Aid:** Scholarship; Work/Study **Size-Class:** 17-20 **Degree or Certification:** BFA in Dance **Job Placement:** Yes

THIS HIGH SCHOOL OF the performing arts plus 4-year college of the arts is a cooperative venture of Florida International University, Miami-Dade Community College and Dade County Public Schools. It was established by the state of Florida in 1984 as a center for excellence in the arts. Chaired by Daniel Lewis, former assistant and protégé of José Limón and assistant director of the dance program at the Juilliard School in New York City, the program stresses performance and well-rounded preparation in all dance forms. The dance program is 1 of 4 divisions in the school, which is fast-paced and quickly growing.

In the 10 years since Lewis became dean of dance, the school has grown from 1 studio with 2 teachers and fewer than 40 students to a state-of-the-art facility with 4 spacious studios and more than 200 students. The school awarded its first BFA degree in 1992; since then graduates have joined the Alvin Ailey Company, Twyla Tharp Dance, the Houston Ballet and the San Francisco Ballet.

Faculty members are chosen for their experience with major companies and for their interest and gifts in teaching young people. In addition to Lewis, faculty members include Bambi Andersen, late of the Limón Dance Company, and Gerard Ebitz, formerly with NYCB. The faculty includes 24 full- and part-time teachers and 13 musicians.

Lewis says his goal is to create dancers equally versed in modern dance, ballet and jazz. In addition, students can learn Spanish dance, tap, African and other ethnic dance. He wants students to be able to switch techniques as easily as they change costumes. The program is considered conservative and traditional because it does not include postmodern dance forms like contact improvisation and release work. Lewis defends the conservative approach, saying that he is producing the kinds of graduates that

NEW WORLD SCHOOL OF THE ARTS

Peter London instructs students at the New World School of the Arts, Miami.

major companies want. The New World School is located in downtown Miami in a 10-story building that includes not only a large dance theater, but also a therapy room and facilities for massage, neuromuscular and hydrotherapy techniques, as well as Pilates facilities. Students are accepted by audition only. Florida residents pay very low tuition. In terms of quality for cost, this is one of the best values in the country.

School of Sarasota Ballet

For ballet, jazz, modern, tap dancers, choreographers Central Gulf Coast, S of St. Petersburg — Danto Center for SBF, 5555 N. Trail, Sarasota, FL 34243 **Voice:** 941-359-0099 **Fax:** 813-358-1504 **Contact:** Robert de Warren, Artistic Dir. **Open:** Year-round **Admission:** Written application **Deadlines:** Rolling **Cost:** $85 for 10 classes **Financial Aid:** Scholarship; Work/Study **Size-Attendees:** 100-200 **Size-Class:** 10-25

THIS PROFESSIONALLY operated school and company is headed by Robert de Warren, a man well known in dance circles, and who enjoyed a lengthy career with the Royal Ballet. Besides de Warren, the school has several things going for it. First, it's one of the few schools offering certification in the Cecchetti Method. This is thanks to school principal Deborah Vinton, who is accredited by the Imperial Society of Teachers of Dancing Cecchetti Method. She has instituted a program that offers the necessary exam and certification. Furthermore, the company is a favorite in the region, employing a well-trained group of dancers from the region and outside the state, and often including students from the school in its seasonal productions.

The school offers classes in ballet, pointe, jazz, modern, tap and character, Monday through Saturday, in its 3 main studios located at the Florida State University Center for the Performing Arts. There are 10 teachers on the faculty, many of whom have enjoyed international careers with the likes of the Kirov and Les Grands

Ballets Canadiens. Definitely a school and a company to keep your eye on!

School of Southern Ballet Theatre

For ballet, jazz, modern dancers, choreographers East central Florida, in the land of Disney — 1111 N. Orange Ave., Suite. 4, Orlando, FL 32804 **Voice:** 407-426-1733 **Fax:** 407-426-1734 **Web Site:** www.800net.com/ballet/2.html **Contact:** Alexia Nassis, School Admn. **Founded:** 1981 **Open:** Year-round **Admission:** Written application, audition **Deadlines:** Rolling **Cost:** $920 for 4-week summer program, $39-$210 for classes from August through June **Financial Aid:** Scholarship; Work/Study **Size-Attendees:** 150-200 **Size-Class:** 10-30

SOUTHERN BALLET THEATRE is poised to take the reigning title of Florida's top regional ballet company. It might not have the magnetism of an Edward Villella calling the shots, but it does have sound management, a top company of dancers and a school that has been offering superior classical training in the central Florida region for more than 15 years.

The school's syllabus is based on the Vaganova method and is maintained thanks to faculty member Alla Chernova, a graduate of the Vaganova Ballet Academy in Leningrad, who continues to teach in-house seminars to other faculty members. An apprentice program is offered to aspiring professionals. The entire operation is housed in the recently renovated, historic Dr. Phillips Center for the Performing Arts, so students can mingle with company members to gain insight into a professional dancer's routine. The 11 faculty members include Vasile Petrutiu, artistic director of the company and former dancer with the Alberta, Pittsburgh, Dallas and Cleveland/San Jose ballets. Also on staff is choreographer Nathalie Krassovska, former ballerina with the Ballet Russe, who has enjoyed the company of such famed dancers as Massine, Lifar, Youskevitch and Dolin. The cele-

73

brated Broadway, film and television choreographer Peter Anastos serves as a resident choreographer. With names like these how can you lose?

University of Florida College of Fine Arts

🏠 📧 ☀️ *For ballet, ethnic, jazz, modern, tap dancers, choreographers* Northern Florida — Dept. of Theater and Dance, P.O. Box 115900, Gainesville, FL 32611 **Voice:** 352-392-2038 **Fax:** 352-392-5114 **E-mail:** milotaj@nervm.ufl.edu **Web Site:** www.arts.ufl.edu **Contact:** Kevin Marshall, Chair **Founded:** 1853 **Open:** Year-round **Admission:** Written application, audition, resume, interview, transcripts **Deadlines:** Each semester **Cost:** $11,000 per year for state residents, $17,000 for nonresidents **Financial Aid:** Loans; Scholarship; Fellowship; Stipend; Work/Study **Size-Attendees:** 100-200 **Size-Class:** 10-25 **Degree or Certification:** BFA in Dance **Job Placement:** Yes

T HE UNIVERSITY OF Florida–Gainesville boasts one of the most imaginative dance programs in the country, probably because, still in its infancy, it is exploring new and inventive ways of servicing its students of dance. For those students who don't want to deal with the usual party line and politics of more established programs, and are less likely to bend the rules, this might be just the ticket.

As the department's mission statement states, "This innovative degree program includes choreography and performance, multicultural dance studies, and dance and medicine. The purpose of the program is to train dancers and choreographers to be prepared to meet the challenge of the 21st century." This challenge includes the Diversity Artists Project, which has featured artist-in-residence Chuck Davis and the African American Dance Ensemble, Mohamed Da Costa from West Africa and Jawole Zollar of Urban Bush Women. The program also offers a unique course of study in Dance in Medicine in cooperation with Shands (the University's teaching hospital), it has summer programs both on campus

and in West Africa, it has a joint degree program with New World School of the Arts in Miami, and it plays host to the Center for World Arts and the Center for the Arts and Public Policy, 2 service organizations for the students and for the community at large. In 1997 the College of Fine Arts inaugurated its BFA degree in dance. This program offers courses in modern dance, ballet, jazz and tap and also includes world dance and intercultural performance. Floridance, the student performing company, presents 15 programs a year in a variety of formal and informal settings. The 2,000-acre campus is located within the limits of a 90,000-population urban area. The northeastern area of the campus is listed as a historic district on the National Register of Historic Places. Open spaces, small ponds, picnic areas, shady nooks and an 81-acre wildlife sanctuary are all part of the campus.

University of South Florida

🏠 📧 *For ballet, modern dancers, choreographers* Dance Dept., 202 E. Fowler Ave., FAD 204, Tampa, FL 33620 **Voice:** 813-974-2614 **Fax:** 813-974-2026 **E-mail:** mkraack@satie.arts.usf.edu **Web Site:** www.arts.usf.edu/dance/ **Contact:** Timothy Wilson, Dept. Chair **Founded:** 1956 **Open:** Year-round **Admission:** Application, audition, transcripts, interview, writing sample **Cost:** $8,190 per year tuition and fees for state residents, $14,100 for nonresidents **Financial Aid:** Loans; Scholarship; Fellowship; Stipend; Work/Study **Size-Attendees:** 100-250 **Size-Class:** 10-30 **Degree or Certification:** BAs in Modern Dance, Ballet, Dance Ed. **Job Placement:** Yes

B OTH THE FACILITIES and the faculty make this rather young program a worthy choice. The USF Dance Centre is a $1.8-million, 3-story facility that houses three 40 x 50-foot studios, observation rooms, a lounge, a reference library, and makeup rooms. Adjacent production facilities include a 550-seat theater and a 350-seat blackbox theater, along with scenic and costume shops. The Dance Centre also has the distinction of serving as home to the ever-popular Florida Dance Festival.

The faculty is equally strong: credits include careers dancing for Anna Sokolow and Ruth Currier, with the Pennsylvania Ballet, as ballet mistress for ABT II and teaching at such institutions as Walnut Hill and Interlochen. The dance program offers a course of study leading to a BA with a concentration in ballet, modern or dance education. The strength of the program lies in its emphasis on original choreography. Those of you with choreographic aspirations will find a wealth of support and resources at your disposal, from classroom work to interaction with guest artists. Unlike many programs, this one offers 4 levels of composition in addition to junior and senior choreographic-project courses. If you are interested in teaching, the program is designed to meet the requirement for certification in Dance Education K-12 in the state of Florida.

Applicants should make note of the program's stand on body type. Weight and physical appearance are major considerations in the field of dance in any case; the USF actually puts it in writing: "A dance major is expected to keep his/her weight at a level that is aesthetically acceptable for classroom training and all performances."

During free time, students can bask on miles of beautiful beaches or visit the nearby Busch Gardens, Florida Aquarium, Lowry Park Zoo, Museum of Science and Industry, St. Petersburg Salvador Dali Museum, and Tampa Bay Performing Arts Center.

Georgia

Atlanta Ballet Centre for Dance Education

For ballet, ethnic, jazz, modern, tap dancers, choreographers Midtown, behind the Woodruff Arts Center — 1400 West Peachtree St., Atlanta, GA 30309 **Voice:** 404-873-5811 **Fax:** 404-874-7905 **Web Site:** www.207.69.239.54/season/summer.htm **Contact:** John McFall, Dir. **Founded:** 1996 **Open:** Year-round **Admission:** Written application, audition **Deadlines:** Rolling **Cost:** $8 per class, $25 application fee for summer program **Financial Aid:** Scholarship; Work/Study **Size-Class:** 22

MORE THAN A MERE dance studio, ABCDE is a veritable cottage industry. A recently expanded facility has enabled this cultural hub in the south to offer year-round classes, 12 hours a day, 6 days a week. Everything from creative movement to hip-hop is offered along with the staple program, ballet. Affiliated with one of the most well-known regional ballet companies, the school has attracted an international array of artists who offer their particular area of expertise to the local community. The mission of promoting the classical art form of ballet is skillfully balanced with the general interests of the community. Open classes are available, in addition to the professional program for student dancers. Ballroom, West African, yoga, tai chi, tap and acting are the more unusual choices offered, as well as the more standard jazz, flamenco and modern. Guest faculty has included such ballet luminaries as Fernando Bujones.

In order to expand both studio space and faculty size, the school has joined forces with Robert Barnett's former Atlanta School of Ballet. It is administered by John McFall, former San Francisco Ballet dancer, choreographer for such companies as the

American Ballet Theatre and Hubbard Street Dance, and now artistic director for the Atlanta Ballet. Sharon Story serves as dean of the school. Her career has included dancing with the Boston Ballet, the Atlanta Ballet and the New York City Ballet. Barnett, who ran the Atlanta Ballet from 1962 to 1994, still serves as master teacher at the school, along with 22 other professional instructors with credits including careers in the Feld Ballets, the Royal Ballet, the National Ballet of Canada, the Bolshoi Ballet and the San Francisco Ballet. In 1997 the school joined the MasterCard Broadway Series in launching Atlanta on Broadway. Held at the Atlanta Ballet studios, this masterclass series brings professional dancers touring through Atlanta as part of the Broadway Series into the community. The inaugural class was presented by *Chicago— The Musical*'s dance captain Gregory Butler; subsequent classes have included shows such as *Showboat, Riverdance* and *Tap Dogs*.

Augusta Ballet School

For ballet, jazz, tap dancers, choreographers Off I-20 in eastern Georgia — *3328 Washington Rd., Augusta, GA 30907* **Voice:** 706-733-5511 **Fax:** 706-826-4716 **Contact:** Ron Colton, Dir. **Founded:** 1962 **Open:** Year-round **Admission:** Written application, registration fee **Deadlines:** Rolling **Cost:** From $45 for one class per week each month **Financial Aid:** Scholarship; Work/Study **Size-Attendees:** 100-150 **Size-Class:** 10-25

FOR SUCH A SMALL community, this school is highly professional and classy. In operation for more than 35 years, it is headed by former New York City Ballet dancer Ron Colton, who is known for identifying and nurturing talented young professionals. The mission of the school is "to develop the individual student to his or her fullest potential physically, mentally and artistically." Within this framework, the school teaches etiquette, tradition and standards of deportment, which are intrinsic elements of dance discipline.

The school is an affiliate of the Augusta Ballet Company, which has a respectable reputation as a regional ballet company. The ballet curriculum is very well developed; jazz and tap are also offered. In addition to Colton, principal faculty includes Zanne Beaufort, who trained at the School of American Ballet and danced with the Charleston Ballet and the Atlanta Ballet; and Renee William Toole, a product of the Augusta Ballet School and a principal dancer with the affiliate company.

Ballethnic

For ballet, ethnic, jazz, modern dancers, choreographers South end of Fulton County — *P.O. Box 7749, Atlanta, GA 30357* **Voice:** 404-762-1416 **Fax:** 404-762-6319 **E-mail:** ballethnic@msn.com **Contact:** Ivye Wright-Arnold, Artistic Admn. **Founded:** 1990 **Open:** Summer **Admission:** Written application, audition **Deadlines:** July 19 **Cost:** $87-$125 per month, $600 for 5-week summer session **Financial Aid:** Work/Study **Size-Attendees:** 60-100 **Size-Class:** 20

TAKING UP WHERE Arthur Mitchell of Dance Theatre of Harlem left off, Ballethnic provides young African-Americans an opportunity to seriously study classical dance in an updated and socially relevant manner. The company and the school blend the traditional discipline of ballet with modern, jazz, African and ethnic dance. The company's mission is to involve the community, especially youth and those who are financially less advantaged, in an appreciation of a dance form to which they are not usually exposed. The organization was founded in 1990 by dancers Nena Gilreath and Waverly Lucas, both former members of DTH and the Atlanta Ballet. The company has been quite successful in its idealistic goal of providing performance opportunities to those who, because of race and in spite of proper ballet training, are often overlooked in the majority of ballet companies.

The school has two separate programs meeting the diverse needs of the community. The Ballethnic Youth Ensemble is a preprofessional training program. Its mission is to provide a more professional study of dance for youth who, based on talent and potential, would benefit from advanced instruction. The Danseur Development Project directed by cofounder Waverly Lucas recruits young men in urban neighborhoods and provides them with positive, black-male role models and athletic dance training. The school also offers the Gregory Mix Scholarship to a student who exhibits exceptional talent and potential. All these good efforts have not gone unrewarded. The company has received universal praise for its unique brand of classic modern dance, performing recently at the prestigious Lincoln Center Out-of-Doors Festival and Aaron Davis Hall in NYC. And it has earned the praise of leading dance critics, such as Jennifer Dunning, who wrote of the Lincoln Center performances, "The Ballethnic dancers are skillful technicians and engaged performers, but they also know how to make every moment count through serene rather than the more common hard-sell dancing, creating striking imagery made visible through their clarity and simplicity." And, like any ballet company worth its salt, Ballethnic has produced a successful version of *Nutcracker*; this one, called *The Urban Nutcracker*, is set in Atlanta and is complete with a cast of characters called Brown Sugar, Leroy and Friends and Big Mama.

Georgia Ballet

For ballet, jazz, modern dancers, choreographers 31 Atlanta St., Marietta, GA 30060 **Voice:** 770-425-0258 **Web Site:** www.georgiaballet.simplenet.com **Contact:** Iris Hensley, Artistic Dir. **Founded:** 1963 **Open:** Year-round **Admission:** Written application, registration **Deadlines:** Rolling **Cost:** $10-$15 per class **Financial Aid:** Scholarship; Work/Study **Size-Class:** 8-12

ALTHOUGH OPERATING somewhat in the shadow of the Atlanta Ballet, the Georgia Ballet has as much going for it, just on a smaller scale. It has been in existence for more than 35 years; the company presents 35-40 performances a year.

The curriculum at the school focuses on classical training. The 4 levels of instruction offered include pointe work and repertory for advanced students and additional classes in modern, character, jazz and tap and an adult program for those who just like to sample. A new class in drama covers basic acting, creating a character, theater games, makeup, hair, costuming and props. The school is headed by Michele Ziemann-DeVos, a former Pennsylvania Ballet dancer, who also dances with the company. The school has a dozen faculty members in all, each with extensive performing and teaching credentials.

The company has both an apprentice and a preprofessional student

Dancers in line at Ballethnic Dance Company, Atlanta.

ensemble attached to it, so young dancers and students at the school can wet their feet doing onstage work. This is a very professional operation, especially for those who want a diverse and well-rounded curriculum.

Ruth Mitchell Dance Studio

For ballet, jazz, modern, tap dancers, choreographers Off I-75 in suburban Atlanta — 81 Church St., Marietta, GA 30060 **Voice:** 770-426-0007 **Contact:** Ruth Mitchell, Dir. **Founded:** 1957 **Open:** Year-round **Admission:** Written application **Deadlines:** Rolling **Cost:** $120 for 12-class card **Financial Aid:** Scholarship; Work/Study **Size-Attendees:** 50-150 **Size-Class:** 5-25

IN EXISTENCE FOR more than 40 years, the Ruth Mitchell Dance Studio is a professional studio operating on a small scale. The studio's namesake is also something of an institution, having studied in New York at the School of American Ballet and at Ballet Arts. She appeared in numerous Broadway shows, worked for leading choreographers and toured with the Ruth Page Company.

Despite the quantity of classes offered, the faculty numbers only 6 full-time members. Advanced students can take a morning class each weekday, and have the opportunity to train professionally with the affiliated company. The summer intensive seems to be the best deal from this studio-cum-performing-ensemble. Here students are offered a variety of programs; guest faculty includes such names as Trinette Singleton of the Joffrey School and Princeton Ballet School and Winthrop Corey. Besides the 6-week basic program, there are several week-long workshops at the intermediate and advanced levels, including a concentrated course in pointe and variations. Jazz and tap are offered in addition to the regular ballet-technique classes.

Hawaii

Ballet Hawaii

For ballet dancers, choreographers 3 mi from Waikiki and 1.5 mi. from the University of Hawaii — P.O. Box 61940, Honolulu, HI 96839 **Voice:** 808-988-7578 **Fax:** 808-988-3623 **E-mail:** ballethi@ pixi.com **Web Site:** www.hcc.hawaii.edu/ artweb/performing/ballethawaii/ **Contact:** Pamela Taylor-Tongg **Founded:** 1975 **Open:** Year-round **Admission:** Written application, audition **Deadlines:** Rolling **Financial Aid:** Scholarship; Work/Study **Size-Attendees:** 100-150 **Size-Class:** 10-25

BALLET HAWAII IS the state's premier professional ballet company, in operation over the last 2 decades. The company produces full-length ballets, such as *Romeo and Juliet, Swan Lake* and *Nutcracker,* with guest artists from such companies as ABT and the Bolshoi and by auditions held in Hawaii and New York. The company commissions new ballets, including works by mainland and local choreographers and composers, so there's a nice mix of native culture interspersed with the classical influence of ballet.

Ballet training is offered at all levels from preballet to professional. The program also features master teachers from the international ballet world, including such names as Shamil Yagudin from the Bolshoi and Finis Jhung and Alaine Haubert from ABT. The ballet is newly relocated in Manoa Valley, with 2 buildings serving as workshop and rehearsal space for the company and the school.

Dances We Dance

For modern dancers Program takes place in a rented studio at the Moiliili Community Center, located near the University of Hawaii — Moiliili Community Center, 2535 S. King St., P.O. Box 22657, Honolulu, HI 96826 **Voice:** 808-537-2152 **Fax:** 808-537-2152 **Contact:** Fritz Ludin, Artistic Dir. **Founded:** 1964 **Open:** Year-round **Admission:** Open **Deadlines:** Rolling **Cost:** $60 for 8-class card **Financial Aid:** Scholarship; Work/Study **Size-Attendees:** 50-150 **Size-Class:** 10-25 **Handicapped Access**

THE LIMÓN LEGACY is alive and well and flourishing on the island of Oahu, thanks to Betty Jones and Fritz Ludin. Jones was an original member of the Limón Dance Company, originating such roles as Desdemona in *The Moor's Pavane* and the Hosanna solo in *Missa Brevis*. Especially when there are so many studios and teachers claiming to offer Limón technique, students can be assured that they are receiving the real McCoy at the Dances We Dance studio.

The studio is located in the Moiliili Community Center. When Jones and Ludin are away, which is about 6 months out of the year, their former star pupils take over, keeping the studio running throughout the year. Classes are offered daily, Monday through Saturday. The level is primarily mixed, with a beginner class taught Friday mornings.

Honolulu Dance Theatre

For ballet, jazz, modern dancers 3041 Manoa Rd., Honolulu, HI 96822 **Voice:** 808-988-3202 **Fax:** 808-988-5519 **E-mail:** hdt@pixi.com **Web Site:** www.pixi.com/~hdt/ahdt.htm **Contact:** Matthew Wright, Artistic Dir. **Founded:** 1993 **Open:** Year-round **Admission:** Written application, placement audition **Deadlines:** Rolling **Cost:** $9-$12 per class **Financial Aid:** Scholarship; Work/Study **Size-Attendees:** 100-200 **Size-Class:** 8-24

THIS YOUNG OPERATION is led by gifted dancer and choreographer Mathew Wright, who enjoyed a lengthy career with such companies as the Hamburg and Atlanta ballets. Because of his connections both the company and the school have grown quite rapidly, employing such guest artists as Erika Fischbach of American Ballet Theatre and Pascual Benichou, principal dancer with San Francisco and Joffrey. Alaine Haubert, ballet mistress for ABT, has also served as guest teacher for the company and the school. One can expect only the best from this ambitious operation.

School of Hawaii State Ballet

For ballet dancers, choreographers 1418 Kapiolani Blvd., Honolulu, HI 96814 **Voice:** 808-947-2755 **Web Site:** http://ourworld.compuserve.com/homepages/bstevens/school.htm **Contact:** John Landovsky, Artistic Dir. **Founded:** 1983 **Open:** Year-round **Admission:** Written application, placement audition **Deadlines:** Rolling **Cost:** $13 per class **Financial Aid:** Scholarship; Work/Study **Size-Class:** 16

UNDER THE ARTISTIC direction of John Landovsky, the Hawaii State Ballet has a reputation for producing dancers that go on to enjoy careers in some of the top companies around the world. Landovsky can take much of the credit for this, thanks to a varied and illustrious career performing, teaching, choreographing and directing dance companies in places such as Minnesota and Oklahoma.

For those interested in a professional career, the junior company offers 6 levels of advanced study, coached exclusively by Landovsky, and ample performance opportunities in monthly concerts. The curriculum is standard fare for a ballet school, including technique, character, partnering and pointe. Classes are offered Monday through Saturday; adults can also sample open classes offered at intervals throughout the week. The Hawaii State Ballet boasts several success stories, including those of Elizabeth Mertz, soloist with the Washington Ballet; Romi Beppu, who has danced with ABT and is currently with the Boston Ballet; and Gred Zane, who dances on Broadway.

University of Hawaii–Manoa

For all dancers, dance educators, choreographers Manoa Valley, a residential section near Honolulu — College of Arts and Humanities, Dept. of Theater & Dance, John Fitzgerald Kennedy Theatre, 1170 EW Rd., Honolulu, HI 96822 **Voice:** 808-956-2464 **Fax:** 808-956-4234 **E-mail:** uhmdance@ hawaii.edu **Web Site:** www2.hawaii.edu/ ~uhmdance/uhmdance.html **Contact:** Gregg Lizenbery, Dept. Chair **Founded:** 1920 **Open:** Year-round **Admission:** Written application, audition, video of choreography, transcripts, writing samples **Deadlines:** Feb. 1 for fall, Aug. 1 for spring **Cost:** $17,412 per year for state residents, $23,480 for nonresidents **Financial Aid:** Loans; Scholarship; Fellowship; Stipend; Work/Study **Size-Attendees:** 420 **Size-Class:** 10-25 **Degree or Certification:** MAs in Dance, Dance Education, Dance Ethnology; MFA in Dance Choreography and Performance **Job Placement:** Yes

A MIX OF TRADITIONAL, academic dance training and the strong influence of dance customs native to the region makes this university rather unique. Drawing much of its inspiration from the diversity and melding of cultures characteristic of the Hawaiian Islands, the dance department offers courses covering dance traditions of Asia and the Pacific, as well as those of Western Europe and the United States. The department is quite large, with a faculty of 15. You're bound to find something to love in this extensive program. And you just can't beat the locale!

Idaho

Ballet Idaho Academy of Dance

For ballet, jazz, modern, tap dancers, choreographers Downtown — 516 South 9th St., Suite A, Boise, ID 83702 **Voice:** 208-336-3241 **Fax:** 208-342-7566 **E-mail:** balletidaho@aol.com **Web Site:** www.balletidaho.org **Contact:** Sarah Arnold Phipps, Dir. **Founded:** 1972 **Open:** Year-round **Admission:** Open **Deadlines:** Rolling **Cost:** $8-12 per class **Financial Aid:** Scholarship; Work/Study **Size-Attendees:** 525 **Size-Class:** 20-30

B ALLET IDAHO IS AN all-in-one dance center, complete with school, company, preprofessional ensemble and related educational and outreach activities. The company's mission is to provide quality training for its students, as well as to educate and expose the community to dance as an art form. Students train alongside the professional dancers in the company, and the school has grown to serve more than 500 students.

Director Sarah Phipps has dedicated more than a decade of her career to bringing dance to Boise. Since 1983 she had already owned 2 successful dance studios before signing on as director of the Ballet Idaho in 1995. Before settling in the region, Phipps performed professionally with the San Francisco Opera Ballet and the Oakland Ballet. Committed to bringing dance into the community, she has designed an educational program with her dancers, offering members of the community of all ages everything from lecture demonstrations, to artist residencies. Rounding out the artistic leadership profile is artistic director Toni Pimble, who studied in London and danced professionally in Germany, and now earns respect as a successful choreographer, commissioned by the New York City, Atlanta, Washington and Pacific Northwest ballets, to name just a few.

University of Idaho

 For ballet, jazz, modern dancers, dance educators, choreographers The Palouse area of northern Idaho — Div. of Health, Phys. Educ., Recreation and Dance, Moscow, ID 83844 **Voice:** 208-885-2189 **Fax:** 208-885-5929 **E-mail:** edhperd@ uidaho.edu **Web Site:** www.uidaho.edu **Contact:** Diane B. Walker, Prof. **Founded:** 1889 **Open:** Year-round **Admission:** Written application **Deadlines:** July 1 **Cost:** $9,750 per year for state residents, $15,750 for nonresidents **Financial Aid:** Loans; Scholarship; Fellowship **Size-Attendees:** 40 **Size-Class:** 10-15 **Degree or Certification:** BA in Dance, BS in PhysEd, MS or MEd in Dance Pedagogy, MA or MS in Interdisciplinary Studies, K-12 Teaching Cert. **Job Placement:** Yes **Handicapped Access**

THIS UNIVERSITY SETS itself apart with a personal touch that is sure to benefit the student looking for a smaller dance department with a comprehensive and diverse course listing and a strong desire to provide quality training and broad opportunities. The department's specialty is its pedagogy program related to physical education, sport and dance. If education is your area of interest, this might be the program for you. The 14 full-time faculty members bring their expertise in pedagogy, dance, health and exercise physiology.

"We have produced research examining...hemispheric preferences and instructional styles in dance teachers, the effect of attribution theory on self-esteem and performance outcomes in dancers, and the effect of creative

movement on social competence and school adjustment in at-risk students." This is how the department defines its attributes. But fear not; all the standard requisites of any good dance program are here, complete with opportunities to choreograph and perform, 2 large studios, 5 theaters, a collaborative partnership with the Lionel Hampton School of Music, site-specific performances and a major presenting venue that brings in professional dance companies, which, in turn, teach masterclasses. Moscow is a college town dubbed the "Heart of the Arts." It combines city sophistication with rural charm and scenic beauty.

Illinois

Barat College

 For ballet, modern dancers, choreographers On the shores of Lake Michigan — 700 E. Westleigh Rd., Lake Forest, IL 60045 **Voice:** 847-604-6263 **Fax:** 847-604-6300 **Web Site:** www.barat.edu **Contact:** Rory Foster, Dean **Founded:** 1854 **Open:** Year-round **Admission:** Written application, audition, transcript, personal statement **Deadlines:** Rolling admissions **Cost:** $13,500 per year for tuition, plus $5,250 for room and board **Financial Aid:** Loans; Scholarship; Fellowship; Stipend; Work/Study **Size-Attendees:** 150 **Size-Class:** 15-20 **Degree or Certification:** BFA in Dance, BAs in Dance, Dance/Psychology **Job Placement:** Yes

A SOLID AND COMPREHENSIVE dance program is offered at Barat. Covering all the bases, the college offers degree options in performance, choreography, therapy and teaching, and is one of the few to specialize in a dance/therapy program at the undergraduate level. Rory Foster, dean of the conservatory of dance at the college, has been a member of the American Ballet Theatre and principal dancer with the London Ballet Theatre, and has worked with such legendary dance figures as Antony Tudor, George Balanchine, Agnes de Mille, José Limón, Alvin Ailey, and Elliot Feld. The faculty also includes Eileen Cropley, former member of Paul Taylor, and Linda Spriggs, former member of Alvin Ailey and Joyce Trisler Danscompany. The full-time staff is rounded out by 6 other teachers. Guest faculty have included the likes of Maria Youskevitch, Armgard von Bardaleban (Martha Graham), Gerald Otte (Alwin Nikolais), Colin Connor (José Limón) and Amy Schwartz (Lucinda Childs, Mark Morris, Bill T. Jones, Joyce Trisler). Alumni of the school are now with such companies as Alvin Ailey, Hartford Ballet and Dayton Contemporary.

The conservatory offers 3 degree programs. The BFA in Dance is a professional dance degree with an emphasis on performance and choreography. The BA in Dance is designed for students wishing to combine a strong liberal-arts education with conservatory training. The BA in Dance/Psychology is an interdisciplinary major. In accordance with the guidelines of the American Dance Therapy Association, Barat's course of study for dance/psychology is designed for students who want to pursue dance therapy at the Master's degree level or to work in the field at the preprofessional level.

Columbia College of Chicago

For ballet, ethnic, jazz, modern dancers, choreographers Downtown — Dance Dept., 600 S. Michigan Ave., Chicago, IL 60605 **Voice:** 312-663-1600 **Fax:** 312-271-7046 **E-mail:** smordine@popmail. colum.edu **Web Site:** www.colum.edu/ home.html **Contact:** Shirley Mordine, Dept. Chair **Founded:** 1969 **Open:** Year-round **Admission:** Written application, audition, transcripts, writing sample **Deadlines:** Rolling **Cost:** $9,544 tuition per academic year **Financial Aid:** Loans; Scholarship; Fellowship; Stipend; Work/Study **Size-Attendees:** 100-150 **Size-Class:** 15-25 students **Degree or Certification:** BA in Dance, MAT in Dance Ed. **Job Placement:** Yes

FROM THE SELECTION of its faculty, the majority of whom are working professionals, to its course offerings, which point up the current trends in modern dance, Columbia College focuses on the practical. Although it's not a well-known department, the college compensates by providing its dance majors with solid training in the concentration of their choice: teaching, choreography or performance. If you are ambitious and enterprising, and are not looking for a prestigious conservatory to open doors for you, this college will serve you quite well.

The core curriculum includes dance technique, improvisation, choreography, history, theory and music, with additional courses offered in tai chi, yoga, jazz and ethnic dance. Students can also complete requirements for an interdisciplinary major in musical-theater performance. The college is a major presenter of contemporary dance, bringing students in close contact with companies from here and abroad.

Dance Crazes—What Causes Them?

The human race has always danced. During every epoch, certain terpsichorean delights have taken the populace by storm. These dances have whipped people into a frenzy or near madness and become the "craze" of a particular decade, generation or nation. In past centuries there have been the Minuet, the Polka, the Waltz and the Virginia Reel, and in the twentieth century the Charleston, the Jitterbug, the Twist, Line Dancing, Break Dancing, the Tango and the Macarena. Entering the new millennium, we have the phenomenon of Irish step dancing, such as "Riverdance," Hip-hop and Capoeira all the rage. Each of these dance forms has become wildly popular not only as entertainment, but also as participatory dance because of its accessibility to the public.

What makes each of these dance forms so popular? They appear to be radically different with their own distinctive movements, which come from quite different cultural and social origins. Irish Step Dancing, with its fast, intricate footwork is light, airy and clean. Hip-hop is streetwise and NOW, with wild moves that can verge on the dangerous. Capoeira is earthy, often primitive, sensuous and virile. Though distinct from each other, they all use energy in a high-powered way that creates a spectacular event, generating even more energy and enthusiasm from the audience or participants.

Perhaps this energy has thrust these dances into today's spotlight. Through not readily apparent, at the heart of this highly charged popularity these dances are united by a deeper aspect, which is distinctly cultural. It is the need and desire to discover the roots of their cultures or common humanity that adds poignancy and power. The passion and energy that each dance offers communicate a rare state of shared feeling that instantly and intuitively attracts followers like a magnet. Dance can bring us to an intuitive understanding of our common humanity.

The great Mexican-American choreographer José Limón believed wholeheartedly that "Dance is all things to all men. It is religion. It is joy. It is pleasure. It is art. It is a human necessity, profound and not to be denied." Limón also said, "I believe that we are never more truly and profoundly human than when we dance." The next dance craze will not be just another frenzy. It will be, as always, the human spirit in motion.

Giordano
Dance Center

For jazz, ballet, ethnic, modern, tap dancers, choreographers Metropolitan Chicago — 614 Davis St., Evanston, IL 60201 **Voice:** 847-866-9442 **Fax:** 847-866-9228 **Contact:** Kathryn T. Larsen, Dir. **Founded:** 1953 **Open:** Year-round **Admission:** Open **Deadlines:** Rolling **Cost:** From $10 per class **Financial Aid:** Scholarship; Work/Study **Size-Attendees:** 150 **Size-Class:** 10-20

FOR THOSE OF YOU IN the Chicago area with a passion for jazz dancing, the grandfather of the movement is right at your doorstep. The history of Gus Giordano is the stuff of legend. During the Depression years, he gave dance lessons in his basement for 15 cents a class. Later on, when the Marines found out about his training as a dancer, they put him into a performing group called the Marine Corps Troupers, which performed at the Hollywood Canteen and featured such stars as Tyrone Power and Spike Jones and His Band.

After a successful career as a performer on Broadway, in the movies and on television, Giordano moved to Illinois to form his Chicago-based company and dance center. He returned to the teaching world in 1953 when he opened his dance studio in Evanston and built it, with the help of his wife, into the institution it is today. Today, Nan Giordano (Gus's daughter) serves as artistic director of the company and helps oversee the school. Giordano remains in worldwide demand as a teacher and is recognized as one of the top jazz dance teachers in the world. In its 4 studios the center offers beginning through professional-level training in jazz, ballet, modern, tap and hip-hop.

Lou Conte
Dance Studio

For modern, jazz, ballet, ethnic dancers West Loop Gate neighborhood — 1147 W. Jackson Blvd., Chicago, IL 60607 **Voice:** 312-850-9744 **Fax:** 312-455-8240 **E-mail:** hsdcbase@aol.com **Contact:** Julie Nakagawa Bottcher, Associate Dir. **Founded:** 1977 **Open:** Year-round **Admission:** Open **Deadlines:** Rolling **Cost:** $100 for 10 classes, $190 for 20 classes **Financial Aid:** Scholarship; Work/Study **Size-Attendees:** 100-200 **Size-Class:** 10-25

THIS SCHOOL IS BETTER known as the school to Hubbard Street Dance Chicago, the hip, nationally recognized company that serves as a second home to such choreographers as Twyla Tharp, Margo Sappington and Kevin O'Day. The studio supports the distinctive style of the company, which is a mix of theatrical jazz, contemporary-dance and classical-ballet technique. The facility recently underwent a transformation, moving from its old location on Wabash Avenue where it had resided for more than 20 years, to a new 56,000-square-foot, 2-story building that houses both the company and the school. The new facility has 5 spacious dance studios, ample dressing rooms, lockers, showers, central heating and air-conditioning.

Former and current Hubbard Street dancers make up some of LCDS's faculty. Josef Patrick, a 12-year veteran of HSDC, teaches jazz and ballet. Patrick is joined by company members Alberto Arias, Ginger Farley and Jeff Hancock. More than 50 classes in jazz, ballet, modern, tap and hip-hop are offered daily. Ballet and jazz are offered at 6 levels, beginning to advanced. Tap has 4 levels, modern has 2 advanced levels and funk classes meet once a week, at either the beginning or the intermediate level.

Ruth Page Foundation School of Dance

For ballet, ethnic, modern dancers, choreographers Chicago's urban sprawl — 1016 N. Dearborn Pkwy., Chicago, IL 60610 **Voice:** 312-337-6543 **Fax:** 312-337-6542 **Contact:** Larry Long, Dir. **Founded:** 1971 **Open:** Year-round **Admission:** Written application **Deadlines:** Rolling **Cost:** From $63 for 6 classes, $525 for 6-week summer program, $90 per class card for professionals **Financial Aid:** Scholarship; Work/Study

THOSE UNAWARE OF THE reputation of its namesake might poke fun at this studio's title. In fact, it is a small but illustrious haven for ballet and jazz artists, thanks to Larry Long. Long has been ballet master with the Harkness Ballet and the National Ballet of Washington, as well as artistic director of England's Ballet International and codirector of the Chicago Ballet. The faculty also includes such performers as Julie Burman, who has performed with Hubbard Street, and Kenny Ingram, dance captain for Hal Prince's *Showboat*. The summer intensive includes such guest artists as master teacher David Howard and Russell Sultzbach, formerly of the Joffrey.

In its 5 studios the school offers classes 11 A.M.-9 P.M., Monday through Saturday, in ballet, tap, jazz, Pilates, character and pointe.

School of Ballet Chicago

For ballet dancers Overlooking Lake Michigan — 185 N. Wabash, Ste. 2305, Chicago, IL 60601 **Voice:** 312-251-8838 **Fax:** 312-251-8840 **Contact:** Patricia Blair, Dir. **Founded:** 1995 **Open:** Year-round **Admission:** Open except audition for preprofessional division **Deadlines:** Rolling **Cost:** $110 for 10-class card **Financial Aid:** Scholarship; Work/Study **Size-Attendees:** 150-200 **Size-Class:** 15-20

THIS BALANCHINE-ORIENTED ballet academy is the heir to 2 previous professional ballet companies in Chicago and the direct successor to Maria Tallchief's Chicago City Ballet. Headed up by Daniel Duell, talented former member of the New York City Ballet, its strong connections with the New York City Ballet are further evidenced by the faculty and by the fact that the Balanchine Trust has granted performing rights to the newly formed Chicago Ballet Youth Company.

In addition to Duell, the faculty includes former NYCB dancer Heather Hawk, SAB-trained Gretchen Klocke, former Eglevsky Ballet dancer Patricia Blair, Ballet Chicago principal Patti Eylar and Christine DuBoulay, who danced with the Royal Ballet and heads the teaching of classical repertory. Balanchine Trust reconstructor Suki Schorer frequently teaches masterclasses at the school and is part of the faculty during the summer season. The school's preprofessional training program is available by audition. Students begin by taking a minimum of 12 classes per week and progress to 15 classes as they enter the advanced division. The facility in downtown Chicago features 3 studios and is actually located in the same building as the Joffrey Ballet. The Joffrey Ballet has a school in New York City but not in Chicago. Ballet Chicago, on the other hand, has no *Nutcracker*, whereas the Joffrey does; Chicago students get to participate in the Joffrey's production of this perennial favorite.

85

University of Illinois, Urbana–Champaign

🏠 *For ballet, modern dancers, choreographers* E central Illinois — Dept. of Dance, 907 1/2 W. Nevada , Urbana, IL 61801 **Voice:** 217-333-1010 **Fax:** 217-333-3000 **E-mail:** graduate@admissions.uiuc.edu **Web Site:** www.grad.uiuc.edu/ **Contact:** Patricia K. Knowles, Dir. **Founded:** 1949 **Open:** Year-round **Admission:** Written application, audition, resume, minimum 3.0 GPA **Deadlines:** Mid-Apr. for BFA, Feb. 15 for MFA **Cost:** $1,704 per year tuition for state residents, $5,112 for nonresidents, summer program from $1,065 **Financial Aid:** Loans; Scholarship; Fellowship; Stipend; Work/Study **Size-Attendees:** 60 **Size-Class:** 15-20 **Degree or Certification:** BFA in Dance, MFA in Dance **Job Placement:** Yes

ALTHOUGH IT IS relatively small, the dance program here is included in many Top Ten lists of the nation's best, and can boast that 78 percent of its alums are currently employed as dance professionals. The university offers both undergraduates and graduates a dance program emphasizing choreography, performance and teaching.

Artists in residence in recent years included choreographers Joe Goode, Rachel Lampert, Victoria Marks and Janis Brenner; master teachers Jackie Villamil and Lynn Simonson; Eddie Taketa of Doug Varone and Dancers; and Cynthia Harvey, ballerina with the ABT. The affiliated Krannert Center for the Performing Arts brings in world-class companies and performers, such as Trisha Brown and Bill T. Jones, who teach residencies and masterclasses here.

A university-circulated newsletter highlights the many events, awards and other newsworthy tidbits relating to the dance program, such as how an Urbana native, who had been involved in the early modern-dance movement at Bennington College in the 1930s, donated her scrapbook of memorabilia to the department's archives; or that dance critic/historian Marcia B. Siegel was on campus to give 2 lectures (one about the Riverdance phenomenon) and to teach improvisation. With a steady stream of activities and events to keep students continually engaged the university seems able to meet the demands of students looking for more than just classes in theory and technique.

DON CLEGG

Performance of *Once Removed* at the University of Illinois, Urbana–Champaign Dance Department.

Von Heidecke' s School of the Chicago Festival Ballet

👣 *For ballet dancers, choreographers* Just outside Chicago — Market Meadows, 1239 S. Naper Blvd., Naperville, IL 60540 **Voice:** 630-527-1052 **Contact:** Kenneth von Heidecke **Founded:** 1991 **Open:** Year-round **Admission:** Open **Deadlines:** Rolling **Cost:** $10 per hr. **Financial Aid:** Scholarship; Work/Study **Size-Class:** 8-10 **Job Placement:** Yes

FASHIONED AFTER Balanchine's School of American Ballet, Von Heidecke's School of Ballet offers young trainees a rigorous and regimented schedule of classes, supported by an impressive faculty and an operation that ranks with some of the finest training institutions.

By the school's own definition the Balanchine technique is a combination of the Russian Vaganova technique combined with the lyrical Paris Opera technique. Von Heidecke's School of Ballet promises its students that with this type of training, they will be prepared to follow many pathways in a ballet career.

Indiana

Academy of Ballet Internationale

 *For ballet dancers* Metropolitan Indianapolis — 502 N. Capitol Avenue, Suite B, Indianapolis, IN 46204 **Voice:** 317-635-6080 **Fax:** 317-637-1637 **Contact:** Vladilen Semenov, Principal **Founded:** 1959 **Open:** Year-round **Admission:** Open **Deadlines:** Rolling admission **Cost:** $650 for 16-week session **Financial Aid:** Scholarship; Work/Study **Size-Class:** 6-10

BALLET INTERNATIONALE is Indianapolis's own Cinderella story. The company's humble roots date back to 1959 when the company recruited advanced student dancers from the area to conduct educational outreach programs in the local schools. In 1973 it emerged as the first professional ballet company in the state, changing its name to Indianapolis Ballet. And 2 decades later, with a third name and a third artistic director, Eldar Aliev, a former Kirov Ballet star, the company seems to have hit its stride.

Today, Ballet Internationale is a mix of transplanted Bolshoi and Kirov stars, as well as American recruits from such companies as the Boston, New York City and Joffrey ballets. But the atmosphere is decidedly Russian. Aliev has recreated the Kirov Academy where he was a leading dancer. Even the teaching staff is the same as he had at the Kirov, notably Semeyonov, who was balletmaster at the Kirov and now serves as principal for the school.

Classes from beginning to advanced levels are available year-round for the local residents. A special training program is offered for those students who do wish to pursue a professional career in ballet. The trainee program enables students to take class and perform alongside the professional dancers in the company.

Butler University

For ballet, modern dancers, choreographers Jordan College of Fine Arts, Dept. of Dance, 4600 Sunset Ave., Indianapolis, IN 46208 **Voice:** 317-940-9346; 800-368-6852 **Fax:** 317-940-9658 **E-mail:** laurent@butler.edu **Web Site:** www2.butler.edu/www/dance/ **Contact:** Stephan Laurent, Artistic Dir. **Open:** Year-round **Admission:** Written application, audition, writing sample, transcripts, test scores **Deadlines:** Rolling **Cost:** $8,500 per semester **Financial Aid:** Loans; Scholarship; Fellowship; Stipend; Work/Study **Size-Attendees:** 85-95 **Size-Class:** 15-25 **Degree or Certification:** BFA in Dance Performance; BAs in Dance/Pedagogy Concentration, Dance Performance, Arts Administration/Dance Concentration **Job Placement:** Yes

THE DANCE PROGRAM at Butler offers the best of both the academic and the professional world of dance. Within the University's Jordan College of Fine Arts exists the Butler Ballet, a preprofessional company composed of dance majors. The company presents a full season of 3 to 5 different programs each year, fully staged and costumed, and performed with live orchestral accompaniment. The repertoire consists of a variety of full-length classical ballets, such as *Swan Lake, Giselle* and *Cinderella*, as well as contemporary and jazz works. Artistic director Stephan Laurent is also chairman of the university's dance program. He is joined by a faculty of 13, including Larry Carpenter, formerly with Martha Graham; Debra Knapp, formerly of Bill Evans Dance Company; Rochelle Zide-Booth, formerly with the Joffrey, Nederlands Dans Theater and Ballet Russe de Monte

Carlo; and Larry Attaway, formerly with Bella Lewitzky.

The program's focus is primarily classical, with additional instruction in modern, jazz and character. Students can focus their studies in the areas of performance, pedagogy and arts administration, and minor in both music and theater.

Indiana University

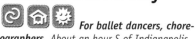 **For ballet dancers, choreographers** About an hour S of Indianapolis — Music Building, Bloomington, IN 47405 **Voice:** 812-855-6787 **Fax:** 812-855-2753 **E-mail:** blf.cesbronj@indiana.edu **Web Site:** www.indiana.edu **Contact:** Jacques Cesbron, Dept. Chair **Founded:** 1910 **Open:** Year-round **Admission:** Written application, audition, interview, transcripts, writing sample **Deadlines:** Apply each semester **Cost:** $9,770 per year for state residents, $16,520 for nonresidents **Financial Aid:** Loans; Scholarship; Fellowship; Stipend; Work/Study **Size-Attendees:** up to 150 **Size-Class:** 5-25 **Degree or Certification:** BA, MS in Ballet **Job Placement:** Yes

THIS SMALL BUT high-quality program offers both graduate and undergraduate degrees in ballet. The ballet program is an adjunct of the large and highly respected School of Music. The curriculum includes ballet technique, pointe, variations, adagio, men's class and jazz.

Jacques Cesbron, a former principal dancer with the Paris Opera, Pennsylvania and Metropolitan Opera ballets, chairs the dance department. His extensive teaching credentials include Dance Theatre of Harlem, Connecticut College, Joffrey Ballet and American Ballet Theatre. The faculty includes his wife, Virginia; Leslie Peck, former dancer with the New York City, Pennsylvania, Houston and Pacific Northwest ballets; Violette Verdy, an international ballerina with major companies, including the New York City Ballet and former artistic director of the Paris Opera Ballet and the Boston Ballet. Guest teachers and artists include a long-term residency by a noted ballet

troupe, and such guest teachers as Jose Manuel Carreno and Julie Kent, both principals with American Ballet Theatre; Susan Jones, ballet mistress of American Ballet Theatre; and John Meehan, artistic director of Ballet Theatre's Studio Company. The high-quality facility includes 3 spacious studios, including a fully equipped Pilates studio with instruction by Pilates-trained faculty. Performance opportunities abound, with an annual *Nutcracker* and fall and spring concerts. Students also perform with the opera company in residence and participate in a student choreographic workshop.

Iowa

University of Iowa

For ballet, jazz, modern dancers, choreographers Eastern Iowa — Dept. of Dance, E. 114 Halsey Hall, Iowa City, IA 52242 **Voice:** 319-335-2228 **Fax:** 319-335-3246 **E-mail:** helenchadima@uiowa.edu **Web Site:** www.uiowa.edu **Contact:** David Berkey, Dept. Chair **Founded:** 1848 **Open:** Year-round **Admission:** Written application, audition, photo, resume, essay, prepared solo **Deadlines:** May **Cost:** $10,536 per year for state residents, $17,658 for nonresidents **Financial Aid:** Loans; Scholarship; Fellowship; Stipend; Work/Study **Size-Attendees:** 200 **Size-Class:** 15-25 **Degree or Certification:** BA in Dance, BFA in Dance, MFA in Dance **Job Placement:** Yes

ALTHOUGH IT'S A BIT off the beaten path as far as dance is concerned, the University of Iowa still offers its students a wealth of opportunity and a high-quality education. Not focused on one particular style of dance, the department stresses individuality and makes every effort to tailor the program to fit the needs and interests of the student.

"The Dance Department at the University of Iowa is one of the best in the United States. The program is broad, yet professionally detailed, and handled with very experienced skill. The staff is well equipped to carry on the curriculum and administration with warmth, understanding and good grace." That accolade is attributed to choreographer Alwin Nikolais. Exposure to outside dance artists comes in the form of guest performers, choreographers and teachers. Guest residencies have included artists such as Susan Marshall, Bebe Miller, Doug Varone, David Parsons and the Joffrey Ballet. Through the Iowa Center for the Arts and Hancher Auditorium, dancers have the opportunity to experience a wealth of performances and to work in masterclasses and seminars with dance companies from the classical to the avant garde. For advanced students a study-abroad semester is available at Danshogskolan in Stockholm, Sweden. The department has 6 technique studios, 2 classrooms and a Labanotation computer room and video library. The Space/Place Theatre is the department's own performance space for informal concerts and experimental works. Formal concerts are produced in the 2,600-seat Hancher Auditorium. Performance opportunities abound, from the annual Dance Gala to the dance department's touring company, Dancers in Company. Students interested in pursuing teaching as a career can develop these skills in such programs as the Dance Forum, or through graduate teaching assistantships.

Iowa City is a community of 60,000 in eastern Iowa, combining a cosmopolitan atmosphere with the best of small-town living. The city offers historic neighborhoods, scenic parks and waterways.

Vine Street Ballet

For ballet, jazz, modern, tap dancers, choreographers 1 mi. S of I-235 — 2501 Vine St., W. Des Moines, IA 50265 **Voice:** 515-222-0698 **Contact:** Susan Snider, Artistic Dir. **Founded:** 1997 **Open:** Year-round **Admission:** Written application **Deadlines:** Rolling **Cost:** $120 for 12-class card **Financial Aid:** Scholarship; Work/Study **Size-Attendees:** 100 **Size-Class:** 10-25

UPON THE DEMISE of the Iowa Ballet, Vine Street Ballet came to the rescue, thanks to the community's push to have a professional school and dance company in the area. Time will tell, but it looks as though the residents of West Des Moines will have a company and school of which they can be proud.

The operation is overseen by Susan Snider, who has devoted the last 2 decades to dance in Iowa, first as a student at the University of Iowa and later as a professional dancer and studio owner in the Quad Cities. The Vine Street Ballet opened in September, 1997, in a building that once housed Lincoln Technical School. It has 5 large studios and a 200-seat theater. The school's 100-plus student enrollment complements the youth-oriented Vine Street Ballet II and a professional company with 8 to 12 dancers. Frank Affruntti of the Eugene Ballet has been hired as artistic director for the professional company. Vine Street Ballet II is made up of nonpaid youth, professional guest dancers and accomplished students from other schools in the area. This program, not unlike an internship, enables students to rehearse with professional dancers and see what the career of a professional dancer is really like. Snider knows about young professionals: all 3 of her children are dancers making their living in the field. The school takes an eclectic approach, offering not only ballet, but also tap, jazz, modern, tai chi, ballroom, creative movement for children and Pilates. The objective is to offer a preprofessional program for the serious dance student, as well as open classes for those who want to dance just for the fun of it. Faculty members are professional caliber, with either a degree in dance or a professional performing career behind them. Classes are offered Monday through Saturday.

Kansas

University of Kansas

  For ballet, modern dancers, choreographers NE Kansas, ½ hour E of Topeka — Dept. of Music and Dance, 452 Murphy Hall, Lawrence, KS 66045 **Voice:** 785-864-3436 **Fax:** 785-864-5387 **E-mail:** mcohan@eagle.cc.ukans.edu **Web Site:** www.ukans.edu/~mad/ **Contact:** Muriel Cohan, Assoc. Prof. of Dance **Open:** Year-round **Admission:** Written application, audition, interview, transcripts, test scores, writing sample **Deadlines:** April 1 for fall admission, June 1 for transfer students **Cost:** $2,500 per semester for state residents, $9,100 per semester for nonresidents **Financial Aid:** Loans; Scholarship; Fellowship; Stipend; Work/Study **Size-Class:** 12-40 **Degree or Certification:** BA in Dance **Job Placement:** Yes

T HE UNIVERSITY of Kansas has a great deal going for it: an A-list faculty, a major presenter of world-class dance events and an extensive curriculum.

Associate dance professors Muriel Cohan and Patrick Suzeau worked with such modern dance legends as Mary Anthony, Anna Sokolow and Pearl Lang before forming their own company, Cohan/Suzeau. Other faculty members include Janet Hamburg, a certified Laban movement analyst who specializes in coordination problems in children and adults, movement efficiency for athletes and movement problems for older adults; and Jerel Hilding, who enjoyed a 15-year career with the Joffrey Ballet. The 6 members of the faculty are all from different backgrounds; consequently students can sample a diverse curriculum that runs the gamut from ballet to jazz, and from theory to composition.

Students also have access to the Lied Center for the Performing Arts, which brings in such companies as Bill T. Jones/Arnie Zane Dance Company, Ballet Hispanico, Limón Dance Company and STOMP. The University Dance Company is open to all students in the program by audition. Resident and visiting choreographers create new works on the company members, which can range from ballet, to jazz, to modern, and which are usually presented either at the Lied Center or at the Elizabeth Serbon Dance Theatre. This program has the resources; it's up to the student to make the most of them.

Wichita State University

 For modern, ballet, jazz dancers, choreographers S Central Kansas — School of Performing Arts Dance Program, 118 Heskett, Wichita, KS 67260 **Voice:** 316-978-3530 **Fax:** 316-978-3951 **E-mail:** frazier@ twsuvm.uc.twsu.edu **Web Site:** www.twsu. edu/~fineart/index.html **Contact:** Nick Johnson, Dir. **Founded:** 1926 **Open:** Year-round **Admission:** Open **Deadlines:** Aug. 21 for fall semester **Cost:** $1,020 per semester for state residents, $3,600 per semester for nonresidents **Financial Aid:** Loans; Scholarship; Fellowship; Stipend; Work/Study **Size-Attendees:** 800 **Degree or Certification:** BFA **Job Placement:** Yes

W HAT PUTS THIS rather small department of dance on the map is the fact that it is surrounded by an array of arts programs, all within the College of Fine Arts. As a result students can dabble in a variety of disciplines, including the more than 11 different majors that constitute the fine-arts department, ranging from studio art to music composition. The closest ally for dance, of course, is the theater department; the 2 departments share the same facilities.

Dance majors at WSU put on 4 productions a year in addition to course work. The department emphasizes modern dance, with additional instruction in ballet and jazz. The 3 full-time faculty members are supplemented by guest teachers and companies. Recent guests have included Garth Fagan, the Martha Graham Ensemble, Limón Dance Company and the Cleo Parker Robinson Dance Ensemble. The faculty includes Denise Celestin, formerly of Fort Worth Ballet and Ballet Met; C. Nicolas Johnson, who enjoyed a career with mime legend Marcel Marceau; and Teresa Wylie McWilliams, who has worked extensively in musical theater. The 5 part-time lecturers teach technique classes ranging from country and western to ballroom.

Kentucky

Louisville School of Ballet

  For ballet dancers, choreographers Downtown — 315 E. Main St., Louisville, KY 40202 **Voice:** 502-583-3150 **Fax:** 502-583-0006 **E-mail:** louballet1@ka.net **Web Site:** www.louisvilleballet.org **Contact:** Helen Starr, Dir. **Founded:** 1975 **Open:** Year-round **Admission:** Registration form, fee $15-$25 **Deadlines:** Open admissions **Cost:** From $272 per semester for 2 classes per week **Financial Aid:** Scholarship; Work/Study **Size-Attendees:** 100-150 **Size-Class:** 10-25

ONE OF THE COUNTRY'S hip regional companies, the Louisville Ballet shows off an excellent troupe that fits as easily into *Don Quixote* as it does into a David Parsons work. This is a tribute to the illustrious faculty that has equally illustrious ties to current and former legends in the dance world; one of the most famous of these is Mikhail Baryshnikov, who returns periodically to perform with the company.

When current artistic director Alun Jones took over the company in 1975, he simultaneously started the company's school, which continues to operate today with a faculty of 8. Jones

enjoyed a long and varied career as a performer, teacher, choreographer and even technical director. Helen Starr, director as well as associate artistic director, danced with the Royal Ballet; her teachers included Alicia Markova, Ninette de Valois, Tamara Karsavina, Anton Dolin and Erik Bruhn. Other faculty credits include the Pittsburgh Ballet Theatre, the London Festival Ballet and Ballet West. For students in the trainee and preprofessional division, classes are offered Monday through Saturday. There is also an open program for adults and a separate boys' class. The company and the school recently moved into a new facility with 2 large studios in downtown Louisville; it received the honor award for Excellence in Architectural Design from the Kentucky Chapter of the American Institute of Architects and was featured in *Architecture* magazine.

School of the Lexington Ballet

  For ballet, jazz dancers, choreographers Central Lexington — ArtsPlace, 161 N. Mill St., Lexington, KY 40507 **Voice:** 606-233-3925 **Fax:** 606-255-2787 **Contact:** LuAnn Pelle-Byrum, Dir. **Founded:** 1974 **Open:** Year-round **Admission:** Written application, placement audition **Deadlines:** Rolling **Cost:** From $120 per semester **Financial Aid:** Scholarship; Work/Study **Size-Attendees:** 50-100 **Size-Class:** 5-25

OPERATED ALONG the lines of a community theater, Lexington Ballet is a homegrown affair, relying on the community to keep it in existence. And by all accounts its existence is assured. Already celebrating its 25th anniversary, the school has a nice offering of classes both for the novice and for the serious student of ballet. Levels range from beginning to advanced, with separate classes for boys, including an invitation-only, pas-de-deux class. Creative movement, preballet and beginning and advanced adult classes, along with jazz, are thrown in for good measure.

Students have the opportunity to perform in the school's spring performance and, during the winter season, in *Nutcracker*. Since guest artists are hired from around the country for many of the company's productions, students gain valuable experience. The senior company is composed of the advanced students in the school. Members must be at least 15 years of age or older, and their involvement entitles them to take advantage of the scholarship program. On staff is an eclectic group of professionals, whose careers were predominantly outside of this country. An advisory panel consists of such heavy hitters as Daniel Lewis, dean of the dance department at the New World School of the Arts, and Carlos Accost Jr., former principal dancer for the Royal London Ballet.

Western Kentucky University

For ballet, jazz, modern dancers, choreographers SW Kentucky — Dance Dept., 1 Big Red Way, Bowling Green, KY 42101 **Voice:** 502-745-5845 **Fax:** 502-745-5387 **E-mail:** william.leonard@wku.edu **Web Site:** www.wku.edu **Contact:** William Leonard, Chair **Founded:** 1906 **Open:** Year-round **Admission:** Written application, audition, interview, transcripts, test scores **Cost:** $1,130 tuition per semester for state residents, $3,050 for nonresidents **Financial Aid:** Loans; Scholarship; Fellowship; Stipend; Work/Study **Size-Attendees:** 40-100 **Size-Class:** 5-25 **Degree or Certification:** BFA in Performing Arts/Dance Minor **Job Placement:** Yes

HERE IS A BARE-BONES dance program that nevertheless offers the opportunity to pursue 2 key academic concentrations: performance and choreography. The dance program coexists with the theater department, so make sure your interest lies with both dance and theater. In dance, there is equal emphasis on ballet and jazz, no doubt due to the department's musical-theater productions.

Faculty member Bob Boross heads the department's jazz program, training students in the Matt Mattox style, as well as serving as choreographer for many of the theater department's musical-theater productions. He is joined by Beverly Veenker, who teaches all the ballet courses, along with composition and choreography.

Louisiana

Dancer's Workshop

For ballet, jazz, modern, tap dancers, choreographers About 80 mi. NW of New Orleans — 10745 Linkwood Ct., Baton Rouge, LA 70810 **Voice:** 225-926-6248 **Fax:** 225-767-5814 **Contact:** Molly Buchmann, Sharon Mathews, Dirs. **Founded:** 1973 **Open:** Year-round **Admission:** Open; placement audition **Deadlines:** Rolling **Cost:** $35-$45 per class, depending on level **Financial Aid:** Scholarship; Work/Study **Size-Attendees:** 100-200 **Size-Class:** 10-25

FOR ALMOST 25 years this studio and its companion community ballet company, the Baton Rouge Ballet Theatre, have offered superior dance training, both for those who wish to pursue a career in dance and for those who just want to take a class for the fun of it. The operation is the brainchild of the artistic team of Molly Buchmann and Sharon Mathews. Because of their efforts dance legends, such as Edward Villella, Melissa Hayden, Robert Joffrey and Martine van Hamel, have guested with the company as well as shared their expertise with workshop students. The success rate of the alumni speaks volumes about this local studio. Numerous students have gone on to enjoy careers with ballet and modern companies and on Broadway, as well as to choreograph, teach and direct their own companies.

The workshop employs 6 teachers and 5 assistant teachers, with credits that range from Canada's Royal Winnipeg Ballet to Ballet West. Ballet is taught daily at 8 levels from preballet to advanced. Beginning and intermediate modern-dance classes are offered on a more limited basis. For adults, morning and evening ballet classes are offered, along with 2 levels of tap and beginning modern. The affiliated company maintains both junior and senior companies, providing numerous performance opportunities for the students, as well as the chance to perform alongside professional dancers hired for individual productions.

Giacobbe Academy of Dance

👣 ❄️ *For ballet, jazz, tap dancers, choreographers* Greater New Orleans area — 6925 Veterans Blvd., Metairie, LA 70003 **Voice:** 504-889-0940 **Fax:** 504-456-1307 **Contact:** Joseph Giacobbe, Dir. **Founded:** 1943 **Open:** Year-round **Admission:** Written application, audition **Deadlines:** Apply each semester **Cost:** $16 per class **Financial Aid:** Scholarship; Work/Study **Size-Attendees:** 575 **Size-Class:** 10-30

THIS 56-YEAR-OLD institution came into being simply because Leona and Lawrence Giacobbe were reluctant to expose their 2 eldest daughters to the perils of the dance world of New York City. Instead they turned their backyard into a makeshift dance studio for their 2 gifted offspring. It didn't take long for the neighborhood children and 2 more Giacobbe siblings to get in on the act. Now hundreds of students a year pack the academy's 3 studios, in Metairie, Slidell and Mandeville. The success rate of the students speaks volumes for the training and legacy of the Giacobbes. Over the years students have won numerous scholarships to such schools as the School of American Ballet, the Joffrey School and the Houston Ballet, and many are dancing in professional companies such as ABT, the Joffrey and the London Festival, San Francisco and Boston ballets.

The school's training focuses on the Italian and Russian styles. Junior, intermediate and advanced courses prepare students for the rigors of a professional career. In addition to ballet the school also offers classes in jazz

and tap in its theater-dance arts program. The faculty of 11 still includes 3 Giacobbes on the roster. The academy is the official training center for the Delta Festival Ballet and the New Orleans Youth Ballet. Created in 1969 as a civic organization, the Delta Festival Ballet became a professional ballet company in 1981. The New Orleans Youth Ballet was formed in response to the needs of younger dancers requiring stage experience: they rehearse weekly and perform with the Delta Festival Ballet, the New Orleans Opera, the Louisiana Philharmonic Orchestra and in the company's own productions of *Cinderella, Beauty and the Beast* and *Sleeping Beauty*.

Maine

Bates Dance Festival

♻️ *For modern, ballet, jazz dancers, choreographers* About 45 min. N of Portland — 163 Wood St., Lewiston, ME 04240 **Voice:** 207-786-6381 **Fax:** 207-786-8282 **E-mail:** dancefest@bates.edu **Web Site:** www.bates.edu/summer/ **Contact:** Laura Faure, Dir. **Founded:** 1982 **Open:** 6 weeks in July **Admission:** Written application, resume documenting dance background **Deadlines:** June 12 **Cost:** $675 **Financial Aid:** Scholarship; Work/Study **Size-Attendees:** 325 **Size-Class:** 15-20 **Degree or Certification:** Certificate of completion, which may be presented to academic institutions to obtain credit

LAUNCHED IN 1982, this summer festival has grown into a nationally recognized contemporary dance gathering that boasts a faculty of over 40 with more than 200 students attending from both here and abroad. The program has gained considerable attention due in part to the size of the program offered: 27 classes daily to choose from, and the renown of the festival participants.

"The Bates Dance Festival is a phenomenon in itself … a formidable dance institution ... a New England artistic mecca," says Alan Kriegsman of the *Washington Post*. The names that might have inspired such enthusiasm include those of Danny Buraczeski, Doug Elkins, Rennie Harris, Liz Lerman, Bebe Miller and Kevin Wynn—all fixtures on the New York City modern-dance scene and regular festival participants. The program's 3 major components are the professional training program (for students 18 years and up), the young dancer's workshop (13-17), and the performance and public events series, featuring internationally renowned dance artists. The professional program is a 3-week intensive workshop for serious students of dance. Participants must have had a minimum of 3 years of continuous dance training. Class sizes are limited, and for the full-time program 4 classes a day are required. Students are encouraged to participate in the concerts given at the conclusion of the festival, performing either in their own work or in the work of faculty members. Rehearsal space is available for the creation of new work. Full-time students receive complimentary tickets to all performances and events during the festival—and there are many, from panel discussions to dance jams. Part-time students can purchase tickets to these evening events for $8. There are also 2 scheduled outings: one to the Maine Coast and the other to the Maine Festival, a multidisciplinary arts extravaganza held in nearby Brunswick.

Portland School of Ballet

For ballet, modern dancers
Downtown — Portland Performing Arts Center, 25A Forest Ave., Portland, ME 04101 **Voice:** 207-772-9671 **Contact:** Eugenia O'Brien, Artistic Dir. **Founded:** 1980 **Open:** Year-round **Admission:** Written application **Deadlines:** Rolling **Cost:** $9.50 per class, $727 for summer intensive **Financial Aid:** Scholarship; Work/Study **Size-Attendees:** 100-200 **Size-Class:** 15-25

THIS PREPROFESSIONAL ballet training center offers classes in ballet at all levels by a faculty with a diverse background in the field, including credits with the Ohio and Boston ballets. Taking into account the needs of the serious young dancer, a partnership has been established with a local school, offering those with career aspirations an academic alternative. High-school-age dancers can enroll in Portland High School for their academic classes, with an early-afternoon release to take ballet at Portland School of Ballet, located just a few blocks away. The program is also available to dancers outside the Portland school district.

The school offers classes in preballet, ballet technique, pointe, variations, partnering, contemporary ballet, modern and character. Guest artists from around the country teach masterclasses. Former students in the preprofessional program have gained entrance into such leading schools and companies as the School of American Ballet, Boston Ballet School, Walnut Hill School and Washington Ballet School.

Maryland

Ballet Theatre of Annapolis

For ballet dancers, choreographers 1 hr. from Baltimore and Washington, DC — 801 Chase St., Annapolis, MD 21401 **Voice:** 410-263-8289 **Fax:** 410-626-1835 **E-mail:** btaballet@aol.com **Web Site:** www. BtaBallet.org **Contact:** Edward Stewart, Artistic Dir. **Founded:** 1980 **Open:** Year-round **Admission:** Registration form **Deadlines:** Rolling **Cost:** From $142 for 1 class per week for 15 weeks **Financial Aid:** Scholarship; Work/Study **Size-Attendees:** 50-150 **Size-Class:** 10-30

THE SCHOOL OF BALLET Theatre of Annapolis offers a Russian-based training system to prepare students for careers in classical dance. The school and the company are housed at Maryland Hall for the Creative Arts, an attractive building just beyond the historic district. They share 5 studios and support facilities. Annapolis is one of the most charming cities in America, and despite its small-town accessibility, it has a sophisticated arts scene.

The school and the company are directed by Edward Stewart, a former featured dancer with the Pittsburgh Ballet Theatre and the Chicago Ballet. In addition to training with David Howard, he studied with some of the great Russian dancers, including Igor Youskevitch, Edward Caton and Valentina Pereyaslavec. Along with Stewart, the faculty includes 6 teachers who dance with the professional company. Many members of the faculty studied at Towson State University, and while their professional performing credentials are with minor companies, the curriculum seems solid. Further, many of the school students have gone on to perform with major companies, always a good indication of quality training.

Goucher College

For ballet, modern dancers 8 mi. from downtown Baltimore — 1021 Dulaney Valley Rd., Baltimore, MD 21204 **Voice:** 401-337-6390; 800-goucher **Web Site:** www. goucher.edu/dance/dance.htm **Contact:** Amanda Thom Woodson, Dept. Chair **Founded:** 1885 **Open:** Year-round **Admission:** Written application, audition, transcripts, SATs, writing sample **Deadlines:** Feb. 1 **Cost:** $20,200 for tuition **Financial Aid:** Loans; Scholarship; Fellowship; Stipend; Work/Study **Size-Attendees:** 200 **Degree or Certification:** BA in Dance **Job Placement:** Yes

THIS HIGHLY REGARDED liberal-arts college with a total enrollment of 1,000 offers a good dance program with a 16-member faculty serving 200 students, 60 of whom are majors receiving a lot of personal attention. The faculty has strong credentials in the areas of performance, dance history, notation, dance therapy, education and movement analysis. They include former members of the Limón Dance Company, the Pennsylvania Ballet, Ballet Oklahoma and the Baltimore Ballet. Many guest teachers and guest companies teach and perform at Goucher, including the likes of Violette Verdy, Gary Masters, Jean-Pierre Bonnefoux, Allegra Kent, Patricia McBride, Bebe Miller and Doug Varone.

The current department chair, Amanda Thom Woodson, studied in England and at Ohio State University. Other faculty include Chrystelle Trump Bond, past chair of the department, who studied at the University of North Carolina; Laura Gurdus Dolid, a former member of the Pennsylvania Ballet, Les Grands Ballets Canadiens and the Israel Ballet; and Lester Holmes, who worked with Gower Champion and Michael Bennett performing on Broadway and in various television productions. According to Woodson, the major strength of the program is its double emphasis, which gives students an opportunity to earn a liberal-arts degree while continuing to study dance. Also, she feels that equal emphasis on ballet and modern produces a "well-rounded dancer."

Recent graduates have gone on to performing careers with Taylor II, the David Parsons Company, Shapiro & Smith and the Ballet Theater of Annapolis. The dance facilities include 3 large studios, a 1,000-seat auditorium and a large studio that converts into a small dance theater. All students are encouraged to master both ballet and modern dance, as well as the study of dance as an academic discipline. The specialty of the house seems to be in preparing dance majors for graduate programs in dance therapy. A student can also specialize in performance, dance education, dance science, dance-and-arts administration, dance and theater or dance history and criticism, or a combination of any 2 areas.

Metropolitan Ballet Theatre and Academy

For ballet, ethnic, jazz, modern dancers, choreographers *Suburban Washington, DC — 10076 Darnstown Rd., Suite 202, Rockville, MD 20850* **Voice:** 301-762-1757 **Web Site:** www.erols.com/mbta/main.htm **Contact:** Suzanne Erlon, Dir. **Founded:** 1989 **Open:** Year-round **Admission:** Written application, registration fee **Deadlines:** Rolling **Cost:** $55 for 5 classes **Financial Aid:** Scholarship; Work/Study **Size-Class:** 12-16

THIS ALL-SERVICE BALLET organization can take credit for the start of numerous professional careers. Headed by Suzanne Erlon, who has enjoyed a 35-year career as a performer, teacher and choreographer, the academy offers the same diversity to the students, who often return to teach or choreograph—a good sign for any training facility. In fact, a lot of the star pupils stay close to home since MBT offers dancers a wealth of opportunities that are not always encountered elsewhere. Recent alumni have gone on to careers with such prestigious companies as the American Ballet Theatre; the New York City, Richmond and Atlanta ballets; and Alonzo King's Lines Contemporary Ballet.

Instruction is offered Monday through Saturday in classical ballet technique, pointe, jazz, modern and Spanish character. Young students are encouraged to experiment with their own creativity by taking choreography classes. The facility has 2 studios, with a size limit on classes. Since there is a resident company, students can follow a preprofessional track, performing in the ballet productions, as well as with the community outreach programs.

Towson University

For ballet, ethnic, jazz, modern dancers, choreographers *Close to Baltimore and Washington, DC — Dept. of Dance, 8000 York Rd., Towson, MD 21252* **Voice:** 410-830-2760; 888-TOWSON **Fax:** 410-830-3752 **E-mail:** kbradley@towson.edu **Web Site:** www.towson.edu **Contact:** Karen Bradley, Chair **Founded:** 1866 **Open:** Year-round **Admission:** Written application, audition, transcripts, test scores **Deadlines:** Aug. 27 for fall semester **Cost:** Tuition $3,122 annually **Financial Aid:** Loans; Scholarship; Fellowship; Stipend; Work/Study **Size-Attendees:** 60 majors, 600 students **Size-Class:** 10-35 **Degree or Certification:** BA in Dance Performance, BA in Dance Education **Job Placement:** Yes

ANY DANCE STUDENT seriously considering a career in dance and torn between sacrificing education to pursue a rigorous dance program should look to Towson University. The university touts its fine-arts programs as well as its liberal-arts education, so students are armed with all the necessary tools to achieve whatever goal they might have. The program has enough of a history to give it clout in the dance community, and offer its graduates a solid curriculum in dance.

Located in the Fine Arts Center on the campus, the dance program shares its facilities with the art, music and theater-arts programs, encouraging students to intermingle and experiment with different arts media. The facilities are also quite respectable, including a 346-seat main-stage theater, a studio theater, galleries, studio space and a 520-seat concert hall. The department makes an effort to keep the program to a workable size, allowing for individual attention. And the courses run the gamut, including ballet and modern, jazz and tap, choreography, teacher training and the opportunity to explore the scientific, philosophical and historical foundations of dance. Guest artists who have visited Towson to teach masterclasses have included David Parsons, Ballet Trockadero, Limón Dance Company and Pilobolus. The University Dance Company presents lecture-demonstrations, concert performances, special matinees and residencies in public and private schools, colleges and universities throughout the state and region. These have included appearances with the Baltimore Symphony Orchestra and the Towson Jazz Ensemble. Students are also encouraged to gain practical experience with opportunities to work part-time and during the summer, teaching and choreographing for local institutions and agencies, including local dinner theaters, the Maryland Arts Festival and various theme parks. The program offers students all the necessary resources they need to pursue a career in dance, whether in performance, choreography or teaching.

Massachusetts

Ballet Theatre of Boston

 For ballet dancers 186 Massachusetts Ave., Boston, MA 02115 **Voice:** 617-262-0961 **Fax:** 617-267-1795 **E-mail:** btb@tiac.net **Web Site:** www.btb. org **Contact:** José Mateo, Dir. **Founded:** 1986 **Open:** Year-round **Admission:** Open **Cost:** $384 to $2,900 per year for Young Dancers Program, $80 for 10 adult classes **Financial Aid:** Scholarship **Size-Attendees:** 100-160 **Size-Class:** 20

THE BALLET THEATRE of Boston school operates a 3-studio facility located in downtown Boston on a main thoroughfare: Massachusetts Avenue, between Symphony Hall and the Berklee School of Music. BTB and its affiliate company have gained considerable recognition for its range of classes and for its high-quality faculty. Both the school and the company are directed by Cuban-born dancer and choreographer José Mateo, who founded the organization 12 years ago. In addition to Mateo faculty members include Mary Thompson, a former dancer with Makarova & Friends; Rachel Moore, formerly of American Ballet Theatre; Rebecca Arnold and Juliana Muirhead, both trained at the Ballet Theatre School; and Leo Guerard, who danced with both New York City Ballet and American Ballet Theatre.

The school focuses on developing aspiring young ballet dancers within a structured system and a carefully graded curriculum. The emphasis here, according to the director, is on American-style training, stressing placement, anatomically correct work and athleticism. The school has an ethnically diverse student body. Underserved students are eligible for support through the Massachusetts State Department of Social Services. Young dancers can audition for placement in the intermediate and advanced levels.

Adult classes, available without audition, are also offered.

Boston Ballet Center for Dance Education

 **For ballet, jazz, modern dancers, choreographers** 19 Clarendon St., Boston, MA 02116 **Voice:** 617-695-6950 **Fax:** 617-695-6995 **Web Site:** www.boston.com/bostonballet **Contact:** Anna-Marie Holmes, Dean of Faculty **Founded:** 1989 **Open:** Year-round **Admission:** Audition and teacher evaluations for summer program, preregistration for some classes, interview for Citydance program **Deadlines:** For summer program: Jan.-Dec. for auditions, Mar. for application, financial aid; for Boston Ballet School: rolling **Cost:** $1,950-$3,350 for 6-week summer program, $1,085-$1,930 for 3-week summer program, $90 for 10-class book **Financial Aid:** Scholarship **Size-Class:** 25 **Job Placement:** Yes

BOSTON BALLET IS one of the country's premier ballet companies, and the training-and-education center that was officially established in 1989 to coexist with the company is of equal note. Today more than 2,000 students train at the school, which is just 1 of 3 programs offered through the Center for Dance Education. Also on the center's roster are Citydance, a tuition-free, dance-training program for urban children; the Summer Dance Program, an intensive for advanced-level students; and the Young Dancer's Summer Workshop.

With 3 locations in the Boston area, the Boston Ballet School offers classes year-round for students wishing to pursue ballet professionally (as well as for those who want to dance just for the fun of it or for exercise). After an informal audition the student is placed in the appropriate level according to ability rather than age. The curriculum is based on the Vaganova method, with year-end evaluations by the teachers before advancement to the next level can be made. The opportunity to perform also exists: students can audition for roles in Boston Ballet's productions of *The Nutcracker*. The Summer Dance Program is an intensive 6-week program for serious dance students through college-age. Students are also given the option of a 3-week plan. Faculty has included Boston Ballet directors Bruce Marks and Anna-Marie Holmes, and such legendary performers as Cynthia Gregory and Fernando Bujones. Besides the traditional offerings of ballet, enrichment classes in jazz, modern, Spanish dance, choreography, character, mime, musical theater and music are offered. Class sizes are kept to a maximum of 25 students. Performance experience is an integral part of the program. At the conclusion of the 6 weeks, students perform original choreography by faculty members and excerpts from the classical repertoire, such as *Swan Lake, Don Quixote* and *Etudes*. Some students auditioning for the Summer Dance Program are offered contracts for Boston Ballet II, which serves as an important entry point into Boston Ballet proper, often supplementing the company's performances throughout the year.

A class at the Boston Ballet School, Boston.

Boston Conservatory

For ballet, modern dancers, choreographers *Downtown — 8 The Fenway, Boston, MA 02215* **Voice:** 617-536-6340 **Fax:** 617-536-3176 **E-mail:** admissions@BostonConservatory.edu **Web Site:** www.bostonconservatory.edu **Contact:** Yasuko Tokunaga, Chair **Founded:** 1867 **Open:** Sept.-June **Admission:** Personal essay, artistic resume, repertoire list, audition **Deadlines:** Dec.15 for application, Feb. 15 for audition tapes, Mar. 1 for financial aid **Cost:** $15,300 tuition, $60 application fee **Financial Aid:** Loans; Scholarship; Fellowship; Work/Study **Size-Attendees:** 60 **Degree or Certification:** Conservatory Diploma in Dance, BFA in Dance, MFA in Dance (emphasis in Performance) **Job Placement:** Yes

FOUNDED IN 1867, Boston Conservatory boasts a distinguished faculty and a rich tradition of training artists through performance opportunities. The dance division, initiated in 1943, is the oldest degree-granting program in the United States. It is the second largest program of the conservatory, with 29 dance faculty. The core curriculum includes ballet and modern dance coupled with a program of jazz, tap, Alexander and various ethnic techniques. Conservatory alumni dance in many of the country's most distinguished ballet and modern-dance companies.

With a surprisingly low student-faculty ratio and only 60 students in the undergraduate and graduate programs, the school ranks among the very best in training dancers and choreographers. The faculty are genuine artists; the setting is decidedly urban. The rich cultural activities in Boston do indeed provide substantial opportunities for the conservatory's students to practice their art and hone performance skills. The dance studios are small and are located in the basement of the Boston Conservatory's theater building. However, an additional studio, the Annex on Boylston Street, is sunnier and more airy. The conservatory is located in the Back Bay section near the Prudential Center, the shops on Newbury Street and Copley Square. Occasionally classes are held along the riverfront. A real plus is the student housing, required for freshmen. Attractive row-houses in this residential neighborhood provide comfortable student lodgings at an affordable price. The faculty is headed by Yatsuko Tokunaga, a graduate of the Juilliard School and head of her own company in New York; former Limón dancer Jennifer Scanlon; Donna Silva, formerly of the Joffrey Ballet and First Chamber Dance Company; and Anamarie Sarazin and Denise Pons, formerly of the Boston Ballet. If an intimate environment with other faculty and students appeals to you, look into the Boston Conservatory. Few other degree-granting institutions are able to offer the level of personal mentoring available here.

Five College Dance Department

For ballet, ethnic, jazz, modern dancers, choreographers *Connecticut River Valley of western Massachusetts — Dance Bldg., Hampshire College, 97 Spring St., Amherst, MA 01002* **Voice:** 413-256-8974 **E-mail:** fcdd@helios.hampshire.edu **Contact:** Becky Nordstrom, Prof. of Dance **Open:** Sept.-June **Admission:** Application, application fee, interview **Deadlines:** Feb. 1, Nov. 15 for early admission **Cost:** $28,980 per year for tuition, room and board, as well as transcript and other fees **Financial Aid:** Loans; Scholarship; Work/Study **Size-Class:** 10-25 **Degree or Certification:** BA in Dance, Dance Theater, or a dance concentration; UMass offers a BFA; Smith College, an MFA **Job Placement:** Yes **Handicapped Access**

FIVE COLLEGE DANCE Department is a collaboration among Amherst, Hampshire, Mt. Holyoke and Smith colleges and the University of Massachusetts at Amherst, offering students more than 100 courses annually, taught by a faculty of 25 professional dancers, choreographers and dance educators. While each college maintains its own admission standards and core curriculum, a student in good standing, after completing a semester, can select from a wide array of courses and activities at the other colleges at no extra charge. Students can also use the libraries and other facilities on the other campuses and benefit from free intercampus transportation between the 5 schools, all located within an 11-mile radius.

All 5 schools offer a BA either in dance, in dance theater or in dance concentration. The university also offers a BFA, and Smith offers an MFA. While students can elect courses at a sister school, credits and degrees are awarded by their home school. While each campus mounts its own productions, an additional performing outlet is offered by the Five College Department's own annual production. By pooling resources the colleges are able to attract a great number of acclaimed performing companies, solo artists and dance critics, writers and educators. Recent guests have included Mark Dendy, Adrienne Hawkins, Bebe Miller, Marcia Siegel, Alvin Ailey Dance Theatre, Ballet Bordeaux and Batsheva Dance Company. The advantages to this collaborative arrangement are significant; anyone uncertain about a performing career, but committed to receiving an undergraduate degree from a solid institution, might consider applying to 1 of the 5 colleges.

Jacob's Pillow

For modern, ballet, ethnic, jazz dancers, choreographers Berkshire Hills of western Massachusetts, 8 mi. S of Mass Pike Exit 2 — Rte. 20, Becket, MA 01223; P.O. Box 287, Lee, MA 01238 **Voice:** 413-637-1322 **Fax:** 413-243-4744 **E-mail:** jacobspillow@taconic.net **Web Site:** www.jacobspillow.org **Contact:** J.R. Glover, Education Programs Dir. **Founded:** 1936 **Open:** June-Sept. **Admission:** Written application ($30), audition or videotape **Deadlines:** Apr. **Cost:** $375 tuition per week plus $150 room and board **Financial Aid:** Scholarship; Work/Study **Size-Attendees:** 75-100 **Size-Class:** 6-26 **Handicapped Access**

J ACOB'S PILLOW IS America's dance mecca. This is particularly true in the field of modern dance where literally every important figure performs or teaches at the "Pillow" during his or her career. The School, founded by dance pioneer Ted Shawn in 1936, was envisioned as a "university of the dance," and the Pillow does indeed offer a wide array of workshops in modern, jazz, ethnic dance, choreography and dance education. It also offers internships in arts administration, providing aspiring managers opportunities to work alongside the professional staff. Located in the culturally rich Berkshire Hills of western Massachusetts, the Pillow boasts a distinguished faculty, particularly in the fields of modern dance and jazz. Among the acclaimed teachers are Daniel Nagrin, Donald McKayle, Sara Rudner, Elizabeth Keen, Danny Buraczeski, Milton Myers and Chuck Davis.

Opportunities to attend performances abound, with a full schedule of professional companies featured in the Pillow's 3 performing spaces. Prospective students should take note that the ballet program varies from year to year and that each summer the Pillow tends to emphasize one or more special areas of ballet technique and performance. The Pillow holds mandatory national auditions in the months of February and March in 11 cities across the country. Applicants are required to

The Ted Shawn Dancers at the original Jacob's Pillow, Becket.

attend auditions if they live within 150 miles of an audition site. Otherwise, videos are accepted. Jacob's Pillow is notable for its bucolic setting and the lovely old barns and other rustic structures on its 150-acre campus. The pastoral setting and sheer physical beauty make it a romantic environment in which to study, work and absorb the atmosphere of this magical place. The Pillow is the site of America's first theater designed specifically for dance, the Ted Shawn Theatre, constructed in perfect harmony with the beautiful buildings of this one-time farm. Over the years the site was developed to include an outdoor theater, the black-box studio/theater and Blake's Barn, a visitors' center as well as an exhibition and archival space. The best feature of the Pillow is the open access to the grounds and campus, an innovation of former director Liz Thompson, who also added programs to support contemporary work. There is absolutely no barrier between artists and audience, and this is essential to the Pillow's personality. The rich offerings each summer include about 35 dance companies presenting at least 150 performances, creative residencies by a handful of companies, and a first-rate community and professional education program, including "PillowTalks" providing pre- and post-performance presentations aimed at building dance literacy. Apparently, audiences are hungry for this kind of presentation and interaction with the artists because these presentations are always well attended. For the student all this adds up to a great opportunity for learning about America's dance traditions and the latest innovations in dance in one of the most enriching and beautiful environments imaginable.

Jacob's Pillow—Dance Mecca

New York Times critic Anna Kisselgoff once wrote, "The point of Jacob's Pillow is that it is Jacob's Pillow," and the *New York Post's* Clive Barnes agreed, "There is only one Jacob's Pillow." But what exactly is that? Visitors are first captivated by the mysterious-sounding name. It's a reference to the biblical Jacob, who laid his head upon a rock and dreamt of a ladder to heaven. A nearby road is known as "Jacob's Ladder," and one of the settlers who first occupied the property in the late 18th century derived the farm's name from a prominent cushion-shaped boulder in the backyard.

Modern-dance pioneer Ted Shawn kept the name when he first started presenting performances in the barn-studio in Becket, Massachusetts, in 1933, and it has been known to legions of dancers and dance-goers as "the Pillow" ever since.

The Pillow's dance season is unmatched in length, breadth and in the uninterrupted span of its history. The Pillow is also unique in that is was built specifically for dance by dancers. The site still has the atmosphere of a farm, with stone walls, rustic barn siding on many of the buildings, and a casual air that makes visitors feel immediately at home. The sense of place is unmistakable. At least two former directors have voiced their opinions on the sense of place. Liz Thompson says, "One feels an accumulation of dancers dancing here," and Charles Reinhart senses that, "There are ghosts and spirits, memories of the great achievements of the past."

Ted Shawn was a champion of all kinds of dance, and he believed in educating both dancers and audiences in understanding and appreciating a diverse range of artists. In fact, for more than 30 years the school was known as "The University of the Dance," in reference to its wide-ranging curriculum. The spirit of inclusiveness lives on today in a place that is regarded as the dance world's "Mecca." The 10-week summer festival and school features presentation and education programs that embrace ballet, ethnic, modern and popular dance forms. Performers, students and audience members from far and wide mix and mingle in an informal atmosphere of creativity and sharing.

While the laid back atmosphere is a wonderful antidote to the fast-paced lifestyle of city dancers, there is a palpable energy at the Pillow that makes it possible to accomplish miraculous things during even the briefest of stays. For artists-in-residence, aspiring dancers and leading performers alike, there can be no rest at Jacob's Pillow.

—Norton Owen,
Director of Preservation,
Jacob's Pillow Dance Festival

Jeannette Neill Dance Studio

For jazz, theater, ballet, modern, funk, tap dancers Downtown — 261 Friend St., 5th Floor, Boston, MA 02114 **Voice:** 617-523-1355 **E-mail:** ace@bitwise.net **Contact:** Jeannette Neill, Artistic Dir. **Founded:** 1979 **Open:** Year-round **Admission:** Open for classes, preregistration for workshops **Deadlines:** None, except June for Boston Summer Dance Festival **Cost:** $75 for 10 classes (2-week limit), professional rate available **Financial Aid:** Scholarship; Work/Study **Size-Class:** 15-20

BOSTON SUMMER Dance Festival and its parent studio school, Jeannette Neill Dance Studio, are developing a good reputation for emerging professionals working in musical theater, tap and jazz. Located in downtown Boston, near North Station and across from the Fleet (performing arts) Center, the studio has small, personalized classes throughout the year with 10 jazz faculty and modest offerings in modern dance and ballet.

The main feature, however, is the Summer Dance Festival, which has some of the best guest teachers working in musical theater today. The 3-week intensive program in July includes such guest teachers as Lane Alexander, Brenda Bufalino, 1993 Tony-winner Wayne Cilento, former Alvin Ailey dancer Milton Myers, master teacher Lynn Simonson and Lynne Taylor-Corbett, who directed *Titanic* and *Chess* on Broadway. The goals of the festival are to preserve the tradition of jazz dance and foster an appreciation of its heritage. Informal gatherings of faculty and students provide an opportunity for the legacy of jazz, tap and musical theater to be passed on to future generations of performers, dancers and teachers. The tuition is substantial for a 3-week intensive, but the school has a classy faculty. Take note: plan to spend quite a bit on housing, which is expensive in Boston, whether obtained through the festival or elsewhere.

Lesley College

For all dancers, choreographers Greater Boston — 29 Everett St., Cambridge, MA 02138 **Voice:** 617-349-8444 **Fax:** 617-349-8313 **E-mail:** gresmini@mail.lesley.edu **Web Site:** www.lesley.edu **Contact:** Gilda Resmini-Walsh, Prog. Advisor **Founded:** 1977 **Open:** Year-round **Admission:** Written application, written personal statement, transcripts, interview, slides of artwork **Deadlines:** Rolling admissions **Cost:** $15,000 per year tuition **Financial Aid:** Loans; Scholarship; Fellowship; Stipend; Work/Study **Size-Class:** 10-20 **Degree or Certification:** MA in Expressive Therapies **Job Placement:** Yes

FOR THOSE INTERESTED in applying their career, training or love of dance and movement to the field of dance therapy, Lesley College offers a progressive, broad-based program integrating arts therapies and the field of psychotherapy. Interested in maintaining a diverse student body, the program does not necessarily require a strong dance background as a prerequisite.

Lesley offers an MA in Expressive Therapies with a Dance-Therapy concentration. The program trains therapists who engage in the healing process by working through the arts. More than 20 years ago, when the Expressive Therapies Program was established, Lesley was a pioneer, one of the first graduate schools in the United States to train professionals in this emerging and highly creative field. Today the program is the largest of its kind in the world. The college makes several promises to its students: as they train they will continue to develop as artists and performers; they will be exposed to a variety of arts; extensive field work will be required— 450 hours of practicum and 600 hours of internship. The program has a student body ranging in age from 21 to 65. A good number have had formal training and professional experience as artists. Others have little background in art but nevertheless share the creativity, energy and strong commitment to helping people. Classes are offered in the morning, afternoon and evening to accommodate students' work and field experience schedules. In October, 1997, Lesley opened its extension site in Israel. The college also has a professional affiliation with the International School of Interdisciplinary Studies in Zurich, Switzerland, and the Toronto Art Therapy Institute in Canada. Clinical field work is emphasized in the program. Sites have included psychiatric hospitals, community mental-health centers, adult day treatment programs, geriatric centers and schools. Lesley's location in the Cambridge community, with its lively and acclaimed arts scene, makes for a dynamic learning experience.

School of Albany Berkshire Ballet

For ballet, ethnic, jazz, modern dancers, choreographers *The Berkshire Hills in Western Massachusetts — 51 North St., Pittsfield, MA 01201* **Voice:** 413-442-1307 **Fax:** 413-445-5382 **E-mail:** ruperd@rpi.edu **Web Site:** www.rpi.edu/~ruberd/bb_main. html **Contact:** Madeline Cantarella Culpo, Dir. **Founded:** 1960 **Open:** Year-round **Admission:** Written application, audition **Deadlines:** Rolling **Cost:** $375-$1,200 depending on class frequency **Financial Aid:** Scholarship; Work/Study

LED BY THE ENERGETIC teacher and ballet advocate Madeline Cantarella Culpo, this school has facilities in Pittsfield, Massachusetts, and in Albany, New York. The courses of study offered at the 2 schools mirror one another and the facilities are similar: each has 2 studios in historic buildings. Each school has an academy program for the professionally oriented student, as well as a junior company. The 2 junior companies perform alone or together throughout the Berkshire region and the New York capital district. Culpo also serves as the artistic director of the related professional company, whose *Nutcracker* and other productions often involve students in the school.

The course of study in ballet is rooted in the Cecchetti method passed on through renowned Juilliard teacher

Margaret Craske, with whom Culpo studied. Enrico Cecchetti was the great teacher with the Ballets Russes and trained many famous dancers, including Pavlova, Fokine and Nijinsky. The school also offers modern dance and jazz and intensive summer programs. In addition to Culpo, full-time faculty include 3 alumna of the school: Nancy Ropelewski Piece, principal dancer with the Albany Berkshire Ballet; Deirdre Duffin Swindlehurst, former dancer with the Pennsylvania Ballet; and Alicia Gilbert, a physical-therapy specialist. Andrea Borak has recently joined the faculty as an instructor in modern dance. Graduates of the school have gone on to many of the country's illustrious companies, including the Pennsylvania Ballet, Houston Ballet, Joffrey Ballet, American Ballet Theatre, and Ohio Ballet. For the serious student, the school offers considerable discounts for taking more than 2 classes per week.

Walnut Hill School

For ballet, jazz, modern dancers, choreographers *20 min. W of Boston — 12 Highland St., Natick, MA 01760* **Voice:** 508-653-4312 **Fax:** 508-653-9593 **E-mail:** walnuthill@aol.com **Contact:** Anthony Blackman, Dir. of Adm. **Founded:** 1893 **Open:** Sept.-June **Admission:** Written application, school transcripts, audition, interview **Deadlines:** Feb.1 for financial aid, Feb.15 for application, **Cost:** $14,300 per year **Financial Aid:** Loans; Scholarship **Size-Attendees:** 230 **Degree or Certification:** HS diploma **Job Placement:** Yes

WALNUT HILL SCHOOL'S claim to fame is that it stands as the only independent school for the arts in the East, a New England version of the celebrated *Fame* high school. In 1893, Walnut Hill was originally founded as a preparatory school for Wellesley College. However, in 1971, with the school's academic reputation well established, a cocurricular program was integrated into the academic program, incorporating the fine and performing arts. The school now has an equally good reputation for providing one of the best training programs for young people who want to pursue a professional career in the arts. Students are required to major in one of the 4 art programs: dance, music, theater or visual arts. Part of the school's success lies in its location within 20 minutes of the city of Boston.

Capitalizing on the wealth of cultural resources and master teachers found in the Boston area, the school has fostered cooperative programs with such institutions as the Boston Ballet's Center for Dance Education. Walnut Hill dancers are allowed to attend rehearsals, dress rehearsals, previews and performances of the Boston Ballet Company. Also, workshops and seminars enable students to observe, question and learn from Boston Ballet artistic staff and dancers. Bruce Marks and Anna Marie Holmes of the Boston Ballet teach advanced classes at Walnut Hill on a regular basis, as do many of the other current company members. However, lest you think this is solely a program for aspiring ballerinas, it's not. The program produces equally gifted contemporary dancers, with a program that includes classes in modern dance, Spanish and character, jazz and choreography. Pupils have gone on to top academic programs and companies worldwide after finishing their dance training at Walnut Hill.

Michigan

Interlochen Center for the Arts

  For ballet, ethnic, jazz, modern dancers, choreographers About 4 hours NW of Detroit — P.O. Box 199, Interlochen, MI 49643 **Voice:** 231-276-7472; 616-276-7472 **Fax:** 231-276-7300 **E-mail:** smithdl@interlochen.k12.mi.us **Web Site:** www.interlochen.k12.mi.us **Contact:** Dee Smith, Asst. Dir. **Founded:** 1928 **Open:** Year-round **Admission:** Written application, audition **Deadlines:** Rolling admissions, Feb. 15 for summer session **Cost:** $23,650 per year, $4,150 for summer camp **Financial Aid:** Loans; Scholarship; Fellowship; Stipend; Work/Study **Size-Attendees:** 430 **Size-Class:** 15-25 **Job Placement:** Yes

O NE OF THE NATION'S premier arts academies, Interlochen has made a name for itself by giving young people a head start on their professional careers. The arts academy is the institution's main component, supplemented by 3 other educational programs: the arts camp, public radio, and the arts festival. Interlochen's mission statement is to "serve as an advocate of all the arts, a model and innovative teaching center, and presenter of outstanding artistic achievement in service to a diverse regional, national, and international constituency."

The Interlochen Arts Academy was established in 1962 as the nation's first independent high school dedicated to the arts. It remains the nation's top fine-arts boarding high school today. A recent statement from Juilliard's director of admissions attests to the academy's impeccable reputation: "The Juilliard School accepts more graduates from Interlochen Arts Academy than from any other single school." Young artists from 46 states and 17 other countries make up the academy's student population; 95 percent of the academy's graduates go on to the nation's most distinguished colleges

INTERLOCHEN CENTER FOR THE ARTS

Dancers at the Interlochen Center for the Arts, Interlochen.

School of Grand Rapids Ballet

For ballet dancers, choreographers About 25 mi. E of the Lake Michigan shore — 233 East Fulton St., Suite 126, Grand Rapids, MI 49503 **Voice:** 616-459-8464 **Fax:** 616-454-0672 **Contact:** Gordon Schmidt, School Dir. **Founded:** 1983 **Open:** Year-round **Admission:** Registration form **Deadlines:** Rolling **Cost:** $90-$395 per semester depending on level, summer program $145 per week or $450 for 6 weeks **Financial Aid:** Scholarship; Work/Study **Size-Attendees:** 150 **Size-Class:** 25

and universities. The academy has produced 27 Presidential Scholars in the Arts—more than any other private or public school in the country. The academy offers a ballet-based program emphasizing performance (3 fully produced concerts are presented each year). Classes in jazz, modern and other contemporary styles are also offered. Guest artists over the years have included Gus Giordano, Violette Verdy and Bella Lewitzky. Recent graduates are now dancing with such companies as the Joffrey, Pacific Northwest, San Francisco, and Milwaukee ballets and Hubbard Street Dance. As part of the Interlochen Arts Festival, more than 750 concerts, visual-arts exhibits, theater and dance productions are presented on the campus for students, faculty, staff and guests. The scenic 1,200-acre Interlochen campus is surrounded by glacial lakes and pines.

GRB CAME INTO being with a little help from its friends; it has developed into one of the state's leading ballet schools. The friends were the influential Robert Joffrey and Edith D'Adarrio, director of the Joffrey Ballet School, who encouraged and supported the school's foundation in 1983. As a result, a steady influx of talent comes from the NYC region, teaching, choreographing and performing with the company.

The school is run by Patrick Johnson, former leading dancer with Dance Theatre of Harlem. Other faculty include Amanda Smith, former member of the Joffrey Ballet, and Melanie Anderson, former principal with the Washington Ballet. The school offers classes year-round, and has trained students who have gone on to work with the Joffrey, New York City Ballet, Milwaukee Ballet and numerous training institutions, such as the School of American Ballet and the Boston Ballet School. Located on the banks of the Grand River, the facility is surrounded by cultural riches and natural wonders.

University of Michigan

For all dancers, choreographers Detroit suburb — U of M Dance Dept., 1310 N. University Ct., Ann Arbor, MI 48109 **Voice:** 313-763-5460 **Fax:** 313-763-5962 **E-mail:** delanghe@umich.edu **Web Site:** http://www.music.umich.edu/departments/dance/ **Contact:** Gay Ann Delanghe, Dept. Chair **Founded:** 1818 **Open:** Year-round **Admission:** Written application, audition, transcripts, writing sample, GRE, interview **Deadlines:** Feb. 1 **Cost:** $20,800 per year **Financial Aid:** Loans; Scholarship; Fellowship; Stipend; Work/Study **Size-Attendees:** 50 **Size-Class:** 5-25 **Degree or Certification:** MFA in Dance, BFA, BDA in Dance **Job Placement:** Yes

THE DANCE DEPARTMENT at this university with its international reputation benefits both from the culturally hip town of Ann Arbor and from the university's abundant resources. It's a solid, respectable program boasting a distinguished faculty, as well as a number of successful alumni, among them Christine Dakin of Martha Graham. Many faculty members are transplanted professionals from the Big Apple, having enjoyed success as both performers and directors of their own companies.

Since the dance department is part of the music school, dance students can often collaborate with composers, musicians, theater-lighting specialists, actors and directors. A program in music and technology offers dancers the opportunity to use advanced computer technology in the creation and performance of dance. Projects can be developed in CD-ROM, video dance, dance history and the creation of synthesizer scores for dance. The department serves about 50 students, with 8 full-time and 4 part-time faculty. Advanced students might be selected to appear with Ann Arbor Dance Works, the school's resident professional company composed of dance-department faculty. The company presents occasional concerts in New York City, as well as tours the state of Michigan. The techniques taught in the department range from Graham-based to the more eclectic approach of combining Limón and Cunningham. Graduate students are required to teach undergraduate courses along with developing an MFA-thesis concert. If your interests include teaching as well as choreography, this program provides you with ample opportunity to do both. Faculty members include Gay Delanghe, a former member of the Lucas Hoving and Yvonne Rainer dance companies; Bill DeYoung, who danced with Bella Lewitzky; Peter Sparling, former member of the Limón Dance Company and the Martha Graham Dance Company; and Robin Marie Wilson, who was a member of Urban Bush Women. The dance building houses 4 studios, 1 of which doubles as a theater. Dance performances are showcased at 6 venues ranging in size from a 1,400-seat center to a 145-seat recital hall.

Western Michigan University

For ballet, jazz, modern dancers, choreographers Midway between Detroit and Chicago — Dept. of Dance, College of Fine Arts, 1201 Oliver St., Kalamazoo, MI 49008 **Voice:** 616-387-5845 **Fax:** 616-387-5809 **E-mail:** wendy.cornish@umich.edu **Web Site:** www.wmich.edu **Contact:** Jane Bass, Dept. Chair **Founded:** 1972 **Open:** Sept.-June **Admission:** Written application, audition, resume **Deadlines:** Rolling **Cost:** $100-$230 per semester **Financial Aid:** Loans; Scholarship; Fellowship; Stipend; Work/Study **Size-Attendees:** 100 **Size-Class:** 15-20 **Degree or Certification:** BA in Dance, BFA in Dance **Job Placement:** Yes

IT SEEMS THANKS ARE due to dance legend Agnes De Mille for the present-day dance program here. During a 1967 appearance to receive an honorary degree, De Mille discussed the viability of dance programs on university campuses with Cornelius Loew, then associate dean of the School of Liberal Arts and Sciences. On the way from the airport in Detroit to Kalamazoo she insisted that no significant program could be developed at WMU until dance was accepted as a fine art and moved out of the women's physical-education department in the College of Education. When the College of Fine Arts was established in 1972, dance was 1 of the first 3 departments to be instituted.

The department today has 100 dance majors and minors and more than a thousand other students taking advantage of the classes offered; it is the largest dance program in any university in Michigan. While still a relatively young program at the university, and in comparison to better-known programs around the country, it provides solid opportunities to any degree candidate, and a list of credentials on a par with most other programs. Classes are offered in ballet, jazz and modern-dance technique. Opportunities to perform in formal and informal productions are available monthly, and student choreography is encouraged and presented in department concerts. Regular guest residencies and performances by dance professionals at the university theater expose students to companies from around the country. Alumni have gone on to perform in such companies as Garth Fagan, Margaret Jenkins and Gus Giordano. A permanent faculty of 7, again representing successful careers in ballet, modern and jazz, is supplemented by guest faculty, such as Urban Bush Women, Alwin Nikolais, Billy Siegenfeld, Shapiro and Smith and former New York City Ballet and Lar Lubovitch company members.

Minnesota

Ballet Arts Minnesota

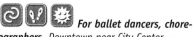 *For ballet dancers, chore-ographers* Downtown near City Center — Hennepin Center for the Arts, 528 Hennepin Ave., Minneapolis, MN 55403 **Voice:** 612-340-1071 **Fax:** 612-332-8131 **E-mail:** dancebam@mtn.org **Web Site:** www.mtn.org/~dancebam **Contact:** Bonnie Mathis, Dir. **Founded:** 1989 **Open:** Year-round **Admission:** Written application, placement audition **Deadlines:** Rolling **Cost:** $55 for 10-class card **Financial Aid:** Scholarship; Work/Study **Size-Attendees:** 140 pre-professional, 40 children, 65 adults **Size-Class:** 5-25

BALLET ARTS IS Minnesota's leading dance studio for those seeking a preprofessional training ground. Although only at the end of its first decade the school has racked up an impressive list of credentials and can already boast alumni dancing in such companies as the San Francisco, Milwaukee and Louisville ballets. This is thanks primarily to the sound vision of codirectors Marcia Chapman and Bonnie Mathis.

Also working in favor of the school is a faculty with strong credentials as educators, not just as former performers. On the other hand the faculty is not without its impressive performing affiliations, including Les Grands Ballets Canadiens and the Bolshoi. Director Mathis herself is no slouch in the career department; she's a former principal dancer with American Ballet Theatre, as well as with Nederlands Dans Theatre, Lar Lubovich, Paul Taylor and the Harkness Ballet. Her connections have paid off: the extensive list of guest teachers includes such eminent names as Martine van Hamel, Helgi Tomasson, Christian Holder, Danny Buraczeski, Edward Villella and Mary Cochran. Performance opportunities are available through the apprentice ensemble, which enables the advanced students in the program to participate in a choreographic workshop with local professionals. One of the state's leading contemporary ballet companies, James Sewell Ballet, is in residence, offering yet another opportunity for students to gain insight into the life of a professional dancer.

School of the Minnesota Ballet

For ballet, jazz, modern, dancers, choreographers Downtown — 506 W. Michigan St., Duluth, MN 55802 **Voice:** 218-733-7570 **Fax:** 218-733-7538 **Web Site:** www.visitduluth.com/Depot/ballet.html **Contact:** Allen Fields, Artistic Dir. **Founded:** 1965 **Open:** Year-round **Admission:** Open; placement class for higher levels **Deadlines:** Rolling **Cost:** $7 per class **Financial Aid:** Scholarship; Work/Study **Size-Attendees:** 200 **Size-Class:** 10-25

A PROFESSIONALLY RUN company and school, the Minnesota Ballet is the state's major classical-ballet training center. It enrolls more than 200 students a semester, with a preprofessional division that periodically feeds into the main-company productions with the corps de ballet roles. Classes in ballet, pointe, adult ballet, jazz, modern, creative dance and "athletic ballet" are offered Monday through Saturday.

Most of the faculty originates with the company, with the exception of artistic director Allen Fields, who enjoyed an eclectic career dancing with such companies as Cleveland San Jose, Ohio Ballet, Hubbard Street and numerous others; and associate artistic director Robert Gardner, who danced professionally with the Joffrey, the Eglevsky Ballet and Cleveland San Jose. The faculty of 10 is augmented for the summer program by guest artists, such as Bonnie Mathis of Ballet Arts Minnesota and Francia Kulchar, formerly with American Ballet Theatre. Both the company and the school have a great deal to offer the

young trainee: 30 years of experience, the company's growing reputation and exposure to working professionals.

University of Minnesota

For modern, ballet, jazz, modern, tap dancers, choreographers Twin Cities metropolitan area — Dance Dept., 106 Norris Hall, 172 Pillsbury Dr. SE, Minneapolis, MN 55455 **Voice:** 612-624-4588 **Fax:** 612-625-2849 **E-mail:** theatre@tc.umn.edu **Web Site:** www.umn.edu **Contact:** Marge Maddux, Dir. **Open:** Sept.-June **Admission:** Written application, audition, writing sample, transcripts, SAT, resume **Deadlines:** May 1 for the fall semester, Oct. 15 for the spring semester **Cost:** $3,800 per year for state residents, $11,000 for nonresidents **Financial Aid:** Loans; Scholarship; Fellowship; Stipend; Work/Study **Size-Attendees:** 70 **Size-Class:** 10-20 **Degree or Certification:** BA in Dance, BFA in Dance **Job Placement:** Yes

R EFLECTING THE HOTBED of cultural activity found in the Twin Cities, the dance department at the University of Minnesota exposes students to a long list of first-rate professionals in the field. Located near the Walker Arts Center, one of the largest arts presenters in this country, the school benefits from the artists who are drawn to this artistic mecca.

The dance program offers 2 undergraduate degrees, which can prepare students for a performance/creative career, teaching or further studies in such areas of dance as history, criticism, ethnology, pedagogy, movement analysis and kinesiology. While the program's emphasis is on modern dance, 4 years of ballet, jazz and modern dance technique are offered, as well as 2 years of tap. There are 4 full-time faculty, 16 affiliated faculty and a full-time visiting professorship through which artists of international renown are invited annually to teach, choreograph and lecture. Faculty members have garnered numerous awards and distinctions, including fellowships from the Bush, Fulbright,

Jerome, McKnight and Rockefeller foundations and from the National Endowment for the Arts. The facility harbors 4 studios and 2 classrooms. Faculty members making use of the local arts scene include Chris Aiken, Danny Buraczeski, Joanie Smith and American Ballet Theatre alumnae Lise Houlton and Bonnie Mathis. The university provides ample performance opportunities for students. On average, nearly 2 dozen performances are given a year, from workshop showings, to fully produced concerts by the University Dance Theatre and the Student Dance Coalition. In addition, UDT often collaborates with a major presenter or guest artist on a work of national significance. Examples include Merce Cunningham's "Changing Steps," as part of the Walker Arts Center's FLUXUS performance event; Bill T. Jones's "The Promised Land"; Kei Takei's "24 Hours of Light"; and Susan Marshall's "Spectators at an Event." Another bonus of the program is the Sage Cowles Land Grant Chair, which, since 1987, has enabled the university to host 4 to 6 dance professionals of international renown in residencies ranging from 1 to 10 weeks. The guests teach, choreograph and lecture in the Department of Theatre Arts and Dance, as well as in the community at large.

Missouri

Ballet Center of St. Louis

For ballet, jazz, modern, tap dancers, choreographers Near downtown — 10 Kimler Dr., St. Louis, MO 63043 **Voice:** 314-991-1233 **Fax:** 314-567-4299 **Contact:** Ludmila Dokoudovsky, Dir. **Founded:** 1984 **Open:** Year-round **Admission:** Written application, placement class **Deadlines:** Rolling **Cost:** $12 per class; from $80 per week tuition for summer program **Financial Aid:** Scholarship; Work/Study **Size-Attendees:** 200 **Size-Class:** 15-25 **Job Placement:** Yes

A HOMEGROWN ENTITY and the brainchild of Ludmila Dokoudovsky and Antoni Zalewski, the Ballet Center of St. Louis provides instruction in classical ballet to the local population from beginning through advanced level-5. With all the trappings of a high-quality training center—school, youth ensemble and a professional company—the center attracts a small but impressive list of guest teachers.

Many of the school's students have been accepted into such leading training institutions as Harid Conservatory, School of American Ballet, the Juilliard School, Pacific Northwest Ballet School and San Francisco Ballet School. The focus is on classical ballet, based on the method of Russian teacher Olga Preobajenska. Classes in tap and jazz are also available. Auditions are not required; all classes are open to students and professionals. The affiliated company has earned its stripes by staging such influential classics as David Lichine's *Graduation Ball*, Bronislava Nijinska's *Les Biches* and such standards as *Sleeping Beauty, Cinderella* and *A Midsummer Night's Dream*. Most of the faculty members have come from the

Ballet Center and are current and former members of the Company. Guest faculty include Deborah Wingert, former dancer with the New York City Ballet, and Hilda Morales, former soloist with the American Ballet Theatre.

5-state area. Students have been accepted into such programs as School of American Ballet, American Ballet Theatre, Pacific Northwest Ballet School, the Rock School of Pennsylvania Ballet and Houston Ballet Academy.

State Ballet School

For ballet dancers *Heart of historic Westport district* — *706 W. 42nd St., Kansas City, MO 64111* **Voice:** 816-931-2299 **Fax:** 816-931-1172 **E-mail:** floken2@coop.crn.org **Web Site:** www.stateballetofmissouri.org **Contact:** Karen Brown, Dir. **Founded:** 1981 **Open:** Year-round **Admission:** Written application, audition **Deadlines:** Apply each semester **Cost:** $8 per class **Financial Aid:** Scholarship; Work/Study **Size-Attendees:** 150 **Size-Class:** 15-25

A TESTIMONY TO THE quality of this organization is the number of dancers who spend their entire careers dancing for the affiliated company. And what goes around comes around: retired company members return as teachers, giving back in some measure the benefit they themselves reaped from the school. A past affiliation with Diana Adams and with director Todd Bolender has also helped keep the school on the map. The school definitely stands as a second home for dancers coming out of the larger training centers of New York, Boston, San Francisco and Pennsylvania.

The State Ballet School offers preprofessional dance training for students who aspire to dance professionally. Annual enrollment is approximately 150 students. The school offers 8 skill levels, from preballet to advanced-level students who attend class 6 days a week. More than 80 students appear in State Ballet's annual production of *The Nutcracker*; students also appear in selected works in the company's 3 repertory programs. A summer program is offered in June and July. In addition to ballet classes, students take classes in nutrition and music, and other forms of dance, such as jazz, tap and modern. The program is open to students in the

Montana

University of Montana

For modern dancers, choreographers *Western Montana* — *Dance Dept., Missoula, MT 59812* **Voice:** 406-243-4481; 800-462-8636 **Fax:** 406-243-5726 **E-mail:** MMBeaulieu@aol.com **Web Site:** www.umt.edu **Contact:** Amy Ragsdale, Head **Founded:** 1893 **Open:** Sept.-June **Admission:** Written application, audition, transcripts, test scores, interview **Deadlines:** Mar. 1 **Cost:** $130 per credit hour for state residents, $334 for nonresidents, plus $988 per semester for housing, $850 for meals **Financial Aid:** Loans; Scholarship; Fellowship; Stipend; Work/Study **Size-Attendees:** 30 **Size-Class:** 20-40 **Degree or Certification:** BFAs in Dance Choreography, Dance Education **Job Placement:** Yes

T HE DANCE PROGRAM here seems to be faculty-driven. The offerings are standard fare for an academic program, with the exception of 2 courses, entitled "Movement for the Disabled" and "Teaching Creative Movement to Children." These courses are taught by faculty member Karen Kaufmann, who specializes in childhood education. Currently running a lab in children's dance at UM, she has devoted a significant amount of time to movement for the young.

Ballet is taught by a former member of the Houston Ballet and the Frankfurt Ballet. Classes in musical-theater and tap are offered by a resident choreographer. Amy Ragsdale, the head of the dance program, made a name for herself performing in Boston and New York with such companies as Ze'eva

Cohen and Fred Benjamin Dance Company. She has also guested with Bill T. Jones/Arnie Zane. Over the years the program has hosted more than 60 guest artists and dance companies. Students have the option of concentrating in either teaching or choreography/performance. For the teaching emphasis, opportunities exist for students to teach college students, young children or the disabled. The university's 200-acre campus is set against the backdrop of Mount Sentinel along the banks of the Clark Fork River, close to miles of scenic wilderness, rivers, national parks and skiing.

Nebraska

University of Nebraska-Lincoln

🏠 *For ballet, modern dancers* Eastern Nebraska — Dept. of Theater Arts and Dance, 215 Temple Bldg., 12th and R Sts., Lincoln, NE 68588 **Voice:** 402-472-5803 **Fax:** 402-472-1712 **E-mail:** lmallett@unl.edu **Web Site:** www.unl.edu **Contact:** Larry Mallett, Chair **Founded:** 1868 **Open:** Year-round **Admission:** Written application, interview, transcripts, test scores, writing sample **Deadlines:** Apply each semester **Cost:** $2,968 for state residents, $6,951 for non-residents **Financial Aid:** Loans; Scholarship; Fellowship; Stipend; Work/Study **Size-Class:** 10-25 **Degree or Certification:** BA in Dance **Job Placement:** Yes

THE DANCE PROGRAM at this 130-year-old university is in transition, having been moved from the theater-and-dance department to the music department. The practical implications for students remain to be seen. But the change in the degree offered, from a BFA to a BA, indicates that there is a shift from a performance-oriented degree to a general, liberal-arts degree. There has been a recent turnover in faculty, with only one long-time faculty member, Lisa Fusillo, re-maining on the staff. Fusillo served as a choreographic assistant and artistic collaborator to Leonide Massine and later served as ballet mistress for the highly regarded company Cloudgate. The faculty also includes Kelly Holcombe, who danced with MOMIX, and Julie Kane, who teaches composition.

This urban university is the largest educational institution in Nebraska. Its Lied Center for the Arts is one of the major presenters of dance in the United States, and many companies that perform there offer masterclasses and other activities to the department's students. This is a definite plus for a program with a small faculty. Recent performances at the Lied Center have included the companies of Mark Morris, Doug Varone and Bill T. Jones. The UNL Dance Ensemble, a resident-student dance company, plans to begin performing in the new arts center in the near future.

Nevada

Nevada Ballet Theatre

🏠 ✳ *For ballet dancers, choreographers* Southern Nevada — 1555 E. Flamingo Road, #112, Las Vegas, NV 89119 **Voice:** 702-243-2623 **Fax:** 702-732-1355 **E-mail:** info@nvdance.com **Web Site:** www.nvdance.com **Contact:** Mark Steivel, Admin. **Founded:** 1972 **Open:** year round **Admission:** Open **Deadlines:** Rolling **Cost:** $36 for 4 classes per month **Financial Aid:** Scholarship; Work/Study **Size-Attendees:** 100-200 **Size-Class:** 5-25 **Job Placement:** Yes

THE LAS VEGAS STRIP isn't all that's putting Nevada on the map these days. But the famous Strip does figure in the history of this 27-year-old institution. NBT was conceived by dancer Vassili Sulich, who was a principal dancer with the Folies Bergere at the Tropicana Hotel, following a successful career dancing for Roland Petit's company. Sulich wanted to create a ballet company in the middle of the desert, and with the support of a single sponsor and a company of Strip dancers who agreed to perform without pay, the initial performances were given to a warm reception by the community.

The company has grown to include 24 resident dancers who, during a 28- to 36-week season, perform such ballets as *Giselle, Swan Lake, Nutcracker* and *La Fille Mal Gardé*. Works by Balanchine have also found their way into the program, along with those of a host of other contemporary classical choreographers. During the company's recent 25th-anniversary celebrations Sulich stepped down as artistic director, passing the torch to Bruce Steivel, who, in the last decade, has led such companies as Hong Kong Ballet, Bern [Switzerland] Ballet, and Ballet de Nord of France. Steivel joins the company as it undergoes some major changes. First, NBT received a $3.6-million grant from the Donald W. Reynolds Foundation to build a new, permanent facility on land in the community of Summerlin donated by the Howard Hughes Corporation. The new facility, the Donald W. Reynolds Cultural Center, was completed in the fall of 1998. All of NBT's operations can coexist under one roof, since the structure is a whopping 35,000 square feet. This stroke of good luck has enabled the company to expand from a regional organization into a world-class ballet company. It also made possible the founding, in 1979, of the School of Nevada Ballet Theatre to "inspire imaginative self-expression through dance." The school teaches and trains more than 250 children annually. The NBT Youth Company, composed of advanced students from the School, is given the opportunity to become familiar with professional performances by appearing onstage with the company. With the completion of the new facility, the school has enough space to teach 2,000 students a week.

New Hampshire

Antioch New England, Graduate School

 For movement therapists Mt. *Monadnock region of southern New Hampshire — 40 Avon St., Keene, NH 03431* **Voice:** 603-357-6265 **Fax:** 603-357-0718 **E-mail:** admissions@antiochne.edu **Web Site:** www.antiochne.edu **Contact:** Susan Loman, Dir. **Founded:** 1852 **Open:** Year-round **Admission:** Written application, group verbal/movement interview, academic history **Deadlines:** Rolling **Cost:** $350 per credit, plus $55 application fee for summer program; $4,000 per semester for fall and spring **Financial Aid:** Loans; Scholarship; Fellowship; Stipend; Work/Study **Degree or Certification:** MA in Dance/Movement Therapy, MEd. in Dance/Movement Therapy **Job Placement:** Yes

DO YOU DANCE TO A different drummer? Antioch will welcome you. Geared for the mature student with more life-experience credits than academic credits, the school prides itself on its nurturing, unconventional, politically correct syllabus and attitude. This is the only program in the country to offer a Master's degree in dance/movement therapy with a minor in counseling psychology. It is also noteworthy for being one of the first academic programs approved by the American Dance Therapy Association (ADTA).

The program stresses both practical and theoretical instruction, and helps graduates meet the requirements for certification as national certified counselors. Certification allows graduates to be licensed as mental-health counselors in most states. Graduates of the program have typically found employment in traditional psychiatric facilities, school systems, prisons, rehabilitation hospitals, drug-treatment centers, crisis centers and wellness and alternative-care centers. A summer intensive in dance/movement therapy is available for those who are undecided; so is a training option in drama therapy for those who want to combine dance and theater in the rehabilitative process.

The 8 core faculty members in the dance/movement program boast credentials showing the scope of career opportunities available to graduates in this field. Faculty members include the chair of the education committee for the American Dance Therapy Association; a specialist at the Group Project for Holocaust Survivors and Their Families; a teacher who integrates cranial psychotherapy, sacred-circle dancing and the expressive arts; and many who run their own private practices and clinics. A testimonial from a former student speaks to the program's vanguard qualities: "Attracted to the program because it honored middle-aged persons with life experience. Antioch is really the only place to go if you want a solid, in-depth background in dance/movement therapy. When I moved to Portland, Maine, in 1984, dance-movement therapy was virtually nonexistent in that area." After establishing her own therapy center and private practice, she now teaches courses on the use of the arts in psychotherapy at the local University of Maine and leads professional seminars in stress management, women's spirituality and tai chi.

Granite State Ballet

For ballet, jazz, modern, tap dancers, choreographers *Southern New Hampshire, 40 mi. from Boston* — *36 Arlington St., Nashua, NH 03060* **Voice:** 603-889-8408 **Fax:** 603-889-6621 **Contact:** Doreen Cafarella, Artistic Dir. **Founded:** 1985 **Open:** Year-round **Admission:** Open **Deadlines:** Rolling **Cost:** $9 per class **Financial Aid:** Scholarship; Work/Study **Size-Attendees:** 200 **Size-Class:** 15-20

COMPANIES AND schools like the GSB provide the sustenance that keeps classical dance alive and well in this country. For experienced as well as novice dancers, they provide opportunities to work, hone their craft and train, without the big budgets and wealth of resources of the larger regional and major dance companies, whose selectivity often discourages young hopefuls.

The school and the company were founded in 1985 under the artistic direction of Doreen Cafarella. In addition to regular classes in ballet, pointe variations and pas de deux, the curriculum includes modern, jazz, musical theater and tap. Students have a chance to be exposed to professional-caliber performances through the company, which employs guest artists and presents a diverse and eclectic repertoire. The company has both an apprentice and a trainee program for students enrolled at the school and upper-level students are invited to audition for both these programs. Among the 6 full-time faculty at the school is Anthony Williams, a charter member of the Boston Ballet, who also danced with the Joffrey.

School of Ballet New England

For ballet, ethnic, jazz, modern dancers Coastal New Hampshire, 60 mi. from Boston — P.O. Box 4501, Portsmouth, NH 03802 **Voice:** 603-430-9309 **Fax:** 603-431-0162 **E-mail:** balletne@tiac.net **Web Site:** www.ballet-new-england.org **Contact:** Angela Sears, School Dir. **Founded:** 1985 **Open:** Year-round **Admission:** Summer program: application, photographs, recommendations; Fall semester: registration **Cost:** $9 per class; $1,000 for 3-week, $1,595 for 6-week summer program **Financial Aid:** **Size-Attendees:** 70-80 **Size-Class:** 20

THE SCHOOL OF BALLET New England is one of the better alternatives for those not willing to travel to Boston. Located in downtown Portsmouth, the school offers classes year-round for all ages, with a program that includes classes in ballet, modern, flamenco and jazz. The affiliated company performs throughout the region. Ballet is based on the Vaganova system while modern is Limón-, Graham- and Cunningham-based, with improvisation thrown in for good measure.

The school has a good track record with regard to its students, many having gone on to train at such prestigious institutions as the School of American Ballet, the Boston Ballet and the Juilliard School. The year-round faculty members have noteworthy credentials, including former principal artists with such companies as the Cleveland Ballet, Les Grands Ballets Canadiens and the Milwaukee Ballet. But it's the summer program that really puts this school on the map, with its strong roster of guest faculty. Summer faculty have included Frank Ohman (former New York City Ballet soloist), Parrish Maynard (soloist with American Ballet Theatre) and William Pizzuto (former principal with Houston Ballet, Boston Ballet and Ballet West). Offered during July and August, the summer program gives the students the option of a 3-week or a 6-week intensive. For advanced students, the summer is dedicated almost solely to classical ballet. Special emphasis is placed on individualized attention: witness the 20-student limit per class.

St. Paul's School

For ballet dancers, choreographers Southern New Hampshire — Dance Department, 325 Pleasant St., Concord, NH 03301 **Voice:** 603-225-3341 **Fax:** 603-229-5591 **E-mail:** rrein@sps.edu **Web Site:** www.sps.edu **Contact:** Richard A. Rein, Dir. of Dance **Founded:** 1974 **Open:** Year-round **Admission:** Written application, audition **Deadlines:** Jan. 31 **Cost:** $22,000 **Financial Aid:** Loans; Scholarship; Work/Study **Size-Attendees:** 500 **Size-Class:** 10-25 **Degree or Certification:** High-School Diploma, Dance Major

IF YOU ARE IN the New England area and are looking for a conservatory specializing in ballet, St. Paul's might be just the place for you. A scaled-down version of Walnut Hill, St. Paul's offers the artistically minded and the serious young professional a venue for training, as well as for completing the academic requirement for a high-school degree.

St. Paul's is an independent, coeducational boarding school, providing students with a strong liberal-arts curriculum, complete with a curriculum in the arts, foreign languages, humanities, religion, mathematics, science and technologies. A variety of levels of ballet are offered, from beginning to advanced, all receiving academic credit. Some recent graduates have moved into professional companies, including New York City Ballet, Feld Ballets/NY, Ballet Chicago, Twyla Tharp, and prominent training schools, such as Juilliard and Tisch School of the Arts. The school's most famous alumnus is principal dancer Philip Neal of NYCB, winner of the silver medal in the 1985 Prix de Lausanne. Part of the school's success is owed to director of dance Richard A. Rein, who received his early training at the School of American

115

Ballet and danced with the American Ballet Theatre and the Pennsylvania Ballet. Rein has also been the coordinator of the National Endowment for the Arts Dance Touring Program. For serious students of ballet who by senior year are clearly heading for a professional career, the independent study program makes it possible to train exclusively. Past projects have included study at professional ballet schools, choreography, an internship at the New Hampshire Commission on the Arts, and the writing of a ballet textbook. Students have ample opportunity to perform, including with the St. Paul's School Ballet Company, which performs throughout the year. The company's repertory ranges from the classical works of Petipa to the modern classics of José Limón. In addition, contemporary choreographers including Lisa de Ribere, Jean-Pierre Bonnefoux and alumna Diane Vivona visit the school regularly to choreograph for the company. Guest performances have been given at the school by members of the New York City Ballet, American Ballet Theatre, Boston Ballet, Dance Theatre of Harlem, Fernando Bujones, Arthur Mitchell and Violette Verdy. The facility has 2 studios, a large one and a smaller one for warm-up and practice, and a 700-seat theater that serves as the dance department's home stage.

New Jersey

New Jersey Ballet School

For ballet dancers, choreographers NE New Jersey, 30 mi. from New York City — 15 Microlab Rd., Livingston, NJ 07039 **Voice:** 973-597-9600 **Fax:** 973-597-9442 **Contact:** Carolyn Clark, Dir. **Open:** Year-round **Admission:** Written application, audition **Deadlines:** Rolling **Cost:** From $335 for 10 months of classes **Financial Aid:** Scholarship; Work/Study **Size-Attendees:** 100-200 **Size-Class:** 10-25

NIPPING AT THE HEELS of the Princeton Ballet School for status of premier ballet school in the state, New Jersey Ballet School has a stellar faculty, but is of slightly more modest size than Princeton with regard to faculty, studio space and courses offered.

Directors of the school include Carolyn Clark, who performed with the American Ballet Theatre, as well as with the Metropolitan Opera Ballet and the New Jersey Ballet; and George Tomal, also a member of the American Ballet Theatre and of Roland Petit's Ballet de Paris. Special guest artist is famed dancer Edward Villella. Other heavy hitters include such ballet stars as Eleanor D'Antuono, principal dancer with ABT; Paul Sutherland, formerly with ABT, Joffrey and Harkness; Natasha Girshov, formerly of the Kirov Ballet; Luba Gulyaeva, formerly of the Kirov Ballet and former teacher at the ABT school at the request of Mikhail Baryshnikov during the 1980s; and Sophia Fatouros, formerly of Ballet Hispanico and the Dayton Ballet. New Jersey Ballet School is the official school of the New Jersey Ballet Company. Students have danced with such companies as ABT, New York City Ballet, Alvin Ailey, Metropolitan Opera, and Twyla Tharp.The school's main studio is located in Livingston, with additional studios in Somerville and Madison.

Princeton Ballet School

For ballet, ethnic, jazz, modern dancers, choreographers W central New Jersey, 40 mi. from Philadelphia — 301 N. Harrison St., Princeton, NJ 08540 **Voice:** 609-921-7758 **Fax:** 609-921-3249 **Contact:** Mary Pat Robertson, Dir. **Founded:** 1954 **Open:** Year-round **Admission:** Written application, audition **Deadlines:** Rolling **Cost:** From $475 per semester; from $1,150 for summer program **Financial Aid:** Scholarship; Work/Study **Size-Attendees:** 1,200 **Size-Class:** 15-30 **Job Placement:** Yes

WITHIN THE LAST 10 years, this school and company have grown into a nationally respected professional regional company providing not only first-class training, but also performing opportunities to many young dancers.

This is the official school of the American Repertory Ballet, founded in 1954 by Audree Estey. In addition to Princeton it also has facilities in Cranbury and New Brunswick. The curriculum also includes instruction in modern, jazz, Spanish and theater dance. The newly opened studio in Princeton has added 4 large dance studios in an 11,000-square-foot space. Besides the student division, the school offers an advanced division, for dancers with 1-2 years of pointe and a strong technique, requiring 3 classes weekly; and a professional training program, which is by audition only and requires a daily class geared to a high level of technical proficiency, seminars in dance-related topics, nutrition, career-preparation seminars, pointe variations, Pilates-based exercise, jazz, modern and Spanish. The school also offers a class for physically challenged adults, including those in wheelchairs, to provide an opportunity for creative self-expression, physical exercise and enjoyment through dance and creative coordination.

Rutgers University

For modern, ballet dancers, choreographers 50 mi. S of New York City — Dept. of Dance, 85 George St., New Brunswick, NJ 08901 **Voice:** 732-932-8497 **Fax:** 732-932-5414 **E-mail:** smayer572@aol.com **Web Site:** www.rutgers.edu **Contact:** Patricia Mayer, Chair **Founded:** 1976 **Open:** Year-round **Admission:** Written application, audition, interview, transcripts, test scores **Deadlines:** Apply each semester **Cost:** $11,778 per year for state residents, $16,502 for nonresidents **Financial Aid:** Loans; Scholarship; Fellowship; Stipend; Work/Study **Size-Attendees:** 80 **Size-Class:** 15 **Degree or Certification:** BFA in Dance, BA in Dance **Job Placement:** Yes

THE MASON GROSS School of the Arts at Rutgers University has an enrollment of approximately 500 undergraduate students, about 80 of whom are enrolled in the BFA or BA in Dance programs. The focus here is on modern-dance technique and performance, supported by regular training in ballet and other dance forms. If you think you would find the artistic and intellectual climate of a major university attractive, Rutgers should be on your list.

The school is actually a separate degree-granting college at Rutgers, and the facilities and environment are of high quality. The faculty consists of 8 full-time and 4 adjunct faculty. Permanent faculty includes Lorn MacDougal,

Modern dance at Mason Gross School of the Arts at Rutgers University, New Brunswick.

who danced with the companies of Martha Graham, Lar Lubovitch, Ron Redlich, Phyllis Lamhut and Daniel Nagrin; Claudia Gitelman, a Fulbright scholar and winner of choreographic competitions, a dance scholar and a veteran performer in both modern dance and on Broadway; and Reagan Wood, who danced for many years with the Paul Taylor Company. The dance department is housed in the Nicholas Music Center, which contains 3 spacious dance studios with excellent floors and natural light. The 350-seat New Performing Theater is used for dance, as is a fully equipped studio theater located in a nearby building. Students perform in semiannual faculty concerts and in their senior year choreographic projects. In addition to its proximity to New York City, another attractive feature is the concert series sponsored by the dance department, which regularly brings in cutting-edge, modern-dance companies both to perform and to give masterclasses. Rutgers also sponsors an annual SummerFest, bringing in some of the most prestigious world-class touring companies.

New Mexico

Academy of Ballet Theatre of New Mexico

For ballet, jazz dancers, choreographers Central New Mexico — 6913 Natalie NE, Albuquerque, NM 87110 **Voice:** 505-888-1054 **Web Site:** www.btnm.org **Contact:** Linda Kennedy, Dir. **Founded:** 1989 **Open:** Year-round **Admission:** Written application **Deadlines:** Rolling **Cost:** $82 for 12 classes **Financial Aid:** Scholarship; Work/Study **Size-Class:** 12-15

THIS SCHOOL WAS begun in 1989 in the belief that a solid base for a professional company is created through quality dance training. I happen to agree, and it seems that this academy and its related professional company are making all the right moves. The organization began with an apprentice company and moved on to a senior company a few years later.

The academy offers a respectable number of classes in ballet with a graded curriculum, and a few jazz classes as well. Fairly intensive training, based on classical Russian technique, is offered at the preprofessional level. Classes for adults are available through the open program, and two levels of preballet are offered as well. The company offers the customary annual *Nutcracker* and other opportunities for the students to work alongside professionals. The school is headed by Linda Kennedy, who performed with the Houston Civic Ballet and attended Southern Methodist University. The faculty is composed primarily of company members.

University of New Mexico

For ballet, modern dancers, choreographers Close to downtown Albuquerque — Dance Program Center for the Arts, University of New Mexico, Albuquerque, NM 87131 **Voice:** 505-277-3660 **Fax:** 505-277-9625 **E-mail:** dance@enm.edu **Web Site:** www.unm.edu **Contact:** Larry Lavender, Head of Dance Dept. **Open:** Year-round **Admission:** Written application, BA, letter of intent, transcripts, writing sample **Deadlines:** Apr. 15 for fall, Nov. 10 for spring **Cost:** $2,241 tuition per year for state residents, $8,461 for nonresidents **Financial Aid:** Loans; Scholarship; Fellowship; Stipend; Work/Study **Size-Attendees:** 45-50 **Degree or Certification:** MAs in Choreography, Dance Criticism **Job Placement:** Yes

THIS PROGRAM IS geared more for the dancer considering a career transition as the idea of retiring from performing becomes more of a reality. The 2 areas of concentration offered are choreography and dance criticism.

The theater-and-dance department maintains 2 theaters. The Rodey Theatre is a 425-seat proscenium space that can be converted to a thrust configuration by means of a hydraulic system. The black-box experimental theater holds more than 100 seats. Also at the disposal of the department are 2 other theaters, Keller Concert Hall and Popejoy Hall, a 2,000-seat roadhouse. The school's 5 dance studios are located in Carlisle Gymnasium, the home of the dance program. The department takes special note of the abundance of nonacademic experiences that students can bring to graduate studies. Professional experience might more than make up for uneven undergraduate preparation. In certain cases, students without an undergraduate degree are considered for graduate admission based on a strong professional record. Other alternatives include a nondegree option, which allows students to take graduate courses even if they are not particularly interested in transferring those credits to a Master's program. Graduate work includes choreography, repertory, criticism, movement analysis, history, pedagogy and teaching courses. The program boasts such faculty members as notable choreographer Bill Evans and Larry Lavender.

New York

550 Broadway Dance

For ballet, ethnic, jazz, modern, tap dancers, choreographers Located in SoHo, between Prince and Spring Sts. — *550 Broadway, 3rd Fl., New York, NY 10012* **Voice:** 212-925-1466 **Contact:** Zvi Gotheiner, Artistic Dir. **Founded:** 1989 **Open:** Year-round **Admission:** Open **Deadlines:** Rolling Admissions **Cost:** $10-$15 per class **Financial Aid:** Scholarship; Work/Study

WITHIN THE LAST 5 years this studio has grown in both reputation and size. This growth is due more to the fact that the studio is located in the heart of New York's downtown dance district than to the actual class offerings. Zvi Gotheiner, who runs the operation, has a loyal following of dancers, primarily from the modern-dance community.

The ballet faculty can easily be seen as the cream of the crop, even by New York standards: it includes Marjorie Mussman, Zvi Gotheiner, Johann Renvall (formerly of ABT) and Douglas Boulivar. Classes are taught in Limón technique with Janie Brendel and theater jazz with Ami Goodheart. Classes are also offered in kung fu, capoeira, swing/jazz, hip-hop and tai chi. This eclectic studio might not be for everyone, but for some it's the only place they will take class. The well-respected company attached to the operation performs the works of Zvi Gotheiner.

92nd Street Y– Harkness Dance Center

🏠 💇 *For ballet, ethnic, jazz, modern, tap dancers, choreographers* Manhattan's Upper East Side — School of the Arts, 92nd Street Y, 1395 Lexington Ave., New York, NY 10128 **Voice:** 212-996-1100 **Fax:** 212-415-5575 **Web Site:** www.92ndsty.org **Contact:** Joan Finkelstein, Dir. **Founded:** 1935 **Open:** Year-round **Admission:** Open **Deadlines:** Rolling **Cost:** $50 for 5 classes, $900 for unlimited 1-year class card **Financial Aid:** Scholarship; Work/Study **Size-Attendees:** 500 **Size-Class:** 15-25 **Degree or Certification:** Certificate **Handicapped Access**

SINCE 1935 THE 92nd Street Y has been a major home for modern dance, having nurtured the talents of many dance pioneers, including Martha Graham, Doris Humphrey, Charles Weidman, Agnes de Mille, Anna Sokolow, Hanya Holm, Alvin Ailey, Merce Cunningham, Robert Joffrey, Jerome Robbins, Pearl Primus and Lester Horton. These artists created new work, performed and taught at the Y. It is no exaggeration to credit the Y with building the foundation for contemporary dance as we know it.

In 1994 the Y added an extensive array of dance classes and expanded its course offerings with the support of the Harkness Foundation for Dance. Course offerings include basic dance education, ballet and modern technique, Isadora-Duncan technique, hip-hop, Afro-Caribbean dance, flamenco and jazz. These classes are taught by some of the best teachers in New York City. Dance-center students receive such special benefits as reduced-rate memberships and daytime passes to the center for health, fitness and sport; invitations to open rehearsals of choreographers working in the dance center studios; free use of the library; and the babysitting services available through the family center. Dance students and the general public can also enjoy lecture series, such as "Breaking Ground, Ballet and Modern Dance: Scenes from a Marriage." In this series, artistic directors of leading ballet companies discussed the influence of contemporary modern-dance choreographers on their dancers and on the repertoire. The speakers included Peter Martins, Balanchine's chosen successor as director of the New York City Ballet; Kevin McKenzie, artistic director of the American Ballet Theatre; and Deborah Jowitt, dance critic of the *Village Voice*.

The Ailey School

🏠 *For ballet, jazz, ethnic, modern, tap dancers, choreographers* Manhattan's Lincoln Center — 211 W. 61st St., 3rd Fl., New York, NY 10023 **Voice:** 212-767-0940 **Fax:** 212-767-0625 **Web Site:** www.AlvinAiley.org **Contact:** Denise Jefferson, Dir. **Founded:** 1969 **Open:** Year-round **Admission:** Written application, audition, 2 letters of recommendation, transcript **Deadlines:** Rolling **Cost:** $10 per class; from $2,775 per semester for certificate program **Financial Aid:** Loans; Scholarship; Fellowship; Stipend; Work/Study **Size-Attendees:** 400 **Size-Class:** 15-25 **Degree or Certification:** BA in Dance **Job Placement:** Yes

BOTH AILEYPHILES and other mortals are likely to find what they're looking for at The Ailey School. This is one of the largest dance centers in New York City and offers a broad range of dance styles from Dunham technique to ballet. The facility trains more than 3,000 students annually, offering more than 150 classes a week, from 9 A.M. to 9 P.M., Monday through Saturday, in its 6 studios. The center's curriculum includes many dance techniques, as well as academics and performing opportunities. There's a reason why Ailey dancers are some of the strongest in the field: the training is intensive.

The certificate program is for advanced and beginning- and intermediate-level dancers who have completed their secondary school requirements. Students may choose to attend the program full time or three-quarter time. The program offers a wide variety of dance techniques, dance academic

MARBETH

Dancers demonstrate strength and flexibility at The Ailey School, New York City.

courses (dance history, music for dancers), repertory workshops and, for those enrolled in the second and third year, the opportunity to gain extensive performance experience through the repertory-and-performance-workshop course. Each term, a guest artist reconstructs a current work or creates a new one on students in this workshop. September, 1992, saw the start of an affiliation between the center and Fordham University. The College at Lincoln Center, with its campus just across the street from the dance center, is a 4-year, undergraduate, liberal-arts college serving about 2,100 full-time and part-time students. Fordham offers a new core curriculum with emphasis on interdisciplinary work. The affiliation enables students enrolled in certain Ailey programs to take courses at Fordham with reduced tuition, irrespective of matriculated status. Fordham and The Ailey School jointly offer a BFA in dance. The 46 faculty members at the school include master teachers, such as Milton Myers and Ana Marie Forsythe.

Ballet Academy East

For ballet, tap dancers, choreographers Midtown Manhattan — 1651 Third Ave., 3rd Fl., New York, NY 10128 **Voice:** 212-410-9140 **Fax:** 212-369-2723 **E-mail:** bae@aol.com **Contact:** Julia Dubno, Dir. **Founded:** 1979 **Open:** Year-round **Admission:** Open **Deadlines:** Rolling **Cost:** $110 for 10 classes **Financial Aid:** Scholarship; Work/Study **Size-Class:** 15

THIS RELATIVELY YOUNG East Side studio is achieving a major coup by wooing dancers away from the larger studios on the West Side, such as the megalith Steps on Broadway. It's not hard to figure out why: classes are not as crowded as at the more established studios, but you still get to take classes with master teachers like Espen Giljane, Dick Andros and Francis Patrelle, many of them transplants from Steps.

Ballet Hispanico School of Dance

For ethnic, ballet, jazz, modern dancers, choreographers Manhattan's Upper West Side — 167 W. 89th St., New York, NY 10024 **Voice:** 212-362-6710 **Fax:** 212-362-7809 **Contact:** Valerie Cruz, School Dir. **Founded:** 1970 **Open:** Year-round **Admission:** Open **Deadlines:** Rolling **Financial Aid:** Scholarship; Work/Study **Size-Attendees:** 300 **Size-Class:** 10-20

ESTABLISHED IN 1970 as an important aspect of Tina Ramirez's vision for a professional company and school drawing on diverse Latino cultural influences, this school now has more than 300 students in its regular programs. The school and the Ballet Hispanico company share 4 studios in what used to be an old stable on Manhattan's Upper West Side. Rather than an ethnic dance company, Ballet Hispanico is better defined as a modern company, although Ramirez has infused the repertory with a unique and distinct Latino flavor.

The program of study includes modern-dance training using the Horton technique, as well as Afro-Cuban, classical ballet and flamenco. Although there is an adult program, where dancers of all levels can sample the open-class offerings, the focus is primarily on young students. There is a 12-member year-round faculty, as well as guest artists who teach during the 4-week summer intensive.

Broadway Dance Center

 For all dancers, choreographers *Midtown Manhattan — 221 W. 57th St., 5th Fl., New York, NY 10019* **Voice:** 212-582-9304 **Fax:** 212-977-2202 **E-mail:** rol@ bwydance.com **Web Site:** www.bwydance. com **Contact:** Allison Ellner-Teitelbaum, Dir. **Founded:** 1984 **Open:** Year-round **Admission:** Open **Deadlines:** Rolling **Cost:** $115 for 10 classes **Financial Aid:** Scholarship; Work/Study **Size-Class:** 20-50

THIS SCHOOL IS GROUND zero for Broadway dancers. The jazz faculty fairly bristles with working professionals, and the latest brochure lists 26 jazz faculty, including Frank Hatchett, Phil Black, Cecilia Marta, Chuck Kelley, Chet Walker and Robb Sapienza. If Hatchett represents the more conservative, old-school approach, the center also provides instruction at the other end of the spectrum with A.C., who works with such artists as Madonna; he has choreographed music videos, as well as the Broadway production of *Footloose*.

There is a sizable ballet faculty with outstanding credentials, among them 2 popular teachers who previously ran their own studios: Finis Jhung and David Howard. Apparently, their devotees have followed them to Broadway Dance Center. Also on the faculty is Madame Gabriela Darvash, the Kirov-trained teacher whom Mikhail Baryshnikov calls "one of the finest ballet pedagogues in America." The school advertises that its teachers "tend to stress audition tips and tricks." The school offers discounted rates to

groups of out-of-town dancers and to professionals who are union members. This is a good thing since the class rates tend to be on the high side. The center has recently relocated to 5 floors of posh new studios above the Hard Rock Café. This is certainly in the thick of things for Broadway gypsies.

Chautauqua Institution

For ballet, jazz, modern dancers *SW New York — P.O. Box 28, Chautauqua, NY 14722* **Voice:** 716-357-6250 **Fax:** 716-357-9014 **E-mail:** info@ chatauqua-inst.org **Web Site:** http://www. chautauqua-inst.org/home.htm **Contact:** Jean-Pierre Bonnefoux, Artistic Dir. **Founded:** 1874 **Open:** Year-round **Admission:** Registration **Deadlines:** Aug. for fall, May for summer **Cost:** $24-$65 per week, $6-$13 per class **Financial Aid:** Scholarship; Work/Study **Size-Class:** 10-20

THIS ORGANIZATION takes its name from an old word meaning "tied in the middle." The word describes the shape of Chautauqua Lake: large at both ends and thin at the center. The natural surroundings are beautiful with many trees and wildlife. The grounds include memorable buildings registered as national historic landmarks, such as the clocktower by the lake and a replica of the Parthenon.

Chautauqua's 9-week summer programs offers literally hundreds of courses from film, computer studies and music, to business and ethics. The 80-page summer catalog provides detailed listings for each of its dance programs, directed by former ballet star Jean-Pierre Bonnefoux. Chautauqua has gained a reputation for presenting quality programs with substantial intellectual content in a vacation setting. The institution was founded as a vacation school for Protestant Sunday-school teachers. While religious courses are still offered, secular concerns have taken center stage. The list of guest speakers features an impressive array of American intellectuals. With its scenic lake, resident symphony, theater, opera and other first-rate entertainment options, the institute provides a unique and stimulating environment unrivaled in the United States. The dance program includes courses in ballet, modern dance, ethnic dance, dance programs for seniors and even line dancing. In addition to Bonnefoux, the faculty includes Jill Keating, a former dancer with the Pittsburgh Ballet Theatre; jazz teacher Fred Walton from Indiana University; William Beck, a mathematician and ethnic-dance expert; and Kathy Wildberger, a faculty member of the Limón Institute in New York. Lodgings, especially in the 19th-century houses, are in great demand, so plan well in advance for accommodations.

Dance Space

For all dancers, choreographers
Just N of Manhattan's SoHo — 451 Broadway, 2nd Fl., New York, NY 10013 **Voice:** 212-625-8369 **Fax:** 212-625-8213 **E-mail:** dsi@dancesspace.com **Web Site:** www.dancespace.com **Contact:** Jana Hicks, Managing Dir. **Founded:** 1984 **Open:** Year-round **Admission:** Open **Deadlines:** Rolling **Cost:** $95 for 10-class card **Financial Aid:** Scholarship; Work/Study **Size-Attendees:** 200-300 **Size-Class:** 15-30

Y OU MIGHT CALL Dance Space the yin to Steps on Broadway's yang. Steps caters more to the ballet community and the uptown dance scene, while Dance Space is designed more for the modern-dance community and the downtown scene. The two are arguably the largest studios in Manhattan, offering the most choices, the largest selection of teachers and a host of workshops, masterclasses and performance initiatives to suit the needs of most people in the business. Their specialty is Simonson jazz, the technique of codirector Lynn Simonson. It includes a set warm-up that goes for about an hour (to music that has not changed in the 14 years the technique has been offered!) and then a combination that goes on for as long as the instructor and the willing

disciples are in the mood. Classes sometimes run close to 3 hours.

Besides Simonson jazz, more than 80 classes a week are held in a variety of disciplines, including modern, jazz, ballet, floor barre, Pilates, yoga, Afro-Haitian and Argentine tango. The studio has a faculty of 30 teachers, 5 spacious dance studios (1 of which can be turned into a black-box theater for the numerous performances) and a massage center. The studio now offers an International student visa program, as well as a Simonson-technique teacher-training program. One of the biggest draws, which a lot of other studios including Steps have copied, is the Modern Guest Artist Series consisting of monthly classes taught by artistic directors, choreographers and master teachers from well-known companies. Guest artists have included Ron Brown, Sean Curran, David Dorfman, Doug Elkins and Jennifer Muller. In an effort to support some of the more practical needs of dancers, the studio developed Evolving Arts, which sponsors a wide variety of performances, including summer workshops, faculty showcases, monthly works-in-progress concerts and theatrical productions fully staged in the studio theater.

Dance Theatre of Harlem

🏠 ☀ ♻ **For ballet, ethnic, jazz, modern, tap dancers, choreographers** Manhattan's Harlem — 466 W. 152nd St., New York, NY 10031 **Voice:** 212-690-2800 **Fax:** 212-690-8736 **E-mail:** dnceharlem@ aol.com **Contact:** Arthur Mitchell, Artistic Dir. **Founded:** 1969 **Open:** Year-round **Admission:** Open, auditions for placement **Deadlines:** Rolling **Cost:** $80 for 10 classes; from $102 for summer program **Financial Aid:** Scholarship; Work/Study **Size-Attendees:** 1,000 **Size-Class:** 20 **Degree or Certification:** Preprofessional Certificate

FOUNDED BY DANCE visionaries Arthur Mitchell and Karel Shook, this school offers general and preprofessional programs to more than 1,000 students. Mitchell was a featured dancer at the New York City Ballet for many years, and George Balanchine and Lincoln Kirstein were instrumental in assisting Mitchell in his efforts to form a company and school in Harlem.

In addition to ballet, the curriculum includes modern, ethnic, jazz and tap, as well as music appreciation and dance history. The school is housed in the Everett Center for the Performing Arts, an award-winning facility on West 152nd Street. The center is also home to the professional company and boasts 4 large studios, a classroom, men's and women's dressing rooms, a parent/visitor lounge with kitchen facilities and an outdoor terrace. A distinguished faculty numbering 18 includes Frederic Franklin, a legend in American dance, as well as a specialist in children's movement, classical European ballet, choreography and musicology. Many of the faculty had notable performing careers at companies as diverse as the Royal Ballet, Martha Graham Dance Company, Ballet Russe de Monte Carlo, and Kirov Ballet. The permanent faculty is supplemented by professional dancers from the Dance Theatre of Harlem. There is also a staff of 9 accompanists. The school offers a preprofessional, certificate program, which is completed in a minimum of 3 years and is designed for students intending to

pursue a professional career. Admission requires a high-school diploma and significant prior training. A 6-to-8-week summer intensive program provides students with daily ballet classes and classes in tap, pas de deux, pointe/men's work, Pilates method and jazz. The program includes workshops in nutrition and injury prevention. Advanced students form an ensemble that presents lecture demonstrations and, on occasion, full-scale performances in school and community centers. The ensemble is considered a steppingstone to the professional company and provides students with a chance to learn the standard repertoire while receiving a full-tuition scholarship and a stipend to boot.

Harlem School of the Arts

🏠 ☀ **For all dancers, choreographers** Manhattan's Harlem — 645 St. Nicholas Ave., New York, NY 10030 **Voice:** 212-926-4100 **Web Site:** www.erols.com/hsoa/ **Contact:** Stephanie Rae Parker, Chair **Founded:** 1964 **Open:** Year-round **Admission:** Written application, audition, essay, interview **Deadlines:** Apply each semester **Cost:** From $130 for 14 weeks **Financial Aid:** Scholarship; Work/Study **Size-Class:** 15-20

THIS VENERABLE institution, which was founded by singer Dorothy Maynor to foster a positive self-image for young African-American and Latino children, offers a strong preprofessional-training program and summer intensive, as well as ongoing classes in a variety of dance forms. Chair Stephanie Rae Parker studied at the Boston Conservatory and later danced with a number of modern companies. She formed and choreographed for her own company, Rae Dance, before joining the Harlem School 7 years ago.

What began as a modest after-school program to teach ballet and modern dance to teenagers has blossomed into a small conservatory that includes jazz, tap, choreography, dance history and dance video, West African dance history, Pilates and even a course in using the computer choreography software

Life Forms. Harlem School has spawned the ensemble Renaissance II to give aspiring young artists an opportunity to study intensively, create and perform in preparation for a professional career or for entrance into a professional performing-arts college. The company has performed the works of many renowned choreographers, including Jawole Willa Jo Zollar of Urban Bush Women, Lygia Barreto of Roots of Brazil, Nai-Ni Chen, Keith Michael and Rod Rogers.

Juilliard School

For ballet, modern dancers, choreographers Manhattan's Lincoln Center — 60 Lincoln Center Plaza, New York, NY 10023 **Voice:** 212-799-5000 **Fax:** 212-724-0263 **Web Site:** www.juilliard.edu **Contact:** Benjamin Harkarvy, Dir. **Founded:** 1951 **Open:** Year-round **Admission:** Written application, audition, transcripts, interview, photos, videotape, test scores **Deadlines:** Dec. 1 **Cost:** $25,000 per year **Financial Aid:** Loans; Scholarship; Fellowship; Stipend; Work/Study **Size-Attendees:** 80 **Degree or Certification:** BFA in Dance **Job Placement:** Yes

FOUNDED BY THE LATE, legendary Martha Hill, the dance division at Juilliard has set the standard in advanced dance training for 3 generations of American dancers. Under the visionary leadership of Hill and Juilliard President William Schuman, Juilliard was the first major educational institution to combine the teaching of modern dance and ballet with equal emphasis. This idea was considered heretical in its day but is now broadly accepted. Hill envisioned a new future for American dance in which the best of the past and the present would be combined, dancers would be well rounded and prepared for any and all choreographic possibilities, and ballet and modern dancers would routinely cross over into one another's territory.

This approach is personified today in the fusion dancer, equally skilled in ballet and modern dance. As faculty member Carolyn Adams puts it, "We expect our students to develop versatility, a keen stylistic sense, and an ease when working with choreographers—all of which makes them inspiring and desirable collaborators." The training gives dancers the essential tools that enable them to cross the bridge from the dance studio to the stage. The core curriculum includes intensive study in ballet and modern dance, dance composition, Labanotation, anatomy, dance-history production and stagecraft and music. Clearly, the emphasis at Juilliard is on crafting talented performers. Throughout the 4-year BFA program a student will participate in up to 80 performances a year, including 8 fully staged concert and workshop presentations in the marvelous Juilliard Theater. In informal concerts and in workshop showings, masterworks of dance are performed in addition to new works developed by the students.

The extraordinary faculty at Juilliard has an extraordinary director, Benjamin Harkarvy, one of the most distinguished teachers of ballet and respected choreographers and artistic directors in the world. The 30 faculty members for only about 80 students make for a dynamite faculty-student ratio. Members of the faculty have been associated with many of the world's greatest companies and institutions, including the Paul Taylor Dance Company, Limón Dance Company, Alvin Ailey Dance Theater, Martha Graham Company, Royal Ballet, Dutch National Ballet, Royal Danish Ballet, Joffrey Ballet, Netherlands Dance Theater and Metropolitan Opera Ballet.

All of the faculty remain active on the world dance scene in such varied capacities as coaches, adjudicators, choreographers, restagers of works, writers and guest teachers. Juilliard brings in some of the world's great choreographers to work directly with its students. Recent visiting artists included Pina Bausch, Paul Taylor, Donlin Foreman, Margie Gillis, Judith Jamison, Ellen Kogan, Jiri Kylian and Glen Tetley. These guests artists and choreographers have restaged many of their own major works or in some cases staged major revivals or new

The Juilliard School: America's Premiere Dance Conservatory

For many years Juilliard has been widely considered America's leading dance conservatory. What is it that makes Juilliard such a prestigious institution? Why is admission to this program so coveted by young dancers and their teachers? To find out, I interviewed some recent Juilliard graduates to get a personal view about what makes this school tick.

It apparently begins with the audition process. The Juilliard faculty sees hundreds of dancers in regional auditions to select an annual entering class that numbers a mere 20. Subsequent auditions are also held in New York in a very well-run, professional manner. One recent graduate was part of a group of 46 applicants (40 women and 6 men) auditioning in the spring for fall admission. Following a ballet class, students were asked to present their ballet solos. This was followed by a modern-dance class. The applicant pool was then cut to 6—1 woman and 5 men. Disappointment for most, but exhilaration for a lucky few.

Various repertory was set on the dancers, and they were then coached to see how they took direction. Following this session, Benjamin Harkarvy, who became Director of the Juilliard Dance Program in 1992, addressed the dancers and faculty members, saying that the goal was to produce not the next ballet superstar but the well-rounded artist who would exhibit individuality

and a distinct voice—in sum, the "multi-faceted" dancer. One alumnus felt that Director Harkarvy was looking for potential and presence, not technique. He said, "While Juilliard is a sheltered place, I don't understand why there is a general perception that it is snobbish and elitist. It is a closed environment, but there is a lot of excellence there and a sense that there is always more to learn. The fact of the matter is that Ben Harkarvy's door is always open. He may be adamant about what he wants, but he tells you why he makes certain decisions and does certain things."

Another student contrasted the organized and business-like way she was received at Juilliard with that of another noted school, which had a more casual, less professional feel. The students I met at Juilliard felt the 4 years of training here were strict and demanding, but the process always enabled them to grow and to find a personal niche. A male alumnus told me "Once you find your direction you are backed 100 percent. The faculty at Juilliard worked hard to get there, and the feeling is that they are the very best teachers in dance. Mr. Harkarvy is a wonderfully ethical person, a good businessman and a great politician. Ben knows how to talk to people, and he really knows his work. At Juilliard I received a 4 years of education and 8 years of information."

works on the student company. There are few companies in America that Juilliard has not influenced to some degree, particularly in modern dance. Just consider some of the distin-

guished alumni: Pina Bausch, Martha Clarke, Lar Lubovitch, Paul Taylor, Mercedes Ellington, Francis Patrelle and Saecho Ichinoe.

Laban/Bartenieff Institute of Movement Studies

   For all dancers
Manhattan's East Village — 234 Fifth Ave., New York, NY 10001 **Voice:** 212-477-4299 **Fax:** 212-477-3702 **Contact:** Lucy Rumack, Dir. **Founded:** 1978 **Open:** year-round **Admission:** Written application, personal essay, transcripts, interview **Deadlines:** Rolling **Cost:** $7,800 per year **Financial Aid:** Work/Study **Size-Attendees:** 125 **Size-Class:** 10-20 **Degree or Certification:** Certificate in Laban Movement Studies

For anyone interested in taking their training a step further or looking for an alternative to the usual ballet-modern-jazz route, the certificate program in Laban Movement Studies might be for you. Founded in 1978 by Irmgard Bartenieff, this program has graduated more than 600 certified movement analysts worldwide.

Not just for dancers, the program attracts professionals in such varied fields as bodywork, therapy, fitness, acting, directing, ethnology and teaching. The principles of Laban Analysis can be applied in any field in which body language plays an essential role. Specifically, dancers use it to clarify their technique and style, but it can also be put to other use. Laban Theory is best known as the source of Labanotation, a written language of movement. The certificate program couples Laban Theory with Bartenieff Fundamentals, which claim to reeducate one's movement patterns so that one can move more efficiently. A devoted group of followers swear by these 2 methods. Besides the year-long certificate program the institute also offers 1-day and 1-week workshops introducing novices to Laban Movement Analysis, Bartenieff Fundamentals and basic anatomy and kinesiology, as well as eclectic courses ranging from "Butoh: Embodying the Spirit" to "Introduction to Connective Tissue Therapy." Courses are also offered on a one-to-one tutorial basis.

Limón Institute

 For modern, ballet dancers, choreographers *SoHo district of Manhattan — 611 Broadway, 9th Fl., New York, NY 10012* **Voice:** 212-777-3353 **Fax:** 212-777-4764 **E-mail:** limondance@aolcom **Web Site:** www.limon.org **Contact:** Alan Danielson, School Dir. **Founded:** 1985 **Open:** Year-round **Admission:** Open **Deadlines:** Rolling **Cost:** $90 for 10 classes **Financial Aid:** Work/Study **Size-Attendees:** 500 **Size-Class:** 20-40

The Limón Institute is the educational arm of the Limón Dance Foundation, which also supports the acclaimed Limón Dance Company, a professional repertory company now in its 52nd year. The Institute has grown rapidly and now offers 12 classes a week at the intermediate and advanced levels at its main facility, 2 beginner classes a week at Dance Space and 5 intermediate classes a week at Peridance. The resurgence of interest in the Humphrey-Weidman-Limón technique has undoubtedly contributed to this growth in recent years.

The faculty includes school director Alan Danielson, as well as former and current dancers from the Limón Dance Company, among them Risa Steinberg, Jim May, Daniel Charon, Janice Brenner, Nancy Bannon, Malou Thein, Colin Connor, Betty Jones, Sue Bernhard, Michael Blake, Pamala Jones and Laura Glenn. In addition to the ongoing classes a number of intensives are taught by former company members Risa Steinberg and Betty Jones. The Limón Institute offers summer workshops both in New York and at its second home in San Jose. All teachers at the summer workshops are former or current company members and expert in the technique, which both Humphrey and Limón insisted should not be codified and made rigid in any way. But the enduring theories of "breath" and "fall and recovery" have persisted and demonstrated their value in the study of modern dance.

Luigi's Jazz Center

For jazz dancers Midtown Manhattan
— *300 W. 56th St., New York, NY 10019*
Voice: 212-262-4434 **Contact:** Luigi, Dir.
Open: Year-round **Admission:** Open
Deadlines: Rolling **Cost:** $85 for 10-class
card **Financial Aid:** Scholarship; Work/Study
Size-Attendees: 100-250 **Size-Class:** 15-30

THE FAMOUS SEPTUAGENARIAN, who needs to go by only his first name, can still be found kicking his legs and inspiring others to do the same 6 days a week at Studio Maestro. If you want the experience of being taught by someone who is considered New York's premier jazz-dance instructor, you're in luck. Luigi teaches a beginning class each morning and intermediate classes throughout the week.

Martha Graham School of Contemporary Dance

For modern dancers, choreographers
Manhattan's Upper East Side — 316 E. 63rd
St., New York, NY 10021 **Voice:** 212-838-
5886 **Fax:** 212-223-0351 **E-mail:** cwmgdc@
aol.com **Contact:** Christine Dakin, School
Dir. **Founded:** 1953 **Open:** Year-round
Admission: Placement audition **Deadlines:**
Apply each quarter **Cost:** $700 per quarter
for training program, $100 for 10 classes.
Financial Aid: Scholarship; Work/Study
Size-Attendees: 500 **Size-Class:** 15-20

THE GRAHAM SCHOOL represents an important area of study in contemporary dance. It is the only school authorized to teach the Martha Graham technique and, of course, is the official school of the Martha Graham Dance Company.

More than 500 students from at least 34 companies currently study at the school, directed by long-time Graham company member Christine Dakin. The 2 dozen faculty include such notables as Terese Capucilli, Kenneth Topping, Diane Gray, Kazuko Hirabayashi, Pearl Lang and Dudley Williams. Guest faculty include Jane Dudley, Donlin Foreman, Peggy Lyman, Sophie Maslow and Donald McKayle. One could make a compelling argument that study of the Graham technique—at this school in particular because it is the only official school—is essential for anyone considering a serious career in contemporary dance. To be sure, there are other traditions, but there is no denying the fact that Graham's influence is profound. One critic described her technique as a "pylon" of modern dance. The technique she developed is as complex and rigorous as ballet technique; unlike ballet technique, however, it was developed over a relatively short period of time.

Graham wrote eloquently about dance and dancing, and her choreographic output remained prodigious throughout her long life. Consider her statement, quoted in the school's international program brochure: "I am a dancer. I believe that we learn by practice. Whether it means to learn to dance by practicing dancing or to learn to live by practicing living, the principles are the same." Her impact on modern dance was all the more profound because she commissioned important compositions and designs for her work, and gave everything she created a distinctive look. Let it be said that at least some study of Graham technique by a recognized Graham teacher is *de rigeur* for a professional performer..

Note: Until June, 2000, the Graham school is located at 440 Lafayette St., New York, NY 10003.

Nurturing Dance—A Home Away from Home

For more than 30 years, Dance Theater Workshop (DTW) has been the home and principal support for scores of individual dancers and small-budget, single-choreographer companies in the New York metro area. It takes more than a great number of dance companies to make New York City the dance capital of the United States. It also takes presenting and service organizations like DTW and its sister organizations, the Joyce Theater, the Kitchen and Danspace, to make a vibrant dance community. David White, DTW's director for the last 23 years, says that their mission is "to contribute to building a functional community at a grass-roots level. "

DTW boasts a membership of approximately 600 artists and artist-driven companies. It provides basic services like press resources, mailing lists and book-keeping services on an as-needed basis. "Our goal," White says, "is to empower individuals who have to manage their own affairs." White believes that DTW and the other spaces taking risks in supporting new work provide "a multiplicity of judgment centers" for the emerging dance community and even for some mid-career and established artists. The Joyce Theater annually presents an "Altogether Different" series, displaying the work of lesser-known artists, and artists can rotate into other spaces like the JoyceSoho, Danspace and the Kitchen as well. "Artists can go back and forth in this environment, and it makes for a healthy dance community," White says.

DTW holds biannual "Fresh Tracks" auditions to identify new talents, and White notes that the 60 slots available for auditionees are filled within 20 minutes, once they open enrollment. The Bessie Schönberg Theater presents more than 200 performances, 50 to 60 of which are artists sharing the space or performing in stand-alone events, and most were discovered in the Fresh Tracks auditions.

If a program can serve the emerging or lesser-known dance artist or performance artist, DTW has probably thought of it. The National Performance Network, established to encourage the performance of new works, now includes 61 sites in 40 cities involving 25 artists and companies. NPN is so successful that it will soon stand alone as an independent organization. However, DTW has moved into other new areas. Its New York State Task Force, supported by the New York State Council on the Arts, encourages the presentation of new work and tours by professional companies in upstate New York; its Public Imaginations series teams artists interested in constructive social change with communities; and its recent retreats for dancers and choreographers have resulted in the formation of a regular Dance Forum for constructive engagement and discussion about key dance issues.

The best thing about DTW is that the services it provides to its membership are available whether the artist or company is being produced at DTW or not. The Joyce Theater plays an important and expanding role in presenting dance by providing a heavily subsidized rental program or by occasionally presenting a company. Danspace also presents companies and provides certain management services, but there is no organization with the reach and impact of DTW.

Merce Cunningham Studio

For modern dancers
Manhattan's West Village — 55 Bethune St., New York, NY 10014 **Voice:** 212-691-9751
Fax: 212-663-2453 **E-mail:** sonya@merce.org **Web Site:** www.merce.org
Contact: Alice Helpern, Studio Dir.
Founded: 1959 **Open:** Year-round
Admission: High-school diploma or equivalent; 10 classes in open program prerequisite for professional-training program
Deadlines: Rolling **Cost:** Open program: $11 per class, $95-$170 for multi-class card, $550-$950 for professional training program
Financial Aid: Work/Study **Size-Attendees:** 150 **Size-Class:** 10-20

THE MERCE CUNNINGHAM Studio's roots date back to 1959 with an impressive roster of charter members, including Trisha Brown, Yvonne Rainer, David Gordon and Viola Farber, all of whom were students in the early 1960s. Today the studio continues that legacy with daily classes taught out of its Westbeth location overlooking the Hudson River.

Classes are taught by present and past company members. Entering students must take an open class to determine their level of proficiency. They must then complete at least 10 open classes before they can be admitted to the professional-training program. This is probably a sign of the times: fewer and fewer dancers are willing to make a commitment to just 1 studio. The studio still has a slightly cultlike flavor, not only because of its prior-enrollment policy, but also because of its off-the-beaten-path location. As a result, the student body is composed of Cunningham aficionados. If you are one of these or are just curious, the studio is probably the place for you since you will get first-rate training in the technique. The studio also offers students enrolled in the professional-training program the chance to work alongside the main company in the repertory understudy group, from which—in theory at least—a hopeful dancer might step in for an injured or departing company member. Some 5 or 10 of the most advanced students are invited to join the Cunningham Company for company class. The main Cunningham studio is a glorious space with windows on the urban landscape. It is one of the largest studios in New York, which is just as well: it serves not only the students at the school and the Cunningham Company, but also solo dancers and ensembles who make use of the facility for evening performances.

Movement Research

For modern dancers, choreographers *Manhattan's East Village — 296 Elizabeth St. BF, New York, NY 10012* **Voice:** 212-477-6635 **Fax:** 212-477-6854
E-mail: movement@pipeline.com **Contact:** Catherine Levine, Dir. **Founded:** 1978
Open: Year-round **Admission:** Open
Deadlines: Rolling **Cost:** $10 per class, $85-$205 per workshop **Financial Aid:** Scholarship; Work/Study **Size-Attendees:** 150 **Size-Class:** 15-20

A CORNERSTONE OF THE postmodern dance movement and of New York City's downtown dance scene, Movement Research represents all aspects of modern dance's current trends. Located in the heart of the funky East Village, of *Rent* fame, the humble space includes 2 studios, one of which is used as a performance space in the evening. For those who come to the city expecting glamour, Movement Research can be a bit of an eye-opener. But the facility does exemplify the very best of what the city stands for in terms of diversity, progressiveness and quality.

This organization is dedicated to creating, maintaining and promoting programs that nurture experimentation in dance performance and education. The programs are designed to expose artists and audiences alike to new work, to facilitate discussions about the changing nature of dance and performance and to promote experimentalism and works with noteworthy content. Programs include a residency project, through which artists are commissioned to create new work; Movement Research at the Judson Church, a free series of informal performances at the pioneering performance space; the Studies Project, a series of panel discussions; Performance Journal, a free publication published by the company; workshops and ongoing classes, such as contact improvisation, release technique and improvisation; MRX, an exchange program for independent choreographers to communicate with their peers nationally and internationally; Dance-Makers in the Schools, pairing dance artists and young children; Open Performances, a monthly series of performances that include a Q-and-A period; and Gentle Movement/Release classes for people with health issues.

New York University-Tisch School of the Arts

For all dancers, choreographers
Manhattan's Greenwich Village — Dance Dept., 111 2nd Ave., New York, NY 10003
Voice: 212-998-1980 **Fax:** 212-998-1981
Web Site: www.nyu.edu/tisch **Contact:** Kay Cummings, Dir. **Founded:** 1831 **Open:** Year-round **Admission:** Written application, audition, writing sample, interview, transcripts **Deadlines:** Apply each semester **Cost:** $10,350 tuition per year **Financial Aid:** Loans; Scholarship; Fellowship; Stipend; Work/Study **Size-Attendees:** 155 **Size-Class:** 15-30 **Degree or Certification:** BFA in Dance, MFA in Dance **Job Placement:** Yes

T HE TISCH SCHOOL of the Arts at NYU offers BFA and MFA degrees in dance to approximately 120 undergraduates and 35 graduate students. The dance faculty is large, with 7 full-time and 14 part-time instructors yielding a handsome student-faculty ratio. Of course the best thing about the program at Tisch is the proximity to all the activity in the dance capital of the world. Some distinguished professional companies and individual artists are in residence throughout the year and in the special summer program as well. Resident companies have included Doug Varone and Dancers, David Dorfman Dance, Bebe Miller Company and Shapiro & Smith.

Tisch students study ballet and contemporary dance and sharpen their choreographic skills in 6 spacious studios equipped with sprung floors and pianos. Many guest choreographers are brought in to choreograph works on the students. Recent guests have included Doug Varone, Bill T. Jones, Ralph Lemon, Bebe Miller, Mark Morris, David Parsons, Paul Taylor and Twyla Tharp. Student performances, featuring both commissioned works from outside choreographers and student work, abound. Tisch dancers give approximately 50 performances each year. Performances by the student company, Second Avenue Dance, are favorably reviewed in major publications. Permanent faculty members include director Kay Cummings, Andre Bernard, Sergio Cervetti, Elizabeth Frankel, Mark Haim, Deborah Jowitt, Phyllis Lamhut, Tere O'Connor, Gus Solomons, Jr. and Linda Tarnay, among others. As an alternative to the regular academic-year schedule, students can choose a 3-year BFA program, which includes intensive work during the summer. Facilities at the school include a recently renovated

Tisch School of the Arts, New York University, New York City.

131

200-seat theater for the presentations of the student company.

Paul Taylor School

For modern dancers, choreographers *Lower Manhattan — 552 Broadway, New York, NY 10012* **Voice:** 212-431-5562 **Fax:** 212-966-5673 **E-mail:** jt@ptds.org **Web Site:** www.nvptdc.org **Contact:** Nicole Vandestienne, School Dir. **Founded:** 1954 **Open:** Year round **Admission:** Open **Deadlines:** Rolling **Cost:** $100 for 10 classes, $300 for 2-week intensive **Financial Aid:** Scholarship; Work/Study **Size-Attendees:** 200 **Size-Class:** 16

WHILE THIS IS A modest operation as far as studio schools go, serious students of modern dance might want to enroll in one of the Taylor intensives or repertory workshops scheduled throughout the year. A morning class given Monday through Friday each week is open to advanced modern dancers. Current or former members of the Paul Taylor Dance Company teach all classes, workshops and intensives. Foremost among them are Nancy Cochran, Susan McGuire, Patrick Corbin, Joao Mauricio and Karla Wolfangle.

At least 2 intensives lasting 2 weeks each are scheduled during the year. The work schedule is 5 hours a day. With an enrollment of 40 or more dancers, the intensives are generally divided into 2 groups. The repertory workshops also last 2 weeks, but the schedule is lighter. The workshops draw 15-20 students who actually learn a Taylor work and perform it in a showing at the end of the workshop. Nicole Vandestienne, who works with Paul Taylor to schedule teachers and workshops, administers the school and is happy to answer any questions a student might have. All classes are taught in the 2 Taylor studio facilities in SoHo. This neighborhood has a great many dance and artistic resources and should be part of your New York City

dance experience. Moreover, it is thrilling to be able to study directly with company members who work with one of America's great modern masters.

Peridance Center

For ballet, modern dancers, choreographers *Lower Manhattan, near SoHo, Greenwich Village, East Village — 132 Fourth Ave., 2nd Fl., New York, NY 10003* **Voice:** 212-505-0886 **Fax:** 212-674-2239 **E-mail:** info@peridance.com **Web Site:** www.peridance.com **Contact:** Igal Perry, Artistic Dir. **Founded:** 1983 **Open:** Year-round **Admission:** Open **Deadlines:** Rolling **Cost:** $11 per class, $100 for 10-class card **Financial Aid:** Scholarship; Work/Study **Size-Attendees:** 500 **Size-Class:** 15-30

THIS IS ONE OF THE CITY's top 5 dance studios, offering classes in everything from tae kwon do to ballet, 7 days a week, morning until evening. In recent years it has found its niche catering to dancers who need a sampling of everything, without the particular emphasis to be found at Dance Space or at Steps on Broadway. Part of what has kept the studio in the shadows is its facility: it lacks the larger studios of a Steps, for example. However, its Visa program and its spring/summer masterclass series have earned it a reputation for solid professional opportunities in contemporary ballet and modern, and this keeps the studios full. Companies, such as Donald Byrd/The Group and Jennifer Muller/The Works, have developed an affiliation with the school that is unique. The school boasts a faculty of 17 with guest artists, such as Donald Byrd, Doug Elkins and Dwight Rhoden, supplementing the faculty.

The center also has a professional ensemble headed by founder Igal Perry, a successful choreographer himself. Always looking for new ways to broaden his facility, Perry founded the ensemble in 1984 to offer students a professional performing outlet.

School of American Ballet

🏠 🌼 **For ballet dancers, choreographers** *Manhattan's Lincoln Center — 70 Lincoln Center Plaza, New York, NY 10023* **Voice:** 212-769-6600 **Fax:** 212-769-4897 **E-mail:** info@sab.org **Web Site:** www.nycballet.com/sab/sabfrm.htm **Contact:** Larry Allan Smith, Pres. **Founded:** 1934 **Open:** Year-round **Admission:** Written application, audition **Deadlines:** Rolling **Cost:** From $186 per month in winter, $750 for summer session, plus $1,285 for room and board **Financial Aid:** Loans; Scholarship; Fellowship; Stipend; Work/Study **Size-Attendees:** 370 **Size-Class:** 20-25 **Job Placement:** Yes

THE PRESTIGIOUS SCHOOL of the renowned New York City Ballet has earned a level of mystique unequaled in the world of dance. Founded in 1934 by the late George Balanchine and Lincoln Kirstein, the school continues under the guidance of artistic director Peter Martins and former principal dancer Kay Mazzo. But the legacies of the 2 founders still loom large in the hallways and classrooms of the school. The training purports to remain faithful to Balanchine's unique brand of classicism, combining the early vocabulary of 19th-century Russia with a deeply American character, recognized for its superior speed, clarity and musicality. The school employs a large number of its faculty from the old school of Russia, former Bolshoi, Kirov and Kiev artists, along with present and former NYCB dancers.

Almost without exception, the entire student body is there to pursue a professional career in ballet, and more specifically to gain a place in the ranks of the company. Nearly all the members of the NYCB have been trained at SAB. This singular mission can leave some young dancers open to disappointment. Take note of the school's words of warning: "It is impossible for every student who receives training at the School to dance professionally. A student may decide ballet is no longer of interest or the School may determine that continued training is no longer appropriate.... The School is extremely selective in admitting new students and renewing their enrollment from year to year. Applicants must be young enough to derive the maximum benefit from their training, enjoy excellent health and have an anatomical structure suited to the demands of classical dance: a well-proportioned, flexible, coordinated body, legs that easily adopt the turned-out condition, and a high instep."

Not all students flourish in the school, but for those who fit the above requirements and are interested in the company, this is without doubt the best place to be. A chance to sample the school's programs is offered each summer during a 5-week course for approximately 200 intermediate and advanced students from around the country. The death of Stanley Williams in 1997 and the retirement, in the same year, of Richard Rapp have created a void yet to be filled for male dancers seeking the exemplary training formerly offered by these noted teachers.

State University of New York–Brockport

🏠 **For ethnic, modern dance, choreography** *15 mi. W of Rochester — Dept. of Dance, Lathrop Hall, 350 New Campus Dr., Brockport, NY 14420* **Voice:** 716-395-2153; 800-382-8447 **Fax:** 716-395-5134 **E-mail:** admit@po.brockport.edu **Web Site:** www.brockport.edu **Contact:** Sondra Fraleigh, Chair **Founded:** 1966 **Open:** Sept.-June **Admission:** audition, resume, interview **Deadlines:** Rolling admissions **Cost:** $225 per credit for state residents, $365 for non-residents **Financial Aid:** Loans; Scholarship; Fellowship; Stipend; Work/Study **Size-Attendees:** 90 **Size-Class:** 15-20 **Degree or Certification:** BA in Dance Studies, BS in Dance Studies, BFA in Dance, MA in Dance/Movement Studies, MFA in Dance **Job Placement:** Yes

SUNY–BROCKPORT is a unique and distinguished program that gains much of its profile from its faculty. Garth Fagan is the most notable mem-

The Educated Dancer

Of all art forms, dance is the most ephemeral, and Seneca's "Vita brevis est, ard longa" doesn't apply: In the case of dance it is art that is short and life that can be long for the dancer, beyond the years of performance. Dancers often used to feel that even thinking about life after performing might inhibit concentration and the ability to give one's all. For women, perhaps survival later in life would be solved by a providing husband, or they might open a dance studio. And in the general populace it was a common assumption that since dancers are so physical, they are surely not very bright and probably could not follow another profession in any case. Even some ballet masters and choreographers preferred dancers who were totally malleable, their individuality effaced, with no personal life or presence that could cause trouble.

Fortunately all that has changed, though sometimes it is an ambitious parent vicariously living through the child's career who most hates to acknowledge the short life span of ballet and is indifferent to the child's education. In fact, the concentration and discipline learned in the dance studio often transfers easily to the classroom. To live in a different world, the academic one, for even a few hours a day, can be a necessary relief from the grueling pace of ballet training. Most serious, committed dance students are so well organized that high-school academics are easily accommodated, if there is some flexibility in scheduling.

A couple of years ago, one senior in the New York City Professional Children's School, who, being only 17, was still living in the School of American Ballet's (SAB) residence hall, received a perfect score in both the math and verbal sections of the SAT (Scholastic Aptitude Test). Since only a few students in the United States had achieved this, she was invited to the White House for a reception. At first she declined because on that date she was listed to perform with the New York City Ballet, but when Peter Martins heard about it, her schedule was changed. She got to go and enjoy the honor of having the other side of her life praised. The applause for her dancing would come the next day.

What ballet-devoted students might be missing is a certain amount of fooling-around teenage time; waste-hours, angst time, and getting into trouble. It

ber of the faculty, having been a member since 1971. Fagan, who choreographed *The Lion King* on Broadway, has developed his world-famous company through the sponsorship of the dance department and the college. Khalid Saleem and Clyde Morgan are 2 other faculty members who have shaped the dance department's focus; both lead Sankofa, the department's African Dance and Drum Ensemble, which tours throughout upstate New York. Still other faculty have their roots in classical modern dance: Limón, Sokolow and Lang. If this is where your interests lie, Brockport might be for you.

The department is fairly large, with 75 dance majors, 15 minors, 10 interdisciplinary arts majors and 15 graduate students. A broad range of degrees is offered: a BA, BS or BFA, and an MA or MFA. The department has its own professionally equipped 500-seat theater; 4 studios; a body-conditioning lab; and computerized music and design studios. Hartwell Hall, the oldest building on campus and the site of the dance program, has recently been renovated. Students of the program have gone on to dance in such top companies as Martha Graham, Paul Taylor, Elizabeth Streb (her-

surprises me, though, how quickly a ballet student can adopt to the normal adolescent mold when opportunity arises. Most of them are missing very little, and from their perspective a lot of the teenage years are merely a holding time and fairly pointless. The difference in attitude from their peers derives from a certainty about goals and the knowledge of exactly what must be accomplished in order to get there. No matter what happens in their dance careers, they will never lose that ability to focus—they have the mental equipment to do anything.

SAB has had a residence hall since 1991, with support systems, programs and counselors. The school is involved in the lives of 65 students for 10 months of the year, and in some cases it is a 5- or 6-year association. A recent study shows without doubt that successful dancers (those receiving contracts from professional dance companies) were also achievers in academics. Clearly, a life that is well rounded is a distinct plus for a dancer.

For the art of ballet, what is even more important is the correlation between dancers who are mentally and esthetically developed, as well as in technique, and what this gives to their dancing, their growth as interpretive artists. They are more interesting to look at. One sees more than just a body in motion; one has the pleasure of perceiving a whole person.

Though dance may be ephemeral, it is finally the quality of the fleeting moment that counts.
—Curtis Harnack, President, School of American Ballet, 1992–1997

self an alumna), Ralph Lemon and Garth Fagan. The department also has several touring companies, including Danscore, a contemporary dance ensemble; and Sankofa. Students can elect to major in dance with an emphasis in African dance and music, dance science and somatics, music for dance, dance performance and choreography. Not exactly a traditional academic program, but that's what makes it special.

State University of New York–Purchase

For ballet, modern dancers, choreographers Westchester County, 15 mi. from Manhattan — Conservatory of Dance, 735 Anderson Hill Rd., Purchase, NY 10577 **Voice:** 914-251-6800 **Fax:** 914-251-6806 **E-mail:** cwalker@purchase.edu **Web Site:** www.purchase.edu/academic/dance/ **Contact:** Carol K. Walker, Dean of Dance **Open:** Year-round **Admission:** Written application, audition, writing sample, test scores, interview **Deadlines:** Dec. 1 **Cost:** $12,225 for residents, $17,125 for nonresidents **Financial Aid:** Loans; Scholarship; Fellowship; Stipend; Work/Study **Size-Attendees:** 140 **Degree or Certification:** BFA, MFA **Job Placement:** Yes

THE SUNY–PURCHASE dance conservatory emphasizes performance and choreography. The recently added MFA program is a 2-year, 60-credit program in which a student can concentrate either in choreography or in performance and pedagogy.

CAROL ROSEGG

Professor Rosanna Seravalli coaches student In-Jung Huh at SUNY–Purchase.

Dean and dance professor Carol Walker studied with Hanya Holm and Alwin Nikolais and at the Graham School before directing her own dance studio for more than a decade. Kazuko Hirabayshi directs the graduate program and brings strong credentials in modern dance and composition to the program. Other distinguished faculty include Elizabeth Sawyer, who teaches music for dance; Gayle Young, former principal dancer with American Ballet Theatre; Bettijane Sills, a former soloist with New York City Ballet; Tarin Chaplin, who teaches composition; and Kevin Wynn, a former Limón Dance Company member and faculty member at the Alvin Ailey School. Overall there is a strong faculty with plenty of personal attention. Other pluses are the school's proximity to New York City and the number of distinguished guest teachers who offer masterclasses and set works on the students. The award-winning dance building at Purchase is one of the largest facilities in the United States specifically designed for dance training and performance. Its 9 well-equipped and light-filled studios are some of the best in the country. The facility also includes a 270-seat dance-theater lab and two Pilates studios. The nearby performing-arts center has 4 great theaters presenting an extensive selection of high-caliber arts events, including a strong dance series as well as student productions.

There is plenty of opportunity for performance through the Purchase Dance Corps, which not only performs works at the college by such luminaries as George Balanchine, Paul Taylor and Merce Cunningham, but also tours the United States and internationally. Like that of Juilliard, the program aims to produce well-rounded performers by giving equal attention to modern dance and ballet. The number of Purchase graduates dancing with professional companies attests to the program's quality. Purchase alumni have gone on to dance with the American Ballet Theatre, Limón Dance Company, Frankfurt Ballet, Houston Ballet, Merce Cunningham Dance Company, Trisha Brown Dance Company, Paul Taylor Dance Company, Bill T. Jones/Arnie Zane Company and Mark Morris Dance Group.

Steps on Broadway

For all dancers, choreographers
Manhattan's Upper West Side — 2121 Broadway, 3rd Fl., New York, NY 10023 **Voice:** 212-874-2410 **Fax:** 212-787-2449 **Contact:** Carol Paumgarten, Artistic Dir. **Open:** Year-round **Admission:** Open **Deadlines:** Rolling **Cost:** $100 for 10 classes **Financial Aid:** Scholarship; Work/Study **Size-Attendees:** 200-400 **Size-Class:** 15-35

PROBABLY NEW YORK City's largest professional dance studio, Steps offers open classes in such standards as ballet, modern, jazz and tap, as well as nonstandards like Pilates, Argentine tango, hip-hop/funk, theater dance, ballroom, flamenco and dance exercise. The faculty can number anywhere from 50 to 75, thanks to a steady influx of guest teachers and substitutes. Most faculty members are still working professionals, so schedules vary daily and weekly. However, a core group of teachers does exist for each of the disciplines offered at the studio. Students benefit from the rotation, gaining exposure to many of the top professionals teaching, choreographing and dancing today.

Steps is also able to boast one of the largest group of master teachers under one roof, with such names as Simon Dow and Wilhelm Burmann (ballet); Charles Goddertz (tap); Zena Rommett, originator of floor barre; Fred Benjamin, Joe Lanteri and Michael Owens (jazz); Milton Myers (Horton); and Randy Skinner (theater dance). The studio is also the first stop for many retiring dancers from companies, such as the ABT and the NYCB, looking to get their feet wet teaching. This might be because during their own careers they took classes at the studio. If your aspiration is to sweat at the barre next to Misha, Paloma Herrera, Susan Jaffe or Wendy Whelan, you might just get your wish at Steps. In the tradition of Dance Space, the studio now runs a workshop series with such guest artists as Dwight Rhoden and Desmond Richardson, Donald Byrd and David Parsons; along with a faculty-showcase performance that grows with each year. A popular scholarship program, operating as a work-study exchange program, offers students free classes in exchange for general upkeep duties around the studio. Steps has 6 main studios, 2 of which are quite large, and the rest of which range from small to medium. The studio remains a place where absolute beginners can come and take class side by side with the top names in the business. Over the years the studio has developed a reputation for a sometimes less-than-warm atmosphere pervading its hallways and studios. But leaving aside the diva mentality—which, truth to tell, can be found to differing degrees no matter where you go—Steps is probably one of New York's and, consequently, the country's best choices.

Teachers College–Columbia University

For dance educators Manhattan's Upper West Side — Box 139, 525 W. 120th St., New York, NY 10027 **Voice:** 212-678-3328 **Fax:** 212-678-4048 **E-mail:** sk413@columbia.edu **Web Site:** www.tc.columbia.edu/~academic/dance **Contact:** Susan Koff, Chair **Founded:** 1918 **Open:** Year-round **Admission:** Written application, placement audition, interview, review of past dance experience **Deadlines:** Jan. or Apr. for audition; Feb. 1 for application, financial aid **Cost:** $640 per credit **Financial Aid:** Loans; Scholarship; Fellowship; Stipend; Work/Study **Size-Attendees:** 30 **Size-Class:** 10 **Degree or Certification:** MA in Dance, MA in Dance with K-12 Dance Teacher Certification **Job Placement:** Yes

THIS DANCE PROGRAM offers graduate degrees to those whose passion is for teaching dance, irrespective of their training or their interest in a particular dance form. The perception of dance ranges from the traditional one of dance as ritual and fine art, to the popular one of dance as mass culture. Using the rich resources of New York City as a kind of dance laboratory and the renowned education faculty of Teachers College, this program offers disciplined students an opportunity to design a program tailored to their interests. Because the program enrolls only about 25 students and has a faculty of 8, a good deal of personal attention is given to each student.

At last count, 13 states, New York among them, require certification for teachers of dance. At this writing, Teachers College is the only program in New York State that offers teacher certification. The philosophy of the department and its chair, Susan Koff, is that this program should be about dance education, not about dance training. Still, training can be part of the education the student receives; Koff believes everyone has a right to experience and enjoy dance. She welcomes individuals who have a love for the spirit of all types of dance. Courses in dance education examine the different populations and settings in which various dance forms reach their audiences. The MA-degree track has the most flexibility and allows students to shape the program with their advisor. This degree can be completed in as little as 18 months. The MA program with teacher certification requires additional courses of study and takes at least 2 years. The 4 areas of study are body sciences, performance practice and analysis, dance pedagogy and theory/research and implementation.

Martha Myers works with a student at the American Dance Festival Choreolab, Durham.

North Carolina

American Dance Festival

For all dancers, choreographers
North central North Carolina, off I-80 — Box 90772, Durham, NC 27708 **Voice:** 919-684-6402 **Fax:** 919-684-5459 **E-mail:** adf@AmericanDanceFestival.org **Web Site:** www.americandancefestival.org **Contact:** Charles and Stephanie Reinhart, Co-Dirs. **Founded:** 1934 **Open:** Summer **Admission:** Written application, resume, 2 evaluation forms **Deadlines:** Apr. 15 **Cost:** $1,610 **Financial Aid:** Scholarship; Fellowship; Work/Study **Size-Attendees:** 350 **Size-Class:** 15-25

ADF IS THE SUMMER mecca for advanced students and professionals who make the annual pilgrimage to Duke University for a modern-dance intensive that has been around since 1934. The 6-week festival attracts students from around the world, as well as master teachers, companies and leading professionals in the field. Along with Jacob's Pillow, this festival stands as 1 of the 2 premier dance gatherings in the country, with a history dating back to the beginnings of the modern-dance movement.

Here's what students get for their money and effort: more than 60 classes a day, special masterclasses and weekend workshops, an opportunity to work with choreographers in residence in the creation of new works and in special student-choreography concerts, faculty mentoring and roundtable discussions, the chance to audition for professional companies participating in and performing at ADF, as well as admission to open rehearsals of those dance companies. Some of the country's top-caliber companies perform here: the likes of Paul Taylor, Merce Cunningham, Pilobolus; so do an eclectic mix of international artists from such countries as Israel and Argentina. The program caters to those seeking an early artistic experience, as well as to those with an eye toward the professional world. The curriculum is geared to exploring both historical approaches and new concepts for dance training. Full-time students receive a complimentary ticket to a performance by each visiting company in the ADF performance series.

North Carolina School of the Arts

🏠 ☀️ *For ballet, modern dancers, choreographers* NW North Carolina — 200 Waughtown St., P.O. Box 12189, Winston-Salem, NC 27117 **Voice:** 336-770-3208 **Fax:** 336-770-3204 **Web Site:** www.ncarts.edu/dance **Contact:** Susan McCullogh, Dean of Dance **Founded:** 1965 **Open:** Year-round **Admission:** Written application, audition, transcripts, interview **Deadlines:** Apply each semester **Cost:** $1,428 tuition for state residents, $10,056 for nonresidents **Financial Aid:** Loans; Scholarship; Fellowship; Stipend; Work/Study **Size-Attendees:** 1,000 **Size-Class:** 20-30 **Degree or Certification:** BFA in Dance **Job Placement:** Yes

L OCATED ON 50 ACRES in downtown Winston-Salem, the school is one of 16 campuses making up the University of North Carolina. Established in 1965, it is the first state-supported school to offer professional training in the performing arts.

According to the school's philosophy the training of a great artist requires emphasis on performance. To this end, the students give hundreds of performances each year at the 4 main theaters on campus and at the Stevens Arts Center. Because it is a state-subsidized school, tuition rates are remarkably low for state residents; even for out-of-state students they are considerably lower than at other arts schools in the country. The school trains gifted young professionals for careers in professional companies. Like the other major conservatories of dance, it aims to turn out well-rounded dancers who "remain flexible to absorb and reflect the current directions in dance." Students benefit from a great student-faculty ratio of 7:1 and from the many distinguished guest artists. The first-rate faculty is headed by Susan McCullogh, former head of the Pittsburgh Ballet Theatre School, former ballet mistress of Netherlands Dance Theatre, a founding member of North Car-olina Dance Theatre and a graduate of NCSA. Probably the best-known faculty member is Melissa Hayden, former superstar of the New York City Ballet and the American Ballet Theatre. Other notable faculty members include Duncan Noble, who has served on the faculty since the school was founded and is a former dancer with Valerie Bettis, Ballet Russe and ABT, and veteran choreographer for Broadway shows and television; former ABT members Fanchon Cordell, Frank Smith and Warren Conover; and assistant dean Diane Markham, who teaches contemporary technique, having trained with Hanya Holm, Alwin Nikolais, Murray Louis and Phyllis Lamhut. The guest faculty reads like a "Who's-who" of American dance, with particularly strong listings in the contemporary-dance area, beginning with Alvin Ailey and including disciples of Graham, Humphrey and Limón. The guest ballet faculty has included Juilliard director Benjamin Harkarvy, and Patricia Wilde, Violette Verdy and Anna-Marie Holmes, to name just a few.

Duncan Noble instructs students at the North Carolina School of the Arts, Winston-Salem.

Raleigh School of Ballet

For ballet dancers, choreographers *Central North Carolina, off I-40 —
3921 Beryl Rd., Raleigh, NC 27607* **Voice:**
919-834-9261 **Fax:** 919-829-1493 **E-mail:**
raleighballet@mindspring.com **Web Site:**
www.raleighballet.citysearch.com **Contact:**
Ann Vorus, Dir. **Founded:** 1981 **Open:** Year-round **Admission:** Written application, audition **Deadlines:** Rolling **Cost:** $42-$300 per
month **Financial Aid:** Loans; Scholarship;
Fellowship; Work/Study **Size-Attendees:**
250 **Size-Class:** 12-25

The Raleigh School offers classes for each stage of a developing dancer. Its children's program nurtures young students. Those who want to pursue a career in ballet can audition for the school's professional division, an intensive training program that offers its students scholarships in the form of reduced tuition rates. An adult program for all levels is also available.

The faculty includes Ann Vorus, founder and director of the school, who was a soloist with the Atlanta Ballet; Nina Jonson, formerly with Ballet Oklahoma; and Mary LeGere, former soloist with the Pennsylvania Ballet. LeGere also serves as artistic director of Raleigh Dance Theatre, the school's affiliate company, which provides performance training to students over age 13.

The facilities are worth noting. The school was designed and built specifically for dance training with 3 spacious studios complete with high ceilings and sprung floors.

University of North Carolina–Charlotte

For ballet and modern dancers,
choreographers *SW North Carolina, off I-85
— Dance and Theater Dept., 9201 University
City Blvd., Charlotte, NC 28223* **Voice:** 704-547-2482 **Fax:** 704-547-3795 **Web Site:**
www.uncc.edu **Contact:** Pamela Sofras,
Coord. **Open:** Year-round **Admission:**
Written application, audition, transcripts,
test scores, writing sample **Deadlines:**
Apply each semester **Cost:** $235 tuition per
credit hour for state residents, $1,144 for
nonresidents **Financial Aid:** Loans;
Scholarship; Fellowship; Stipend; Work/Study
Size-Attendees: 30 **Size-Class:** 10-20
Degree or Certification: BAs in Dance,
Dance Education **Job Placement:** Yes

While this school is not as large as those in Raleigh or in Greensboro, the dance-and-theater department offers a strong professional program accredited by the National Association of Schools of Dance. The emphasis here is on combining theater and dance in unique ways; the program is not geared toward musical-theater artists but toward ballet and modern dancers who seek a solid grounding in theater technique, which they can put to use in their careers as performers and choreographers.

The present facility has 2 theaters: the Rowe, with 300 seats, and a 75-seat black-box theater, both with state-of-the-art computerized light and sound systems. The university has plans to build a new humanities building, opening in 2000, to house the department of dance and theater. The program offers an excellent faculty-student ratio and trumpets the fact that it offers undergraduates more "hands-on" experience because they don't have to compete with the graduate students. There are around 30 dance majors served by 5 full-time and 5 part-time faculty. The faculty includes 2 Fulbright scholars, department chair Sybil Huskey and Karen Hubbard, a specialist on African dance. Delia Neil, a former dancer with the Cincinnati Ballet, is also on the faculty, as is Noel Reiss, who danced with the Nikolais Louis Company. Coordinator Pamela Sofras is a graduate of the Juilliard School. Recent student concerts included performances of historic modern works by Ruth St. Denis, Doris Humphrey, Helen Tamiris and Anna Sokolow. The university has a rich history, but this is a new campus in one of the largest urban centers in the South. Together with the University Research Park the campus comprises the University City area of Charlotte. Charlotte's arts scene has emerged in recent years as one of the liveliest and best in the country, and students can take advantage of the fine theater, dance and music performances available throughout the year. Although the university's 1,000-acre campus is set among rolling hills, forests and streams, it is located just 8 miles from one of the fastest-growing and most prosperous metropolitan areas in the country today.

University of North Carolina–Greensboro

🏠 💥 *For all dancers, choreographers*
North central North Carolina, off I-85 — 323 HHP Building, P.O. Box 26169, Greensboro, NC 27412 **Voice:** 336-334-5570 **Fax:** 336-
E-mail: sue_stinson@uncg.edu **Web Site:** www.uncg.edu/dce **Contact:** Sue Stinson, Dance Dept. Head **Founded:** 1892 **Open:** Year-round **Admission:** Written application, audition, transcripts, test scores, writing samples, interview **Deadlines:** Apply each semester **Cost:** $2,949 per year for state residents, $6,584 for nonresidents **Financial Aid:** Loans; Scholarship; Fellowship; Stipend; Work/Study **Size-Attendees:** 140 **Degree or Certification:** BA in Dance, BS in Dance Education, BFA in Choreography and Performance **Job Placement:** Yes

T HIS PROGRAM OFFERS 3 undergraduate degrees in dance with different emphases, and a graduate program. The BFA permits the study of dance as a creative and performing art with an emphasis on choreography and performance; the BS provides an understanding of dance as an art form and as an important aspect of a well-rounded education; and the BA provides a general education in dance and an opportunity for a double major at the university. Either an MFA or an MA is offered to graduate students. Undergraduate enrollment is 120; graduate enrollment, 20.

As part of the university's School of Health and Human Performance, the dance program encourages young artists to be "total dancers," stressing creativity, confidence and resourcefulness. While training is offered in all genres and forms, for performers the stress is on modern dance. The program also asks students to consider alternative forms of work and training to supplement their meager earnings as a dancer. One goal is to train new teachers in dance to meet the scarcity of certified dance educators in North Carolina and elsewhere. This approach seems extremely practical and considerate of the students' needs, and in no way disparaging of the students' talents. Greensboro's facilities are first rate, with 5 state-of-the-art studios, a fully equipped dance theater and a complete library.

Performance opportunities abound, with at least 9 concert programs during the year, and former students give Greensboro high marks for offering opportunities to choreograph and develop young talents. The full-time faculty includes department head Sue Stinson, who is a highly regarded dance movement specialist and teacher of dance to young children; Jan Van Dyke, a Fulbright scholar and author of *Modern Dance in a Post Modern World,* as well as artistic director of the Van Dyke Dance Group, a local performing ensemble; John Gamble, who formerly codirected the Zero Moving Company and chaired the dance department at Temple University; Rick McCullough, who danced with North Carolina Dance Theater and Netherlands Dance Theatre and choreographed dances for modern and ballet companies. The faculty also includes 9 full-time regular faculty and a full-time guest artist, as well as some part-time faculty and dance companies who perform in the university's performing-arts series.

Ohio

BalletMet Dance Academy

🎵 ☀️ *For ballet, ethnic, jazz, modern, tap dancers, choreographers* Central Ohio — *322 Mt. Vernon Ave., Columbus, OH 43215* **Voice:** 614-224-1672 **Fax:** 614-229-4858 **Contact:** David Nixon, Dir. **Founded:** 1978 **Open:** Year-round **Admission:** Application **Deadlines:** Rolling **Cost:** From $48 for 4 classes per month **Financial Aid:** Loans; Scholarship; Work/Study **Size-Attendees:** 100-150 **Size-Class:** 10-25

U NDER THE STEWARDSHIP of David Nixon, BalletMet is Ohio's leading dance center, with a national reputation as one of the country's top regional companies. The academy has it all: a professional division that attracts preprofessionals from around the country, outreach and performance opportunities.

The rigorous professional training program is divided into 2 levels. Level A students dance 4 hours a day, 6 days a week. Their curriculum includes ballet technique, pointe, variations, men's class, partnering, jazz, Afro- Caribbean, modern, choreography and rehearsals. Level B students dance 3.5 hours a day, 6 days a week, with a schedule similar to that of Level A, and is meant to prepare students for eventual promotion into that level. The director of the professional program is faculty member Yoko Ichino, internationally acclaimed prima ballerina with the American Ballet Theatre, the National Ballet of Canada, the Stuttgart Ballet and a host of others. Ichino is joined by such dancers as April Berry, formerly of Alvin Ailey; George Boft of the Bolshoi; Catherine Yoshimura of the Milwaukee Ballet; and Billy Bruce, who enjoyed a career on Broadway. The dance center houses 7 fully equipped studios; the 3 largest studios measure 60 x 60 feet. A bonus for students in the professional division is the career-counseling program. During the students' senior year, advice is given on developing resumes and photographs for auditions. Even for students not enrolled in the professional program, the course offerings are numerous and varied. Besides the standard classes in ballet, modern, character, tap and jazz, the school offers street jazz/funk, jazz/Ailey Technique and Afro-Caribbean.

WILL SHIVELY

Kristen Stevens performs at the BalletMet, Columbus.

Dayton Ballet School

🎵 ☀️ *For all dancers, choreographers* Downtown — *140 N. Main St., Dayton, OH 45402* **Voice:** 937-449-5060 **Fax:** 937-461-8353 **Contact:** Dermot Burke, Dir. **Founded:** 1937 **Open:** Year-round **Admission:** Written application, placement audition **Deadlines:** Rolling **Cost:** $55 for 8 classes **Financial Aid:** Scholarship; Work/Study **Size-Attendees:** 50-150 **Size-Class:** 5-25

O NE OF OHIO's premier regional companies, along with Ballet-Met, Cleveland Ballet, Cincinnati Ballet and Ohio Ballet, the Dayton Ballet School offers students quality training with faculty members who have almost all spent their careers training, dancing or teaching at the company-affiliated school. The 9-member faculty has extensive experience.

Professionally minded students can join the junior company, Dayton Ballet II, or the senior company, for those enrolled in their final year at the school. Gregory Robinson, who spent much of his performing career with Dayton Contemporary Dance Company, codirects the junior company, along with Karen Russo, who also serves as the main company's rehearsal assistant and as a school faculty member. The entire operation is overseen by Dermot Burke, who was a principal dancer and associate ballet master with the Joffrey Ballet and resident choreographer for Milwaukee Ballet for several seasons.

Jeraldyne's School of the Dance

For modern, jazz, ballet dancers Downtown — 126 N. Main St., Suite 240, Dayton, OH 45402 **Voice:** 937-223-5312 **Fax:** 937-223-6156 **Contact:** Jeraldyne Blunden, Dir. **Founded:** 1960 **Open:** Year-round **Admission:** Open **Deadlines:** Rolling **Cost:** $40 for 4 classes per month **Financial Aid:** Scholarship; Work/Study **Size-Attendees:** 100-200 **Size-Class:** 10-25

THIS SCHOOL IS home to one of the country's top black dance companies, Dayton Contemporary Dance Company, a powerful group of dancers following in the footsteps of Alvin Ailey. Small wonder that many of the students end up dancing with the Ailey Company. Both the company and the school are led by the indefatigable Jeraldyne Blunden, one of America's national dance treasures. The school's mission statement points to the rigorous demands of the kind of repertory usually performed: "Our staff strives to create an atmosphere of strenuous intellectual, physical and mental labor, competition, cooperation and dedication to the pursuit of excellence and pride in the arts."

Classes focus on equal amounts of modern, jazz and ballet. The modern is a combination of the Horton and Graham techniques. Jazz follows the Nat Horne style, which stresses isolations, body placement and syncopated movement. The School offers a single technique on certain days of the week, with jazz taught on Tuesday, modern on Wednesday and ballet on Thursday. No classes are offered on Monday and Friday.

Ohio State University

For ballet, modern dancers, choreographers Central Ohio — 1813 N. High St., Columbus, OH 43210 **Voice:** 614-292-7977 **Fax:** 614-292-0939 **E-mail:** Giffin.1@osu.edu **Web Site:** www.ohio-state.edu **Contact:** John R. Giffin, Chair **Founded:** 1968 **Open:** Year-round **Admission:** Written application, audition, transcripts, test scores, writing samples **Deadlines:** Rolling for BA, Dec. 15 for MA/MF **Cost:** $13,900 tuition per year for state residents, $22,200 for nonresidents **Financial Aid:** Loans; Scholarship; Fellowship; Stipend; Work/Study **Size-Attendees:** 120 undergrad, 30 grad **Degree or Certification:** MA in Dance, MFA in Dance **Job Placement:** Yes

THIS WELL-RESPECTED school is a real bargain for Ohio residents, especially for those interested in a varied and rich graduate program in dance. The dance department is contained within the College of the Arts, 1 of 18 colleges in this large university. The beautifully landscaped urban campus features excellent facilities in Sullivant Hall, including 6 studios, dressing rooms, production facilities and an extensive library. The city of Columbus has become decidedly more lively in recent years with a much-improved, professional-arts scene.

While the undergraduate programs offers either a BFA in performance or dance education, the graduate program offers many alternatives, including an MA in dance, considered an intermediary degree that can lead to either an MFA or a PhD. MFA degrees are offered

Dance Preservation

Dance is, with little argument, the most difficult of the arts to document. A tradition handed down from generation to generation, teacher to student, dancer to dancer, the ephemeral art often leaves few tangible records. Documenting dance has challenged both performers and historians alike; quite often, when the dancers leave the stage, the work is gone. As Marcia Siegal observed in her book, *The Shapes of Change,* "Continuity in dance must be worked at. Preservation—or the losing battle we fight with it—may be the basic issue of American dance. The immediacy and the ephemerality of dance are its most particular qualities."

The issues surrounding preservation span the imagined boundaries of ballet, modern, jazz, tap, ritual and traditional dance. Typically, dance and dancers are recorded and preserved through a variety of methods, including videotape, motion-picture film, photographs, documents on paper (programs, news clippings, correspondence, business records), oral and video histories, and notation scores (Laban and Benesh are two systems for writing dance).

Those who create documentation include not only choreographers and performers, but also dance presenters, videographers, historians, critics and notators, as well as archivists and librarians in dance repositories.

In recent years, dancers and dance companies have become increasingly aware of the value of their historical materials. Throughout the dance community, a family which had lost so many members to both age and AIDS in the 1980s, the desire to acquire and maintain archival documents became intense. Responding to this crisis, Preserve, Inc., a national service organization, was formed in 1987 to provide archival education to the dance community. In mid-1990,

in choreography, performance, lighting and production; directing from Labanotation scores; and dance technology. Of the 22 faculty, 15 are full time, with about 80 undergraduate students and 30 graduate students. Visiting artists and major dance companies are regularly invited to the university for concerts, masterclasses and lecture demonstrations. Much of this activity is produced in conjunction with the Wexner Center for the Arts. Recent visitors have included the Trisha Brown Dance Company, Ann Carlson, Eiko & Koma, Garth Fagan Dance, Karen Finley, the Mark Morris Dance Company and Twyla Tharp. The dance department frequently hosts professional conferences, courses and workshops, such as the Dance Notation Bureau Teacher Training Course, the Dance History Scholars' Conference, the Congress on Research in Dance Conference, the American College Dance Festival Association, the Laban/Bartenieff Institute for Movement Studies certification program, the International Council on Kinetography Laban and the Multimedia Workshop in Dance Documentation and Preservation. Ohio State is one of the leading centers in the exploration of new technologies for recording and preserving dance. Among its projects are the development of a Multimedia Prototype for creating an interactive multimedia model for documenting dance on CD-ROM. It has the largest collection of dance scores of any university library. No other university can match the training Ohio State has in dance documentation, so if this is your interest, OSU is the place to be.

the Andrew W. Mellon Foundation and the Dance Program of the National Endowment for the Arts initiated a study of the national issues surrounding dance documentation and preservation. Entitled *Images of American Dance: Documenting and Preserving a Cultural Heritage,* the report concluded that "Creation in the absence of documentation and preservation only denies the future. It is the conveyance of a history, the continuity of an art form, and the preservation of works through which our own renaissance becomes more likely."

Subsequent to that report was the publication of Preserve's *Dance Archives: a practical manual for documenting and preserving the ephemeral art,* and the launch of *afterimages,* a quarterly newsletter on the subject. The Dance Heritage Coalition was formed by the heads of major repositoires and dance festivals to address cataloging issues at the national level. Several other initiatives furthered the preservation of dance and dancers, including the Repertory Etudes Project of the American Dance Legacy Institute, archival documentaries created by the George Balanchine Foundation, and the Legacy Oral History Project.

At the close of the 20th century, new technologies are emerging to create, document and preserve dance. Development of the software programs *Lifeforms, Poser, LabanWriter* and other movement-generation packages, allow choreographers to work at a computer instead of in a studio. Presently, new CD-ROMs are being developed, notably the Ohio State University Multimedia Dance Prototype (OSU-MDP), in which several digital technologies are integrated to create a composite picture of dancers and their work. New Internet technologies create universal on-line access to dance companies, library catalogs and preservation resources.

—Leslie Hansen Kopp,
Executive Director, Preserve, Inc.

School of Cleveland San Jose Ballet

For ballet dancers, choreographers Cleveland's "Over the Rhine" neighborhood near the city; the California facility is in the Santa Clara Valley, 45 mi. S of San Francisco — 1375 Euclid Ave., #110, Cleveland, OH 44115; P.O. Box 1666, San Jose, CA 95109 **Voice:** 216-621-3633 (OH); 408-288-2820 (CA) **Fax:** 216-621-7039 **Contact:** Dennis Nahat, Artistic Dir. **Founded:** 1972 **Open:** Year-round **Admission:** Written application, audition **Deadlines:** Rolling; May 1 for summer program **Cost:** Summer program starts at $280 for Level I for 3 weeks **Financial Aid:** Scholarship; Work/Study **Size-Attendees:** 100-200 **Size-Class:** 10-25

B ECAUSE OF A unique circumstance, this dual-named, dual-housed company has developed into a universally admired and respected regional company. It all began with the School of Cleveland Ballet in 1972, which engendered the Cleveland Ballet. In 1985 the operation underwent a change, thanks to the enthusiasm and sponsorship of a single community: San Jose, California. When in California the company and the school go by the name "San Jose Cleveland Ballet." While both cities maintain separate administrative staffs, they share the vision of one artistic director, Dennis Nahat, who along with a single company of dancers travels between both cities. The success of the venture owes much to the skillful leadership of Nahat, who has earned the respect of colleagues as a performer with Joffrey Ballet and American Ballet Theatre and as teacher and choreographer.

Both schools are dedicated to training students in the rigors of classical dance, with 2 programs fulfilling the needs of the community at large: the professional division and the community program. For the professional division other dance forms are offered that enhance the study of classical movement, including contemporary dance, ethnic dance and mime. The syllabus is eclectic, drawing from the best of the American, Russian, French, Italian and Danish schools of training.

In Cleveland, students and company members share the same studio facilities, giving students the opportunity to observe personally the lives and work of professional dancers, which is integral to the success of any program training young professionals. Performance opportunities are available to students at the school who augment the company performances at both sites. The facilities in both San Jose and Cleveland are relatively new. The spacious and airy studios in San Jose were renovated in 1997, and the newly located and expanded facilities in Cleveland were opened in 1998.

provided at the School for Creative and Performing Arts.

School director Dennis Poole has excellent credentials, including previous positions with the company as resident choreographer, acting artistic director and ballet master. Before joining Cincinnati, Poole was artistic director of the Ballet de Santiago, ballet master of the Houston Ballet, resident choreographer and ballet master of the Oklahoma Festival Ballet and a principal dancer with the Joffrey Ballet, Houston Ballet, Pittsburgh Ballet Theatre and the National Ballet. Victoria Morgan, the company's energetic artistic director, is also an important figure in the school. Before joining the Company, she served as Ballet Mistress of the San Francisco Opera and as a Principal Dancer with the San Francisco Ballet and Ballet West. The faculty is rounded out by more than a dozen current and past company members. The enrollment is approximately 200, and many of the students participate in *The Nutcracker* and in special productions mounted for the school. Plans are underway to launch a satellite school in Northern Kentucky.

School of the Cincinnati Ballet

For ballet dancers, choreographers SW Ohio — 1555 Central Pkwy., Cincinnati, OH 45214 **Voice:** 513-621-5219 **Fax:** 513-621-4844 **E-mail:** ballet@one.net **Web Site:** www.cincinnatiballet.com/schl19899.htm **Contact:** Victoria Morgan, Artistic Dir. **Founded:** 1963 **Open:** Year-round **Admission:** Open **Deadlines:** Early Aug. **Cost:** From $185 per semester **Financial Aid:** Scholarship; Work/Study **Size-Attendees:** 200

THE CINCINNATI Ballet perceives its 3-year-old school as the lifeblood of the affiliated company. It envisions a significant number of the company's members will be coming from the school, which in turn is staffed by current and former dancers with the company. Emphasis is on a graded syllabus and on training leading to professional status. The school shares 2 studios with the professional company; additional studio space is

University of Cincinnati

For ballet dancers, choreographers SW Ohio — College-Conservatory of Music, Cincinnati, OH 45221 **Voice:** 513-556-5463 **Fax:** 513-556-1028 **Web Site:** www.uc.edu/www/ccm/dance/ **Contact:** Carol N. Iwasaki, Head, Dance Div. **Founded:** 1870 **Open:** Year-round **Admission:** Audition, transcripts, test scores, interview **Deadlines:** Aug. 1 **Cost:** $3,900 per year for state residents, $13,280 for nonresidents **Financial Aid:** Loans; Scholarship; Fellowship; Stipend; Work/Study **Size-Attendees:** 100 **Size-Class:** 25 **Degree or Certification:** BFA in Ballet **Job Placement:** Yes

WHILE THE DANCE division of the University of Cincinnati offers the artistic environment of a real conservatory of music and related arts, it profits from the facilities and advantages of a major, comprehensive university. It is strictly for ballet dancers, understandably when one learns that it is both the founding institution and the affiliate of the Cincinnati Ballet, one of America's finest regional ballet companies. The university was the first music school in the nation to offer a degree in classical ballet.

The dance program has 3 large dance studios, observation booths for faculty and visitors, dressing rooms and a therapy room. Dance performances are held in the Cincinnati Conservatory's 400-seat Corbett Theatre, with the Ballet Ensemble offering works by faculty and guest choreographers. Naturally, live music is offered for the dance performances. Alumni of the program have joined many leading companies, including the Atlanta, Cincinnati, Cleveland, Dallas, Joffrey, New York City and Vienna State Opera ballets. Auditions are required through an advanced classical-ballet-technique class and scholarships are awarded solely on the basis of ability as demonstrated through this admissions audition.

Of special interest to the prospective student is the community, which prides itself on its support of the arts, with a host of first-rate arts organizations. Another item of interest is the conservatory library, with more than 100,000 books, scores and tapes, including the Chujoy Memorial Dance collection of books and historic memorabilia.

Wright State University

🏠 ☀️ *For ballet, jazz, modern, tap dancers, choreographers* Suburban Dayton — Dept. of Theatre Arts, 3640 Col. Glenn Hwy., Dayton, OH 45435 **Voice:** 937-775-3072; 800-247-1770 **Fax:** 937-775-3787 **E-mail:** jon.rodriguez@wright.edu **Web Site:** www.cola.wright.edu **Contact:** Jon Rodriguez, Dance Chair **Founded:** 1968 **Open:** Year-round **Admission:** Written application, audition, transcripts, interview **Deadlines:** Apply each semester **Cost:** $9,250 for tuition, room, board and fees for state residents; $13,140 for nonresidents **Financial Aid:** Loans; Scholarship; Fellowship; Stipend; Work/Study **Size-Attendees:** 15 **Degree or Certification:** BFA in Dance **Job Placement:** Yes

THIS DISTINGUISHED university offers a unique approach to the teaching of the theater arts by including them in a program that also embraces film. In the Department of Theatre, Dance and Motion Pictures, dance majors are offered a BFA program that requires significant amounts of classes in theater and acting as well as music.

Underpinning the training here is a daily ballet class, but courses are also required in modern dance, jazz and tap. Dance chair Jon Rodriguez aims to integrate the dance with acting and music. To him, dance is more than just movement; dancers need to understand and develop internal emotional responses to enhance their performances. Music, too, is emphasized, and dancers must master basic musical skills and study singing for the musical theater and take private voice lessons for a year. The particularly noteworthy aspect of Wright State is its affiliation with 2 local professional companies in Dayton: the Dayton Contemporary Dance Company and the Dayton Ballet. These so-called exchange programs provide additional training and performance opportunities for exceptional dance majors. Wright State students join the main or the second company of the ballet or DCDC as apprentice dancers or even

147

as company members. Masterclasses and workshops conducted by these companies and their official schools are also available to Wright State students. Enrollment for this program is competitive, as only about 15 students are admitted each year. As a consequence, class sizes are small. The faculty is headed by Rodriguez, former artistic director of the Dayton Ballet and ballet master and principal teacher for the Cincinnati Ballet and the New Orleans Ballet. Other permanent faculty members include Suzanne Walker, a specialist in jazz and theater dance, who performed on Broadway for more than a decade, and Pamela White, a choreographer whose work has been seen at the Kennedy Center.

Oklahoma

Oklahoma City University

For ballet, jazz, tap dancers, choreographers Central Oklahoma — School of American Dance and Arts Management, 2501 N. Blackwelder, Oklahoma City, OK 73106 **Voice:** 405-521-5322 **Fax:** 405-521-5971 **E-mail:** jvfl01a@prodigy.com **Web Site:** www.okcu.edu **Contact:** Jo Rowan, Dance Chair **Founded:** 1901 **Open:** Year-round **Admission:** Written application, transcripts, interview, writing sample, test scores, auditon **Deadlines:** Early Sept. for fall, late Jan for spring **Cost:** $9,320 per year **Financial Aid:** Loans; Scholarship; Fellowship; Stipend; Work/Study **Size-Attendees:** 240 **Size-Class:** 10-25 **Degree or Certification:** BPA in Dance; BSs in Dance Management, Entertainment Management; MBA in Arts Management **Job Placement:** Yes

WITH MORE THAN 100 dance majors in its BPA program, 70 dance management majors in its BS program, 50 majors in its entertainment-management degree program, and 15 students in its arts-management MBA program, the School of American Dance and Arts Management ranks as one of the largest programs in the country focused on theater dance and the commercial-entertainment area of dance.

The curriculum at this newest department in this American-heartland university includes ballet, tap, jazz, theater dance, American-dance history and special courses on auditioning and surviving as a performer. Experienced arts administrator John Bedford is dean of this unique program that positions itself as the place to come to study the show-business side of dance. The dance faculty is headed by Jo Rowan, a former actress and comedian who has appeared in more than 30 major productions of musical comedies and musicals and also has extensive choreographic experience. She has served as ballet mistress for Dallas Ballet and is a frequent lecturer on American ballet and theater dance. Other faculty members include Kay Sandel, who danced with Chicago Ballet and Liz Reiter, a former member of the Gus Giordano Jazz Dance Company. The arts-administration faculty includes many working professionals from Oklahoma City's major cultural organizations.

Performance opportunities abound, with companies including the American Spirit Dance Company, the Oklahoma Opera and Musical Theater Company, the Spirit of Grace Liturgical Dancers, the OCU Pep Dancers, the Student Choreography Show and a holiday production produced with the Oklahoma City Philharmonic. Although the university is affiliated with the Methodist Church, it is not aggressively religious. Some students, though, elect to express their faith through performance groups with a liturgical focus. The American Spirit Dance Company, while it elects to refrain from participating in the American College Dance Festival, frequently tours internationally. Performing spaces include the 1,100-seat Kirkpatrick Auditorium, the 250-seat Burg Auditorium and a 500-seat recital hall. Guest artists come to the university to set works on the various student companies, and the program frequently honors distinguished artists in American tap, jazz and musical-theater dance.

If you are interested in the show-biz side of dance, either as a performer or a manager, you will want to consider this program.

School of Ballet Oklahoma

For ballet, jazz dancers, choreographers *Central Oklahoma — 7421 N. Classen, Oklahoma City, OK 73116* **Voice:** 405-843-9894 **Fax:** 405-843-9894 **E-mail:** info@balletoklahoma.com **Web Site:** www.balletoklahoma.com **Contact:** Bryan Pitts, Artistic Dir. **Founded:** 1965 **Open:** Year-round **Admission:** Written application, placement class **Deadlines:** Rolling **Cost:** From $69 per month for 2 classes per week **Financial Aid:** Scholarship; Work/Study **Size-Attendees:** 200 **Size-Class:** 20

NOW IN ITS THIRD decade, Ballet Oklahoma takes the training of young ballet dancers very seriously. The school has 7 levels of ballet classes in its preprofessional curriculum, plus classes for young children and adults. Students trained in its school have been accepted into the professional company or have gone on to other professional school and companies, such as Boston Ballet, Houston Ballet, and Pacific Northwest Ballet.

The school and the company are headed by Bryan Pitts, who has served in this capacity for more than a decade, following a distinguished career as a principal dancer with New York City Ballet. He also previously served as ballet master for the Dallas Ballet and his international career included principal roles with the acclaimed Zurich Ballet. He is married to former New York City Ballet dancer Laura Flagg, who serves as his assistant. The 3 spacious studios with sprung floors are shared by the school and the company.

Tulsa Ballet

For ballet dancers *NE Oklahoma — 4512 S. Peoria, Tulsa, OK 75105* **Voice:** 918-749-6030 **Fax:** 918-749-0532 **E-mail:** tulsaballet@webtek.com **Web Site:** www.webtek.com/tulsa/ballet **Contact:** Marcello Angelini, Dir. **Founded:** 1956 **Open:** Summer **Admission:** Written application, audition **Deadlines:** Late spring **Cost:** $175-250 for 1 week, $300-400 for 2 weeks **Financial Aid:** Scholarship; Work/Study **Size-Attendees:** 100 **Size-Class:** 10-20

THIS RESPECTED professional company of 30 dancers was founded by Moscelyne Larkin and Roman Jasinski, who were internationally acclaimed stars with Ballet Russe. Now under the direction of Marcello Angelini, the company offers a 2-week summer program taught by Angelini, Daniela Buson, his wife, company ballet mistress Susan Frei and guest faculty. This intensive is offered in the spectacular 38,000-square-foot facility that houses the professional company. Aspiring professional dancers should consider taking this intensive in order to get a taste of the professional-dance environment.

University of Oklahoma

🏠 ☀ **For ballet, modern dancers, choreographers** Central Oklahoma — 563 Elm Avenue, Room 209, Norman, OK 73019 **Voice:** 405-325-4051 **Fax:** 405-325-7024 **Web Site:** www.uo.edu/class/art4910/ cfa/dance/dance2.shtml **Contact:** Mary Margaret Holt, Chair, Dept. of Dance **Founded:** 1961 **Open:** Year-round **Admission:** Written application, audition, transcripts, test scores, interview, writing samples **Deadlines:** Apr. 30 for undergraduates, Mar. 1 for graduate students **Cost:** $6,950 per year for state residents, $10,700 for nonresidents **Financial Aid:** Loans; Scholarship; Fellowship; Stipend; Work/Study **Size-Attendees:** 80 **Degree or Certification:** BFA in Dance (Teaching or Performance Emphasis), MFAs in Modern Dance, Ballet **Job Placement:** Yes

THE DANCE DEPARTMENT here is highly regarded for its training in ballet and modern, offered at both the undergraduate and graduate levels. With modest tuition costs, especially for state residents, these programs are indeed a bargain. The department had its official beginning in 1961 when Ballet Russe de Monte Carlo principal dancers Miguel Terekov and Yvonne Chouteau were invited to teach at the university. A dance department that incorporates modern dance as well was soon formed. The 2 preprofessional performing ensembles in modern dance and ballet perform regularly at the university and on tour. The size of the repertory (Oklahoma Festival Ballet, the ballet group, has a repertory of 30 ballets) and the number of dance presentations demonstrate that this is a school that puts an emphasis on performance.

Ko Yukihiro is the coordinator in the modern-dance area and artistic director of the Modern Repertory Dance Theatre. As a performer she worked with Paul Sanasardo and Saeko Ichinohe. In the ballet area, Allan Kinzie specializes in training male dancers and also currently serves as Ballet Master of Oklahoma Festival Ballet. Donn Edwards, another accomplished teacher, was a principal dancer with the Boston, Frankfurt and Joffrey Ballet companies. The work of the faculty is supplemented by guest artists, including ballet greats Melissa Hayden, Royes Fernandez, Lupe Serrano, Helgi Tomasson, Patricia McBride, Jean-Pierre Bonnefoux and Luiz Fuente, as well as master modern teachers Takako Asakawa from the Martha Graham Company and Denise Jefferson from Alvin Ailey. The facilities include 4 large studios and a 700-seat performance facility with adjacent scene and costume shops. Former students now dance with major ballet and modern companies, including the Pittsburgh, Houston, Joffrey, Dallas, Tulsa and Boston ballets and The Alvin Ailey Ensemble, Martha Graham Dance Ensemble and Jennifer Muller/The Works.

Oregon

School of Oregon Ballet Theatre

👣 ☀ **For ballet dancers** Downtown — 1120 SW Tenth Ave., Portland, OR 97205 **Voice:** 503-227-0977 **Fax:** 503-227-4186 **E-mail:** school@obt.org **Web Site:** www. obt.org **Contact:** Haydee Gutierrez, Dir. **Founded:** 1984 **Open:** Year-round **Admission:** Placement audition **Deadlines:** Early Sept. **Cost:** $185-$245 per month **Financial Aid:** Scholarship; Work/Study **Size-Attendees:** 300 **Size-Class:** 10-25

UNDER THE DIRECTION of Haydee Gutierrez since 1993, this large school has launched the careers of many young professionals, with recent graduates entering professional companies, the School of American Ballet, Houston Ballet School, American Ballet Theatre and San Francisco Ballet and other prestigious schools.

The operation is currently housed in a renovated museum in downtown Portland and shares 3 studios with the professional company, Oregon Ballet

Theatre. The school will soon move to temporary facilities nearby with 4 studios; plans are afoot to construct a new facility with 7 studios. These changes are indicative of the growth and success of the operation. In the past 5 years, 8 dancers from the school have entered the affiliate professional company. The school currently has 11 faculty and 7 accompanists, more than a good many college programs can boast.

The faculty has excellent credentials. Gutierrez was born and trained in Havana, later training at the American Ballet Theatre School and with David Howard and Benjamin Harkarvy. She danced for many years with the Ballet Concerto Company, and was the founder and director of her own school in Tampa, Florida, before becoming director here. She is assisted by Miguel Campaneria, who has had an international career with the American Ballet Theatre, the Pittsburgh Ballet, Les Grands Ballets Canadiens and the Pennsylvania Ballet. He was twice a medal winner at the International Ballet Competition in Varna, Bulgaria. This is a ballet school with a difference. In a recent annual school performance, it produced nothing less than *La Bayadère.* Other major classical works were presented as well, most of them staged by Campaneria. This kind of programming is indicative of the quality of the training available here.

The facility is located in the heart of Portland's performing-arts scene and within easy walking distance of the Portland Art Museum, Portland State University and the Portland Center for the Performing Arts. During August, Oregon Ballet Theatre holds open-air company classes and rehearsals in a nearby park. A 5-week summer intensive is held in July. Students frequently perform with the affiliate professional company in addition to presenting their own performances.

University of Oregon

For ballet, modern dancers, choreographers Western Oregon — Dept. of Dance, 1214 Univ. of Oregon, Eugene, OR 97403 **Voice:** 541-346-3386 **Fax:** 541-346-0723 **E-mail:** jeraig@oregon.uoregon.edu **Web Site:** www.uoregon.edu **Contact:** Jennifer P. Craig, Chair **Founded:** 1876 **Open:** Year-round **Admission:** Written application, interview, transcripts, test scores, writing sample **Deadlines:** Apply each quarter **Cost:** $1,233 per quarter for resident, $4,266 for nonresidents **Financial Aid:** Loans; Scholarship; Fellowship; Stipend; Work/Study **Size-Attendees:** 40-45 undergrads, 7-10 graduates **Size-Class:** 25 **Degree or Certification:** BA in Dance; BS in Dance; MA in Dance; MSs in Dance, Dance Science; Laban-Bartenieff Certificate **Job Placement:** Yes

THE DANCE DEPARTMENT is part of the School of Music at this public institution. The undergraduate program provides dance training within the liberal-arts framework of the university. Unlike a conservatory program emphasizing performance, this program offers a great deal of world culture-and-theory classes. The department chair Jennifer Craig stresses that this is a broad program for people who want dance in their life, regardless of their ultimate career course. Career opportunities for graduates include teaching and dance-related careers in journalism and physical therapy. The university offers courses as requirements for the dance major that also lead to Laban Movement Analysis Certification sponsored by the Laban/Bartenieff Institute of Movement Studies in New York.

The small faculty of 8 has strong credentials in theory and more advanced degrees than the typical dance faculty. This adds strength to their graduate program, which has some features that should be considered by anyone interested in dance science and theory. In addition to the MS and MA degrees, the program will soon offer an MFA degree. The department has just added a visiting assistant professorship, currently held by Pamela Geber, who danced with Sara Rudner and David Gordon in New York and is teaching modern dance at the university. Another recent faculty addition is Amy Stoddart, who danced with Ballet Caravan and the Boulder Ballet. Steven Chatfield, who received his PhD from the University of Colorado at Boulder, coordinates graduate studies and is a specialist in dance sciences and movement analysis. The faculty even includes a specialist in electronic and computer-generated music, Jeffrey Stolet. The campus is extraordinarily beautiful. Eugene is a city of 200,000, and while the university is in the city, it has the feel of a rural paradise, with prodigious stands of pine trees, streams and mountains surrounding the campus. There are 3 spacious studios, one of which can be converted to a performance space seating 500. Recent graduates dance with the Eugene Ballet, have gone on to graduate school and have become physical therapists.

Pennsylvania

Central Pennsylvania Youth Ballet

 For ballet dancers, choreographers S central Pennsylvania — 107 Meetinghouse Rd., Carlisle, PA 17013 **Voice:** 717-245-1193 **Fax:** 717-245-1189 **E-mail:** wingard@Dickinson.edu **Web Site:** http://physics.dickinson.edu/CPYB **Contact:** Maurinda Wingard, Exec. Dir. **Founded:** 1955 **Open:** Year-round **Admission:** Written application, audition **Deadlines:** Apply each semester **Cost:** $13-$107 for monthly tuition; summer program: $2,530 for tuition, room and board, $920 for local students **Financial Aid:** Scholarship; Work/Study **Size-Attendees:** 100-200 **Size-Class:** 15-30

OVER THE PAST 40-odd years, the Central Pennsylvania Youth Ballet, with studios in Carlisle and Harrisburg, has grown from a small, local dance studio to a widely respected classical ballet school and performing company. For students seeking a professional career in ballet, CPYB offers the necessary building blocks and encouragement to achieve this goal, as well as scholarship support.

CPYB is noted for being the only youth company and the only regional ballet to whom the Balanchine Trust has granted the right to perform Balanchine's *Nutcracker*—and one of the few that does so using only its own dancers. Of course, it helps that Darla Hoover, who is a restager of ballets for the Balanchine Trust, is also the associate artistic director at CPYB.

Anyone who doubts the professionalism of the troupe need only read Jennifer Dunning's recent summary of the company in the *New York Times*: "Marcia Dale Weary and her Central Pennsylvania Youth Ballet have been much talked about but little seen in New York City.... Ms. Weary's dancers more than lived up to their legend...with strongly centered bodies and an aplomb rare in far more experienced performers." Further evidence of the level of training at CPYB is the fact that many students have graduated to such top companies as New York City Ballet, American Ballet Theatre, Boston Ballet, San Francisco Ballet and Paris Opera. This success can largely be attributed to artistic director Weary, who has been called "one of the country's foremost ballet teachers." Weary has masterminded a complete dance program, including the regular school program offered September through June; a summer program developed in cooperation with Dickinson College, enrolling more than 350 students from across the United States and abroad; and a performing company that has an impressive repertoire of ballets performed in the fall, spring and June of each year.

Several years ago, CPYB opened its doors to the community at large with its new open program, offering classes in various disciplines, such as ballet and creative movement, tap, jazz, body conditioning based on the Pilates method, yoga and ballet for gymnasts. Located in a red barn, the Carlisle facility is not large, comprising 3 small studios and a much larger one used for rehearsals.

Dance Alloy School

For all dancers, choreographers 5530 Penn Ave., Pittsburgh, PA 15206 **Voice:** 412-363-4321 **E-mail:** alloy@tellerama.lm.com **Contact:** Mark Taylor, Artistic Dir. **Open:** Year-round **Admission:** Open **Deadlines:** Rolling **Cost:** From $110 for 12 sessions **Financial Aid:** Loans; Scholarship; Work/Study **Size-Attendees:** 200 **Size-Class:** 10-20

M ARK TAYLOR, artistic director of Dance Alloy and the head of its affiliated school, has become the great modern-dance pioneer in Pittsburgh. In addition to works that he choreographs, he brings in some of the best choreographers working in the field today. Sean Curran is Dance Alloy's current guest choreographer-in-residence, and part of his residency includes teaching a series of intermediate-level, modern-dance classes.

Dance Alloy offers a regular schedule of classes at the Carnegie Museums in Oakland and at the Neighborhood Performance Center in Pittsburgh's Friendship district. The curriculum includes classes in modern, Afro/modern, jazz, Alexander technique, tai chi, yoga, "big band" social dancing and 3 levels of ballet, tap, hip-hop and dance aerobics. Special workshops are given in swing, modern dance and eurythmy (an art of movement based on the sounds of speech and music). An after-school dance and performance lab is also available for young people interested in finding out more about dance as a professional pursuit. The faculty is composed of Dance Alloy company members, professional dancers who perform with other dancers in the Pittsburgh area and specialist teachers in Alexander Technique, yoga, tai chi and African dance. Robert Vickery, who danced with the Joffrey Ballet and San Francisco Ballet and is artistic administrator for the Pittsburgh Ballet Theatre, is the ballet instructor.

Pennsylvania Academy of Ballet

For ballet dancers Greater Philadelphia — 29 N. Narberth Ave., Narberth, PA 19072 **Voice:** 610-664-3455 **Fax:** 610-664-6733 **E-mail:** pabs@pond.com **Contact:** John White, Dir. **Founded:** 1974 **Open:** Year-round **Admission:** Open **Deadlines:** Rolling **Cost:** From $192 for 24 lessons, $432 for 1 weekly class per year **Financial Aid:** Scholarship; Work/Study **Size-Attendees:** 100-200 **Size-Class:** 10-25 **Job Placement:** Yes

T HIS MODEST SCHOOL in the suburbs of Philadelphia is unique both in the quality of the training its provides and in the accomplishments of its graduates. Many of the students studying here with Margarita de Saa and John White, her husband, have gone on to professional companies and, most significantly, graduates have won medals at the International Ballet Competition in Varna and Bulgaria, and at the American Ballet Competition.

The couple took a risk when they left the more established School of the Pennsylvania Ballet in 1974 to begin their own school. But now more than 100 of their former students are dancing in important professional companies. The school also offers classes to nonprofessionals. All the instructors teach the Vaganova method of classical ballet.

153

Pittsburgh Ballet Theatre School

For ballet dancers, choreographers Pittsburgh's urban sprawl — 2900 Liberty Ave., Pittsburgh, PA 15201 **Voice:** 412-281-6727 **Fax:** 412-281-9901 **E-mail:** ashillingpbt@juno.com **Web Site:** www. artsnet.org/pbt/school.htm **Contact:** David Holladay, School Dir. **Founded:** 1987 **Open:** Year-round **Admission:** Written application, placement audition **Deadlines:** Rolling **Cost:** $3,340-$4,580 per year **Financial Aid:** Scholarship; Work/Study **Size-Attendees:** 400 **Size-Class:** 10-30

THIS IS THE OFFICIAL school of the Pittsburgh Ballet, now headed by former ABT principal dancer and ballet master, Terrence S. Orr. The school has a solid reputation as an institution offering quality training and a program that takes into account all the needs of the preprofessional dancer, from housing to stress management.

For intermediate and advanced students aged 13-18, an intensive program has been developed to prepare young dancers for the rigors of professional life. The school has set up an academic program with Schenley High School enabling their preprofessional dancers to take more than 25 hours of ballet and dance training each week, while still attending high school. Classes include technique, pointe, pas de deux, character, modern, jazz, exercise, lecture, repertory studies and rehearsal. In addition to the academic needs of the students, PBT has also taken steps to address the emotional and physical needs of the students, instituting a relationship with the University of Pittsburgh's Western Psychiatric Institute and Clinic, which offers students a stress-reduction program, and the Pittsburgh Sports Medicine Institute, which provides an in-house physical therapist for PBT's professional company and also accommodates students at the school. On-site chiropractic care is also available. Students have opportunities to perform throughout the year in the company's mainstage productions of *Sleeping Beauty, Nutcracker, Jewels* and *Symphony in C.* Students from the school have gone on to become members of the Pittsburgh, New York City, Miami City, Milwaukee and Richmond ballets. Besides Orr, leading members of the dance community are also found teaching at the school, including school director David Holladay, who served as Ballet Oklahoma's school director; ballet mistress Dana Arey, a former member of Eliot Feld and Pennsylvania Ballet; Marianna Tcherkassky, one of this country's foremost ballerinas; Roberto Munoz, formerly of the Hartford Ballet; Kristen Brandt, formerly of ABT, San Francisco Ballet and Metropolitan Opera Ballet; and Nancy Schaffenburg, formerly of the Metropolitan Opera Ballet.

Point Park College

For ballet, modern dancers, choreographers Pittsburgh's downtown Golden Triangle — 201 Wood St., Pittsburgh, PA 15222 **Voice:** 412-392-3430; 800-321-0129 **Fax:** 412-391-1980 **Web Site:** www.ppc.edu **Contact:** Ron Tassone, Dir. of Dance **Founded:** 1960 **Open:** Year-round **Admission:** Written application, audition, photo, resume, questionnaire, interview, SAT **Deadlines:** Aug. 15 **Cost:** From $5,400 per semester **Financial Aid:** Loans; Scholarship; Fellowship; Stipend; Work/Study **Size-Attendees:** 100 **Size-Class:** 15-20 students **Degree or Certification:** BA, BFA in Dance **Job Placement:** Yes

THIS COLLEGE PROMOTES itself as having a conservatory mentality within a liberal-arts setting. This is aided, no doubt, by the fact that it is situated in one of the country's larger cities with many fine points of interest to keep the student body entertained and enriched.

The dance program offers concentrations in ballet, jazz and modern dance. The BFA requires a student to select a dance-performance focus. The BA degree provides an eclectic view of the arts with no performance requirement. The curriculum includes courses in tap, folk, character, Dunham, pointe, pas de deux, jazz, contemporary partnering and 8 levels of ballet. Director

Ron Tassone has a resume stretching from the West Coast to the East. Graduating from Juilliard, he performed in Hollywood with Carol Burnett and Joel Grey, and in such classics as *Gypsy* with Ethel Merman and *Funny Girl* with Barbra Streisand.

Rock School of Pennsylvania Ballet

 **For ballet dancers, choreographers** *Philadelphia's Avenue of the Arts — 1101 S. Broad St., Philadelphia, PA 19147* **Voice:** 215-551-7010 **Fax:** 215-551-8538 **E-mail:** flash@therockschool.org **Web Site:** www.therockschool.org **Contact:** Bojan Spassoff, School Dir. **Founded:** 1963 **Open:** Year-round **Admission:** Written application, audition **Deadlines:** Apply each quarter **Cost:** From $135 per quarter; from $1,700 for 4-week summer program **Financial Aid:** Scholarship; Fellowship; Work/Study **Size-Attendees:** 200-400 **Size-Class:** 10-25 **Job Placement:** Yes

FOR THOSE interested in size and prestige, Rock School has both in spades. This is the official school of the Pennsylvania Ballet, a premier ballet company located in the City of Brotherly Love. Students learn the ABCs of life as a classical-ballet dancer. The school has developed dancers for Pennsylvania Ballet and many other leading dance companies both here and abroad. The company and the school share the same facility, exposing students to the company professionals, a key ingredient of any young dancer's training. The faculty includes distinguished instructors and choreographers, as well as current and former dancers from major companies worldwide.

Besides studying amidst the comings and goings of the company, students are used in productions, such as *Nutcracker, Cinderella, Sleeping Beauty, Romeo and Juliet, Coppelia, Swan Lake,* and *A Midsummer Night's Dream.* The school is the exclusive resource for the company's productions, providing two programs for adult dancers. The professional division, for the intermediate- and advanced-level dancer with 5-7 years of dance experience, requires a minimum of 14 class hours per week. The adult division offers classes for beginner to advanced students with no preregistration or attendance requirements.

The school offers a 10-month residence program for females age 14-18 to live, dance and attend to their scholastics in Philadelphia for the school year. Students train 15-23 hours a week at the school and can pursue their academics at Friends Select School or John W. Hallahan High School or through correspondence study. In the same way that the Professional Children's School in New York City offers a flexible high-school schedule for young people in the arts, the Friends School has worked with the Rock School to provide opportunities for young dancers to pursue a rigorous college-preparatory program while continuing to study dance at the highest level. Members of Friends' faculty work with each student, creating a schedule that balances the need for dance classes with the difficult academic load of high school.

Temple University

For ballet, modern dancers, choreographers Dance Dept., 309 Vivacqua Hall, Philadelphia, PA 19122 **Voice:** 215-204-6282 **Fax:** 215-204-8705 **E-mail:** dance@blue.temple.edu **Web Site:** www.temple.edu/HPERD/dance/ **Contact:** Ann Vachon, Coord. **Founded:** 1970 **Open:** Year-round **Admission:** Written application, resume, audition **Deadlines:** Apr. 1 **Cost:** $308 per credit hour for state residents, $429 for non-residents **Financial Aid:** Loans; Scholarship; Fellowship; Stipend; Work/Study **Size-Attendees:** 125 **Size-Class:** 15-25 **Degree or Certification:** BFA, MFA, MEd, PhD **Job Placement:** Yes

MERELY FOR ITS location and sheer size, this program earns high marks. Temple offers 4 degree programs: BFA, MFA, MEd and PhD. The doctoral program at Temple is a standout. Originally offered in the 1970s, when dance was viewed as a tool for social change, this program continues to maintain that ideal and is widely acknowledged to be one of the finest in the world. The program has undergone some changes of late. Recently appointed faculty include department chair Dr. Luke Kahlich and doctoral coordinator Dr. Joellen Meglin. Kahlich's areas of expertise are dance and technology and dance science and pedagogy. Meglin's background includes dance history and gender studies, and she is review editor for *Dance Research Journal* as well as serving on the board of the Society of Dance History Scholars.

Temple University is 1 of 3 universities in Pennsylvania classified as a Research I Institution, which means that the opportunities for interdisciplinary study are available and extensive. Degree candidates can pursue graduate certificates in feminist studies or create linkages with departments in African-American studies, anthropology, human-movement sciences, as well as religion, philosophy or history, to name a few. Nationally recognized schools at Temple (Tyler School of Art and Esther Boyer College of Music) offer opportunities for inter-arts study and collaboration. In fact, discussion is under way about an academic restructuring, which would bring dance, music and theater together under the aegis of a college of performing arts, allowing even more opportunities for collaboration.

University of the Arts

For ballet, jazz modern dancers, choreographers, dance educators School of Dance, 320 S. Broad St., Philadelphia, PA 19102 **Voice:** 215-875-2270 **Fax:** 215-875-5114 **E-mail:** sglazer@uarts.edu **Web Site:** www.uarts.edu **Contact:** Susan B. Glazer, Dir. **Founded:** 1987 **Open:** Year-round **Admission:** Written application, audition, transcripts, test scores, interview **Deadlines:** Rolling **Cost:** $15,300 per year **Financial Aid:** Loans; Scholarship; Fellowship; Stipend; Work/Study **Size-Attendees:** 200 **Size-Class:** 10-25 **Degree or Certification:** BFAs in Dance, Dance Education **Job Placement:** Yes

THIS DISTINGUISHED Philadelphia institution has a rapidly growing high-quality program offering a BFA in ballet, jazz/theatre dance, modern dance or dance education. The curriculum includes a lively mix of courses, including Brazilian, African, Spanish and tap dance. The campus is literally in the center of the professional-arts scene, as well as the arts-education scene in Philadelphia. The cultural offerings are first rate, and if you like an urban campus setting, you should consider the University of the Arts.

The big news for the program is the new facility that opened in the fall of 1999. A converted former hotel, the new facility offers no fewer than 10 studios, 4 of which are in the former ballrooms of the hotel and give absolutely spectacular. A number of the student dance performances are now presented in the Merriam Theater, the old Shubert Theater on Broad Street. The student dancers perform works by major choreographers, as well as student works. Opportunities to choreograph are offered to all students, and the senior concerts are fully produced by the students. Distinguished faculty include department chair Susan Glazer, who has run the program since 1981 after dancing with companies in the United States, France and Germany. She is co-founder of the Mosaic Repertory Company in Philadelphia and has written a number of books on modern dance. Other faculty members include: Andrew Pap, former principal dancer with the Romanian National Ballet; Peter Bertini, who danced with the companies of Garth Fagan and Jo Jo Smith; legendary hoofer LaVaughn Robinson; former Pennsylvania Ballet principal dancer Barbara Sandonato; former Alvin Ailey Company member Pat Thomas; former Paul Taylor dancer Ruth Andrian; and Gabe Masson, formerly with Doug Varone and Dancers.

Dancers perform at the University of the Arts School of Dance, Philadelphia.

Rhode Island

Roger Williams University

For modern dancers, choreographers About halfway between Newport and Providence — 1 Old Ferry Rd., Bristol, RI 02809 **Voice:** 401-254-3624 **Fax:** 401-254-3634 **E-mail:** kwd@alpha.rwu.edu **Web Site:** www.rwu.edu **Contact:** Kelli Wicke Davis, Dept. Dir. **Founded:** 1958 **Open:** Year-round **Admission:** Written application, audition, transcripts, writing sample **Deadlines:** Rolling admissions **Cost:** $16,690 per year **Financial Aid:** Loans; Scholarship; Fellowship; Stipend; Work/Study **Size-Attendees:** 100 **Size-Class:** 5-25 **Degree or Certification:** BA in Dance/Performance **Job Placement:** Yes

THIS MAVERICK dance program provides dance majors with all the necessary tools they need to make a go of it. The focus is less on formal training and more on movement studies, with a strong modern-dance emphasis and performance concentration. If your affinity is for dance and you have a love of physicality and theater, this program will allow you to explore and blossom.

In the course of their studies, pupils are encouraged to investigate many career avenues. According to department director Kelli Wicke Davis, "...we have a small unique curriculum which allows for individual attention and one that holds many options for students." Alumni go on to professional work not only in dance, but also in theater, performance art, education, arts management, business and advanced studies in graduate work. In keeping with the program's unconventional approach, special offerings include cooperative work/study experiences, internships, study abroad, individualized majors, continuing education and career services. The department not only stresses technical proficiency, but also focuses on original choreography. All levels of modern, jazz and ballet are offered, along with the option of working toward a K-12 teacher certification in dance. Sample course titles are "Mime Workshop," "Creative Athletes," "Choreography for Theatre," "Movement for the Actor," and "British Dance and Performance Art and its Cultural Influences" (London program). Each year 2 major concert series are presented. The university company has performed several times at the National Gala Concert of the American College Dance Festival at the Kennedy Center, as well as touring in New York City, Philadelphia, Boston, New Jersey, New Hampshire and Virginia. The majority of the school's alumni grace the stages of this country's most experimental and innovative performing venues. Most famous among the alumni is Sean Curran, a former Bill T. Jones/Arnie Zane principal dancer, who now heads his own company.

South Carolina

Charleston Ballet School

 **For ballet dancers, choreographers** Coastal South Carolina — 477 King St., Charleston, SC 29403 **Voice:** 843-723-7334 **Fax:** 843-723-9099 **E-mail:** tdominey@charlestonballet.com **Web Site:** www.charlestonballet.com **Contact:** Donald and Patricia Cantwell, Artistic Dirs. **Founded:** 1966 **Open:** Year-round **Admission:** Written application, audition **Deadlines:** Apply each semester **Cost:** $20 per class **Financial Aid:** Loans; Scholarship; Fellowship; Stipend; Work/Study **Size-Class:** 20-40

CHARLESTON BALLET Theatre's official school provides year-round classes and a major summer workshop cosponsored by the professional company. Artistic directors Donald and Patricia Cantwell share responsibility for running both the school and the company, and teach most of the classes in the school themselves. Their work is supplemented by jazz teacher Perry Mauzy. Class size averages no more than 20 students, assuring a good deal of personal attention.

Charleston native Don Cantwell returned to this historic city after a career with the Atlanta Ballet, the American Ballet Theatre and the Joffrey Ballet. His wife, Patricia, is a former principal dancer with the Charleston Ballet Theatre and the Savannah Ballet. She is particularly expert at teaching children and preprofessionals, and has developed summer programs to support emerging young talents. Students at the school are offered opportunities to perform in the professional company's performances. The intensive ballet summer workshop enrolls 40 or more students and draws in some guest faculty. The workshop emphasizes classical-ballet technique with pointe class variations and the classical-ballet repertory; classes are also offered in jazz, modern, musical comedy and Broadway dance. Guest faculty has included former New York City Ballet dancer Mel Tomlinson, Boston Ballet's Arthur Leeth and company resident choreographer Jill Eathorne Bahr. Auditions, required for the summer workshop, are held throughout the southeast early in the calendar year. Students are housed at the Wild Dunes Resort on the Isle of Palms, a barrier island not far from Charleston. Having visited the Isle and the resort myself, I can report that both are absolutely beautiful. It will undoubtedly be difficult for students to tear themselves away from this oceanfront paradise to take class.

Columbia College

For ballet, jazz, modern dancers, choreographers, dance educators Dance Dept., 1301 Columbia College Dr., Columbia, SC 29203 **Voice:** 803-786-3847; 800-277-1301 **Fax:** 803-786-3868 **E-mail:** smcdowell@colacoll.edu **Contact:** Libby Patenaude, Chair **Founded:** 1854 **Open:** Sept.-June **Admission:** Written application, audition, transcripts, interview, test scores, writing sample **Deadlines:** Rolling admissions **Cost:** $12,505 tuition per year **Financial Aid:** Loans; Scholarship; Fellowship; Stipend; Work/Study **Size-Attendees:** 40 **Size-Class:** 10-15 **Degree or Certification:** BAs in Dance, Dance Education; BFA in Dance with emphasis on performance and choreography **Job Placement:** Yes

A 4-YEAR-LIBERAL-ARTS college for women, founded in 1854 by the Methodist Church, Columbia is frequently ranked as one of the top liberal-arts colleges in the South. It is notable for a student-faculty ratio of 14:1. During the first year, faculty members observe a student's talent, interests, work habits and potential, and recommend the program to which they feel the student is best suited.

The dance department offers 3 degrees. The BFA program is for students with performing or choreographic abilities and places emphasis on career preparation or graduate school. BFA students must take 9-12 hours per week of ballet or modern-dance techniques each semester. In addition, 3 semesters of jazz technique and 4 semesters of composition are required. The BA program is for the student who desires intensive study in dance coupled with a broadly based liberal-arts program, perhaps with a career in arts administration or dance therapy in mind. It requires less studio work, and enables the student to adopt a double major. The BA program in dance education is offered for students with performance skills who wish to be certified as dance teachers in grades K-12. All dance majors are expected to participate each semester in every production of the department's student-dance company in some way. Auditions are held for works set by visiting artists; the repertory ranges from classics by Ruth

St. Denis and Doris Humphrey, to new modern and ballet works. The college's newest venture is its SoSoHo, or South of SoHo, a series bringing cutting-edge performances to the college. This is also used as a community-involvement program, with members of the community invited to participate in the masterclasses and workshops. The department is housed in Godbold Gym, which has 3 dance studios. Formal concerts are held on campus in a 376-seat theater. The department has an enrollment of 40 dance majors and 4 faculty plus guest teachers, insuring a good deal of personal attention. Guest choreographers and companies in recent years have included Laura Dean, Randy James, Shapiro and Smith, Dayton Contemporary Dance Company, Joe Goode Performance Group and Dance Alloy.

Tennessee

Dancers Studio

For all dancers Eastern Tennessee — 4216 Sutherland Ave., Knoxville, TN 37919 **Voice:** 423-588-8842 **Fax:** 423-588-8842 **E-mail:** tcde@nxs.net **Web Site:** www.kornet.org/tcde **Contact:** Dorothy Floyd, Dir. **Founded:** 1957 **Open:** Year-round **Admission:** Written application, placement audition **Deadlines:** Rolling **Cost:** $10 per class, or $200 for 5 months **Financial Aid:** Scholarship; Work/Study **Size-Attendees:** 200 **Size-Class:** 10-20

THIS IS THE OFFICIAL school of Tennessee Children's Dance Ensemble, a unique performing group consisting of young women aged 12-16. Dorothy Floyd, who studied with Martha Graham and Mary Wigman, founded the school in 1957, and began the ensemble in 1981 in the belief that children are capable of great sensitivity and wise judgment when given the opportunity to use them. Further, she believes that children are able to give sophisticated, professional performances that have aesthetic value and conviction.

The curriculum includes modern dance, ballet, jazz, children's classes and adult classes. In addition to Floyd, the faculty includes Irene Linn, who also studied with Wigman and works with the ensemble, and Lenette Perra, a medical doctor, who had a career as a professional ballet dancer in Germany. The ensemble is open by audition to children who are residents of Tennessee; it gives 40-50 performances a year and tours internationally. In addition to repertory by Floyd and Linn, the company has commissioned major choreographers, including Ze'eva Cohen, Karla Wolfangle, Eleo Pomare and Peter Pucci.

Memphis Concert Ballet School

For ballet dancers, choreographers P.O. Box 11136, Memphis, TN 38111 **Voice:** 901-737-7322 **Fax:** 901-763-2318 **Contact:** Dorothy Gunther Pugh, Artistic Dir. **Open:** Year-round **Admission:** Written application, audition **Deadlines:** Rolling **Cost:** $80 for 10 classes; from $100 for summer dance camp **Financial Aid:** Scholarship; Work/Study **Size-Attendees:** 100-150 **Size-Class:** 10-25

BALLET MEMPHIS is a company that is gaining a reputation outside its home state, and the Memphis Concert Ballet School is not far behind. Certainly the largest and best-known ballet company in Tennessee, the entire operation is undergoing an impressive facelift that will no doubt benefit the local population, as well as the host of dancers from around the country who come to train and perform with the company. The organization recently completed a $3.1-million capital campaign and moved into a new 19,500-square-foot facility.

The most advanced students at the school are required to take 6 classes a week, including pointe and modern. Adults can take an intermediate/advanced class twice a week at the studio with no registration requirements.

Dorothy Gunther Pugh, the artistic director of the company and the school, studied with David Howard in New York and at the Royal Academy of Dancing in London. She is assisted by Karl Condon, a former principal dancer with the Boston Ballet and the group's resident choreographer.

School of Nashville Ballet

For ballet dancers Central Tennessee — 2976 Sidco Dr., Nashville, TN 37204 **Voice:** 615-244-7233 **Fax:** 615-242-1741 **Contact:** Susan Tolle, School Dir. **Founded:** 1986 **Open:** Year-round **Admission:** Audition (summer), placement class (lower school) **Deadlines:** Mar., Apr. (summer) **Cost:** $10 per class **Financial Aid:** Scholarship

THIS IS PROBABLY the state's largest professional ballet company, complete with a newly acquired international reputation and an equally impressive school operation. The school and the company share the same facility, which houses 3 studios. The school boasts 11 faculty members with credits ranging from the Royal Ballet to Alvin Ailey.

The lower-school program has 8 levels of instruction, from beginning to advanced preprofessional. The school also emphasizes and offers the body-conditioning technique of Pilates. There is an open division for adults and for those who simply want to take class for the enjoyment of it. The open division also offers a range of classes outside the classical vein, such as modern and jazz. A sure sign that a school is geared to the needs of the aspiring professional is the existence of some program that addresses the academic dilemma. The Nashville Ballet School has instituted an out-of-school credit program at the secondary level in Davidson, Rutherford, and Williamson Counties for those dancers who are training full time. A 5-week summer intensive is also offered, which students aspiring to join the ranks of the company can attend as an informal audition period. The curriculum for the summer program is a bit more extensive than during the academic year, including such classes as character, ethnic, stage and theater techniques and dance history, in addition to the regular ballet, modern and jazz offerings.

Tennessee Association of Dance

For all dancers *P.O. Box 2432, Johnson City, TN 37605* **Voice:** 423-929-1129 **Fax:** 423-929-1129 **E-mail:** tndance@mounet.com **Web Site:** www.tennesseedance.org **Contact:** Judith Woodruff, Dir. **Founded:** 1971 **Open:** Mid-Oct. **Cost:** $75

THE TENNESSEE Association of Dance encourages and supports the development of dance in Tennessee. The Association's annual conference offers a weekend of intensive technique classes in ballet, jazz, tap and modern dance. Regional workshops are also given periodically across the state.

Texas

Academy of Dallas Black Dance Theatre

For ballet, ethnic, jazz, modern, tap dancers *NE Texas — 2627 Flora St., Dallas, TX 75201* **Voice:** 214-871-2376 **Fax:** 214-871-2842 **E-mail:** dbdt@gte.net **Web Site:** www.dbdt.com **Contact:** Ann Williams, Dir. **Founded:** 1972 **Open:** Year-round **Admission:** Written application **Deadlines:** Rolling **Cost:** $45 per month for 1 class weekly, $12 per class for professionals **Financial Aid:** Scholarship; Work/Study **Size-Attendees:** 200 **Size-Class:** 20

FOUNDED BY THE visionary Ann Williams in 1972, this academy has developed and trained scores of dancers who have gone on to perform with professional companies, such as Dallas Black Dance Theatre.

The faculty is headed by former company member Milton Tatum, who also studied and danced with Dance Theatre of Harlem and the Alvin Ailey Company. Another principal teacher is Pamela Johnson, also a former company member, who directs the academy's outreach program. The school shares facilities with the company and uses 2 studios. A summer intensive offering modern dance and ballet is offered for 3 weeks in July. Students present an annual end-of-year recital.

Fort Worth School of Ballet

For ballet dancers *NE Texas — 6845 Green Oaks Rd., Fort Worth, TX 76116* **Voice:** 817-731-2779 **Fax:** 817-763-0624 **Contact:** Jeanie M. Hamilton Wilkins, Admin. Dir. **Founded:** 1985 **Open:** Year-round **Admission:** Placement class **Deadlines:** Aug.-Dec. for semester I , Jan.-May for semester II **Cost:** $148-$740 per semester **Financial Aid:** Scholarship; Work/Study **Size-Attendees:** 100-150 **Size-Class:** 15-20

THE COMPANY'S artistic director Benjamin Houk heads this official school of the Fort Worth Dallas Ballet. Houk represents a new generation of visionary young artists who have not only experience in classical ballet, but also energy and a commitment to excellence. Houk was a principal dancer with the renowned Pacific Northwest Ballet where he danced for more than a decade; he then served 2 years as artistic director of the Nashville Ballet. The school was established in 1985 as the only fully professional ballet academy in the Fort Worth/Dallas metroplex.

The school's mission is to train and educate young dancers who aspire to become professionals. The principles of dance and the progressive training methods of the School of American Ballet established by George Balanchine are followed. All students must arrange for placement with the administrative director of the school. Class levels include preballet, 5 levels of preprofessional and professional training. A total of 21 classes are offered each week. Students are given opportunities to perform in the company's annual production of *The Nutcracker* and other ballets.

Houston Ballet Academy

For ballet dancers *Eastern Texas — 1921 W. Bell, Houston, TX 77019* **Voice:** 713-523-6300 **Fax:** 713-523-4038 **Web Site:** www.neosoft.com **Contact:** Clara Cravey, Prin. **Founded:** 1955 **Open:** Year-round **Admission:** Audition (preprofessional, professional divisions) **Deadlines:** Every 2 months, about mid-month **Cost:** $12 per class **Financial Aid:** Scholarship; Work/Study **Size-Attendees:** 350 **Size-Class:** 15-25

UNDER THE LEADERSHIP of Houston Ballet's artistic director Ben Stevenson, the Houston Ballet Academy is the company's official school. Stevenson has been widely hailed both for his choreography and for his gifts as a teacher. New York critic Clive Barnes has declared that "Stevenson must be regarded as one of the most persuasive teachers of our time." Stevenson studied at England's renowned Arts Educational School and at the Royal Ballet School.

The preprofessional division provides 6 levels of training to enable students to progress through a carefully planned syllabus. The professional division imparts advanced and concentrated training in all facets of classical ballet to prepare the school's graduates for a professional career. Students in the professional division who wish to combine their high-school education with dance training are offered special assistance by the school administration. An adult dance program with open classes is available as well. The school, an accredited institutional member of the National Association of Schools of Dance, shares a spacious new facility with the Houston Ballet. The facility features 6 large studios, as well as a physical therapy room, a body-conditioning studio and an audio/video library in addition to lounge

Entering the Dance Marketplace

Recently I was asked to speak to a dozen graduating dance majors at a college in the New York area about the business side of dance. It was surprising to learn that they knew so little about auditioning, preparing a resume, interviewing and the other essentials of the business of dance.

For example, when auditioning you should not wear loose T-shirts, leg warmers and mismatched colors. Whether it's ballet, modern, tap or step-dancing, a solid-color leotard, and neatly groomed hair and appearance are the most beneficial way to present yourself. Directors of companies are looking for a good line and beauty of movements, not for the strangest outfit. You might be noticed at first for your gold-spandex leotard and flying hair, but you will soon be forgotten.

One of the most important things in an audition is to respond to direction. A lot of dancers don't pay attention to details, but with any serious choreographer or artistic director, attention to detail is a primary concern. You may be doing 15 pirouettes, but if they ask for 1, they want 1.

In my opinion no one aged 21 should have more than a 1-page resume. If you have had extensive special training, select some of the most notable programs. When interviewing, be clear and gently assertive. Remember that you are the one who will "hold the stage," and that people will pay for tickets to see you. It is also important to know something in advance about the dance culture or environment you are entering. Audition appropriately, based on your skills—choose companies or styles of choreography that you are passionate about. If it is a not-for-profit ballet, modern-dance or ethnic company you seek to join, try to learn something about the not-for-profit arts world by contacting some of the service organizations listed in this book. Try to cultivate a relationship with a professional mentor, whom you can question about wages and working conditions. If you are seeking a union job, contact the union for information about wages and work rules in its realm.

In general, the more you know about the dance world and how the business of dance is conducted, the more confident and prepared you will be to land a job in this extremely competitive field. And be sure to read Part Three, "The Business of Dance," in this book.

---

areas and dressing rooms. It is certainly one of the most attractive facilities for dance in the United States. Students are offered many opportunities to perform with the affiliate professional company in *Nutcracker* and in other full-length ballets, such as *Sleeping Beauty, Cinderella, Coppelia,* and *Swan Lake.* The most impressive statistic about the school's graduates is that in 1994, 100 percent of its graduating class secured positions with professional companies. Graduates have joined such leading companies as the Australian Ballet, Eliot Feld, the Dutch National Ballet, American Ballet Theatre, San Francisco Ballet, Boston Ballet, Pacific Northwest Ballet and Hubbard Street Dance Company. Furthermore, 85 percent of the current members of Houston Ballet trained at the academy.

Munro Ballet Studios

For ballet, jazz, tap dancers
Gulf Coast — 5610 Everhart St., Corpus Christi, TX 78411 **Voice:** 512-991-6151 **Fax:** 512-993-2233 **Contact:** Cristina Munro, Dir. **Founded:** 1972 **Open:** Year-round **Admission:** Written application **Deadlines:** Rolling **Cost:** $30-$85 per month, depending on number of classes **Financial Aid:** Scholarship; Work/Study **Size-Attendees:** 250 **Size-Class:** 10-25

FOUNDED BY CRISTINA Munro, this school offers a disciplined and high-quality program in classical ballet, jazz and tap. Munro trained in England and danced with the London Festival Ballet, Sadlers Wells Opera Ballet and the Dutch National Ballet before coming to the United States as a founding member of Eliot Feld's original company in New York. She also served as co-artistic director of the Louisville Ballet, as ballet mistress of the Houston Ballet and as a teacher in the Houston Ballet Academy.

The summer program includes classes in theater arts and features distinguished guest teachers, such as Martine Harley, former principal dancer with Houston Ballet and now its ballet mistress; Alan Kinzie, a member of the dance faculty at the University of Oklahoma; and Joe Alegado, a popular teacher in Europe. Munro also serves as artistic director of the Corpus Christi Ballet, and the studios serve as the home for the ballet. This relationship affords students an opportunity to audition for and dance in the CCB annual *Nutcracker* production and in regional ballet festivals. A number of dancers from the school have gone on to professional careers at the Louisville Ballet and Ballet West, among others.

Sam Houston State University

For ballet, modern dancers, choreographers *70 mi. N of Houston, 170 mi. S of Dallas — Dance Program, P.O. Box 2418, Huntsville, TX 77341* **Voice:** 409-294-1875 **Fax:** 409-294-3954 **E-mail:** dance_smm@shsu.edu **Web Site:** www.shsu.edu **Contact:** Dana Eugene Nicolay, Coord. **Founded:** 1940 **Open:** Year round **Admission:** Written application, audition, transcripts, test scores, writing sample **Deadlines:** Aug. 1 for fall semester, Dec. 1 for spring semester **Cost:** $6,360 per year for state residents, $12,750 for nonresidents **Financial Aid:** Loans; Scholarship; Fellowship; Stipend; Work/Study **Size-Attendees:** 50 undergrads **Size-Class:** 10-20 **Degree or Certification:** BFA Dance, BFA Musical Theater, MFA Dance **Job Placement:** Yes

WHILE THIS PROGRAM is located in a small town, Houston and Dallas are fairly close by. Besides, it has some great facilities: its 6 spacious studios and 150-seat dance theater serve fewer than 50 undergraduate and graduate students. There is also a larger theater for major events. The MFA degrees have a concentration in dance performance or choreography. The BFA student can choose either dance performance or musical-theater-dance emphasis. Students in the BA program can major either in dance or in dance with secondary teaching certification.

The student-faculty ratio is not particularly favorable, but there seems to be a good number of quality student choreographic works coming out of the program. Specifically, 25 student choreographic works have been selected for the regional gala concerts or American College Dance Festival, and 5 works have been selected for the national gala at the Kennedy Center. The strong faculty is led by dance-program coordinator Dana Eugene Nicolay, who worked with the Royal Winnipeg Ballet and the Houston Ballet, among others. The faculty also includes John J. McLaughlin, who developed the first undergraduate degree in dance at the Western Australia Performing Arts Academy in

Perth and was artistic director of Share-Sight Dance Ensemble, which explored the fusion of Western and aboriginal Arts. He also won a Bessie Award in performance for his work with Douglas Dunn.

Southern Methodist University, Meadows School of the Arts

For ballet, jazz, modern dancers, choreographers — *P.O. Box 750356, Dallas, TX 75275* **Voice:** 214-768-2951 **Fax:** 214-768-3272 **E-mail:** sberg@mail.smu.edu **Web Site:** www.smu.edu/~meadows/ **Contact:** Shelley Berg, Div. Chair **Founded:** 1911 **Open:** Sept.-June **Admission:** Written application, audition, resume, transcripts **Deadlines:** Mar. 1 **Cost:** $7,820 per year **Financial Aid:** Loans; Scholarship; Fellowship; Stipend; Work/Study **Size-Attendees:** 90-95 **Size-Class:** 20 **Degree or Certification:** BFA in Dance, MFA in Choreographic Theory and Practice **Job Placement:** Yes

THIS WELL-ROUNDED program emphasizes versatility as well as virtuosity in its students. It is well respected among top professionals in the 3 major areas of dance: ballet, modern and jazz. Recent alumni are gaining entry into well-known companies, from the Alvin Ailey American Dance Theater, to the Radio City Rockettes. SMU is the alma mater of Ailey star Nasha Thomas, who graduated from the program in 1984. Accolades have been offered the program from such dance giants as Paul Taylor, in whose view "The dancers at SMU are such a pleasure....The Dance Division is something Dallas can be proud of."

The BFA program provides a comprehensive sequence of technique classes in ballet, modern and jazz, as well as courses in choreography, dance history, stage production, repertory, Labanotation, kinesiology and music analysis. The MFA in choreographic theory and practice focuses on the development of the dance artist/scholar. Coursework emphasizes the development of original choreography, the analysis of repertory masterworks in a variety of dance idioms and styles and the practice of teaching skills in performance coaching and dance directing. Students are expected to present a final creative project of original choreography and/or reconstruction with a written component, such as a project notebook. Faculty members have been affiliated with most major ballet and modern-dance companies, as well as a few dance legends, including the London Festival Ballet, Les Grands Ballets Canadiens, Houston Ballet, Boston Ballet, Martha Graham, José Limón, Merce Cunningham, David Parsons, Bill Evans, Moses Pendleton and Judith Jamison. Guest artists have included Lynn Taylor-Corbett, Mary Cochran and Laura Dean.

Tapestry Dance Company Academy

For ballet, jazz, modern, tap dancers, choreographers *Within a mile of downtown* — *507B Pressler St., Austin, TX 78703* **Voice:** 512-474-9846 **Fax:** 512-474-9212 **E-mail:** dance@tapestry.org **Web Site:** www.tapestry.org **Contact:** Acia Gray, Artistic Dir. **Founded:** 1989 **Open:** Year-round **Admission:** Written application **Deadlines:** Rolling **Cost:** From $10 per class to $150 per month for unlimited classes **Financial Aid:** Scholarship; Work/Study **Size-Attendees:** 100-200 **Size-Class:** 10-30

THIS 10-YEAR-OLD professional company and its related dance academy offer "multiform dance," a unique combination of ballet, jazz, tap, modern and even Irish step dancing. The company and the academy were founded by Deirdre Strand, who trained with Fort Worth Ballet, and Acia Gray, a former performer with Austin on Tap. Gray now heads the company, and Strand directs the academy.

In 1997 the organization relocated its administrative offices, studios and academy to downtown Austin. The new location has 3 studios. Some 80 classes a week are offered, ranging from beginning ballet, to modern and jazz, to rhythm tap, to stomp. There are even courses with such titles as "Power Yoga" and "Cardio-Funk," and it is probably the only school with an Irish step dancer in residence, Eimir Donnellan. The company began with three professionals: Strand and Gray, along with French tap dancer Fred Moritel. It now numbers 7 artists, many of whom also teach in the academy. The company has won considerable praise for the manner in which it blends different dance idioms, sometimes within the same work. If you like dance but aren't certain which style or idiom appeals the most, this is a fine place to immerse yourself in a variety of forms.

Texas Christian University

🏠 *For ballet, modern dancers, choreographers* About 3 mi. from downtown Fort Worth — Dept. of Ballet and Modern Dance, TCU Box 297910, Fort Worth, TX, 76129 **Voice:** 817-921-7615; 800-TCU-3764 **Fax:** 817-921-7333 **E-mail:** e.garrison@tcu.edu **Web Site:** www.tcu.edu **Contact:** Ellen Page Garrison, Chair **Founded:** 1949 **Open:** Year-round **Admission:** Written application, audition **Deadlines:** Feb. 15 for fall semester; Dec. 15 for spring semester **Cost:** $7,130 per year **Financial Aid:** Loans; Scholarship; Fellowship; Stipend; Work/Study **Size-Attendees:** 60 undergrads, 13 grads **Size-Class:** 10-20 **Degree or Certification:** BFA in Dance, MFA in Dance **Job Placement:** Yes

THE DEPARTMENT of Ballet and Modern Dance was founded in 1949 at TCU, the first university in the country to offer a fine-arts degree in ballet. The program, which until 1975 offered ballet training exclusively, was expanded to include the modern-dance major. The university has one of the best reputations among academic institutions as a program specializing in dance.

In 1993 a department dance company was created that performs both ballet and modern-dance repertory. TCU now offers dance certification for grades 6-13, through the Texas Education Association. The program has

separated the 2 departments of ballet and modern, although both share the same facility with 3 very large studios especially equipped for dance. The departments have 5 full-time faculty members, supplemented by guest faculty and visiting companies and artists who teach masterclasses. Among these are Fernando Bujones, who has developed an affiliation with the university as choreographer-and-ballet-master-in-residence. The curriculum includes classes in performance and ensemble work, composition, improvisation, aesthetics, teaching methods, dance history, music, theater, dance kinesiology and jazz. Ballet majors enroll in pas de deux and variations; modern-dance majors enroll in repertory classes.

University of Texas–Austin

  For modern, ballet dancers, choreographers Eastern rim of central Texas's Hill Country — Dept. of Theater and Dance, The Winship Building, Austin, TX 78712 **Voice:** 512-471-5793 **Fax:** 512-471-0824 **E-mail:** hug@mail.utexas.edu **Web Site:** www.utexas.edu/cofa/theatre/index.html **Contact:** Sharon Vasquez, Dept. Chair **Founded:** 1887 **Open:** Year-round **Admission:** Wrritten application, audition **Deadlines:** Feb. 1 for fall semester, Oct. 1 for spring semester **Cost:** $11,980 tuition, room, board and fees per year for state residents; $17,520 for nonresidents **Financial Aid:** Loans; Scholarship; Fellowship; Stipend; Work/Study **Size-Attendees:** 30 **Size-Class:** 10-25 **Degree or Certification:** BFA in Dance **Job Placement:** Yes

FEEDING OFF THE energy of one of this country's hippest and most culturally minded cities, the UT offers a dance program geared more for modern dance than for ballet. In fact, the program leans toward the experimental, giving students the opportunity to explore, train and experience a variety of dance styles and expressions, not only in the classroom but by exposing them to the talent that is presented at the school's major presenting organization, the UT Performing Arts

Center. Artists presented at the venue include Tharp!, James Galway, Chanticleer, Tap Dogs and Voices of Change.

The program boasts 5 fully equipped theaters, ranging from a 3,000-seat concert hall to a 3,600 square-foot black-box performance space. A professional dance company, Sharir Dance Company, is also in residence at the college. Artistic director Yacov Sharir is a member of the theater and the dance faculty, and his company regularly offers internships to UT dance students. He has performed under the direction of such dance luminaries as Martha Graham, Jerome Robbins, José Limón and Anna Sokolow. Other faculty notables include Lathan Sanford, whose work in show business includes the 1959 premiere of *The Fantasticks* in New York; Sondra Lomax, former member of Les Grands Ballets Canadiens; Lyn Elam, former member of Alvin Ailey; Deborah Hay, original member of Judson Dance Theatre and performer with Yvonne Rainer, Steve Paxton, Lucinda Childs and Holly Williams, formerly of Mark Morris. A majority of the company members are UT graduates.

Utah

Ballet West Conservatory

🏠 *For ballet dancers, choreographers* Foothills of the Wasatch Mountains in NW Utah — 110 Marriot Center for Dance, 330 S. 1500 East, Salt Lake City, UT 84112 **Voice:** 801-581-6324 **Fax:** 801-581-5442 **E-mail:** info@balletwest.org **Web Site:** www. balletwest.org **Contact:** Sharee Lane, Asst. Dir. **Founded:** 1989 **Open:** Year-round **Admission:** Written application **Deadlines:** Late Aug. for fall, May 15 for summer **Cost:** $850 for 6-week summer program **Financial Aid:** Scholarship; Work/Study **Size-Attendees:** 75 **Size-Class:** 10-20

B ASED AT THE UNIVERSITY of Utah's ballet department and sharing many of the same resources, this conservatory is one of the best choices for classical training in the region. One of the premier western ballet companies, this nationally recognized regional company is headed by the celebrated Jonas Kage. Besides having been a leading dancer with such companies as the Royal Swedish Ballet, the American Ballet Theatre and the Stuttgart and Zurich ballets, Kage has for the last 10 years served as an artistic director back in his native Sweden. Assistant director Sharee Lane brings to the conservatory more than 15 years as a master teacher both here and abroad. Other faculty include Deborah Dobson-Kage, who also enjoyed a career with the American Ballet Theatre as a soloist and was a permanent guest artist with English National Ballet, and Bene Arnold, formerly of the San Francisco Ballet, who has served as ballet mistress since the inception of Ballet West in 1975. Other members include company artists and university faculty.

For the students, the education includes attending Ballet West rehearsals and performances, as well as being exposed to concerts ranging from the Utah Ballet, to the Repertory Dance

Theatre, the Ririe-Woodbury Dance Company and the Performing Dance Company, all affiliated with the University. For intermediate and advanced students afternoon classes are offered in ballet, pointe and character.

University of Utah

For ballet, modern dancers, choreographers Foothills of the Wasatch Mountains in NW Utah — 110 Marriot Center for Dance, Univ. of Utah, Salt Lake City, UT 84112 **Voice:** 801-581-7327 **Fax:** 801-581-5442 **E-mail:** ed.groff@m.cc.utah.edu **Web Site:** www.dance.utah.edu **Contact:** Scott Marsh, Dept. Chair **Founded:** 1892 **Open:** Year-round **Admission:** Written application, audition, videotape of choreography, statement of purpose, resume **Deadlines:** July 1 for fall, Nov. 13 for winter, Feb. 17 for spring, May 15 for summer; Apr. 10 or May 15 for audition **Financial Aid:** Loans; Scholarship; Fellowship; Stipend; Work/Study **Size-Attendees:** 90 undergraduate students, 25-30 graduate students **Size-Class:** 15-25 **Degree or Certification:** MAs in Dance Education, Kinesiology, Laban/Bartenieff Movement Studies; MFA with emphasis in Performance, Choreography, or Special Projects **Job Placement:** Yes

ONE OF THE MOST respected dance programs in the country, the U of U is exceptional in that it is usually on someone's top 10 list, and has 2 cooperative yet fully autonomous departments within the fine-arts college: a department of ballet and a department of modern dance. The modern-dance department was established in 1949 by Elizabeth R. Hayes. In 1951 the founder of the San Francisco Ballet, William F. Christensen, returned to his home state and to the university to establish a ballet training center. Christensen also founded the nationally recognized company Ballet West—hence the affiliation between the university and the Ballet West Conservatory, which is housed in the department's Marriott Center for Dance and trains dancers ages 12-17.

The conservatory is composed of members of Ballet West and artistic staff and faculty members from the university ballet department. The Ballet West roster includes several former university graduates. Several ballet majors at the university are selected each year to rehearse, learn the repertoire and perform with the company. In return, the university has developed an MFA degree specifically geared toward Ballet West members: the non-thesis, scholarly-research project or performance. The program requires a 2-year residency and a scholarly written research project and/or performance component that is open only to Ballet West or Utah Ballet dancers. Lest you think the program offers professional opportunities for only ballet dancers, the modern-dance department has also established ties to local companies. Graduates of the modern-dance department perform with 2 major Salt Lake City professional companies: the Repertory Dance Theatre and the Ririe-Woodbury Dance Company. The modern-dance department offers an MFA with an emphasis in choreography, performance or special projects, and an MA with 3 areas of focus: education, kinesiology or Laban/Bartenieff movement studies. The ballet department offers an MFA with 3 areas of focus: choreography/teaching, character dance or scholarly research project or performance; and an MA that requires a thesis and scholarly research. Both departments share the Marriott Center for Dance, a large facility including a 333-seat theater, 6 dance studios, academic classrooms, production workshops and a conditioning clinic. The center is 1 of only 3 facilities in the United States designed specifically for dance.

Vermont

Bennington College

For modern dancers, choreographers
SW Vermont — Dance Route 67A, Bennington, VT 05201 **Voice:** 802-440-4547; 800-833-6845 **Fax:** 802-440-4320 **E-mail:** admissions@bennington.edu **Web Site:** www.bennington.edu **Contact:** Terry Creach **Founded:** 1932 **Open:** Year-round **Admission:** Written application, audition, transcripts, test scores, writing sample, interview **Deadlines:** Feb. 1 for fall semester, Jan. 1 for spring semester **Cost:** $13,200 per year **Financial Aid:** Loans; Scholarship; Fellowship; Stipend; Work/Study **Degree or Certification:** BA in Dance, MFA in Dance **Job Placement:** Yes

THIS SMALL BUT venerable liberal-arts college preserves its prestige by staying on the cutting edge of higher education; its performing-and-visual-arts program leads the way. The arts are accorded equal stature with literature and other liberal-arts studies, and the emphasis is on creating new work in a multidisciplinary mode. Thus the focus of the MFA program is on the "continual making of new work." All MFA candidates participate each semester in a graduate seminar designed to encourage cross-fertilization of ideas and creating dialogue between artists. And at some point in their program, students are asked to work outside of their medium or discipline.

Make no mistake: the reputation that Bennington had during the Martha Hill glory days has changed. As a center for dance it is no less interesting, but it is different. There is a small but highly expert faculty, many of whom are still doing fascinating work: Terry Creach, Sara Rudner and Dana Reitz, known by many for her choreography and dancing with Mikhail Baryshnikov. Rudner's work is seen widely on film and through her own performances, and Creach, while no longer part of Creach/Koester, main-tains a performing ensemble. The school is located on a 550-acre campus that was once an old farm, and continues to use some of the farm buildings. But you wouldn't be going to class in a barn. The center for the visual and performing arts is one of the largest woodframe structures in the eastern United States. It has galleries, theaters, exhibition spaces and support areas. For the dance program there are 3 studios and a 10,000-square-foot-black-box theater named for Martha Hill.

Virginia

George Mason University

For modern dancers, choreographers Washington, DC, area — Dance Division, MS 3D4, 4440 University Dr., Fairfax, VA 22030 **Voice:** 703-993-1114 **Fax:** 703-993-1366 **E-mail:** dance@gmu.edu **Web Site:** dance.gmu.edu/ **Contact:** Linda Garner Miller, Dance Dir. **Founded:** 1977 **Open:** Year-round **Admission:** Written application, interview, test scores, transcripts, writing sample, audition for BFA, MFA programs **Deadlines:** Feb. 1 for fall semester **Cost:** $180 per credit for state residents, $510 per credit for nonresidents **Financial Aid:** Loans; Scholarship; Fellowship; Stipend; Work/Study **Size-Attendees:** 120 **Size-Class:** 30 **Degree or Certification:** BA, BFA in Dance, MFA in Dance **Job Placement:** Yes

THE DANCE PROGRAM here has a solid reputation as a center for teaching contemporary dance, with a good faculty and outstanding guest artists. The proximity to the nation's capital and its lively cultural scene make it desirable as well. Director Linda Garner Miller performed with the Cincinnati Ballet and the Chicago Ballet and was nominated for a Helen Hayes Award for her choreography. The faculty also includes the respected dance historian and critic

Suzanne Carboneau, who teaches at the Bates Dance Festival and at Jacob's Pillow Dance Festival. Susan Shields, a former dancer with the Mark Morris Dance Group and the Laura Dean Dancers, adds an important contemporary dimension to the faculty.

Guest artists play an important role, adding sparkle and contributing to what one dance writer termed George Mason's being "tuned into the contemporary scene." Recent guests include Jan Erkert & Dancers, Mark Morris, Donald Byrd, Danny Buraczeski, and the Royal Winnipeg Ballet and Hubbard Street Dance Chicago, providing masterclasses and other residency activities. Every year 2 well-respected companies are in residence for a minimum of 2 weeks.

The dance division offers a variety of degrees. The BA, which does not require an audition, provides a general program of dance study. The performance-oriented BFA offers concentrated study in performance, choreography and teaching; the emphasis, as noted above, is on modern dance. The small and selective MFA program seeks applicants with some life experiences in the field before application, precluding students recently awarded an undergraduate degree. Each year the program produces 4 concerts, 2 informal choreography showcases and a number of MFA-thesis concerts. Campus facilities include 3 theaters: a 100-seat dance performance studio, the 520-seat Harris theater and a 2,000-seat concert hall. Graduates have gone on to dance with a number of important companies, including those of Laura Dean, Rachel Lampert, Ririe-Woodbury and Twyla Tharp.

Richmond Ballet Center for Dance

For ballet dancers — *614 N. Lombardy St., Richmond, VA 23220* **Voice:** 804-359-0906 **Fax:** 804-355-4640 **E-mail:** richmondballet@mindspring.com **Contact:** Stoner Winslett, Dir. **Founded:** 1953 **Open:** Year-round **Admission:** Placement audition **Deadlines:** Apply each quarter **Cost:** $250 per quarter or from $10 per class **Financial Aid:** Scholarship; Work/Study **Size-Attendees:** 600 **Size-Class:** 20

THIS BOOMING operation has more than 600 students enrolled at its 2 locations. The main facility, 2 minutes from the center of downtown Richmond, has 4 studios, and a suburban branch school has 3 studios. The main facility is shared with the professional company, which has been in existence since 1983. Both the company and the school are under the direction of Stoner Winslett, who trained with the American Ballet Theatre and the North Carolina School of the Arts.

Faculty chair Judy Jacob danced with the Memphis Ballet and the Indiana Ballet Theatre and is ballet mistress with the Richmond Ballet. Other notable faculty include Malcolm Burn, ballet master of Richmond Ballet and a former dancer with London Festival Ballet and Ballet West; Jasmine Grace, former ballet mistress of Ballet Arizona; Arnott Mader, who danced with the Royal Ballet and American Ballet Theatre; and Maria Youskevitch, who danced with American Ballet Theatre and was formerly principal teacher for Hartford Ballet, BalletMet, and Nevada Dance Theater. The curriculum includes the usual array of preballet, adult-division and middle-school classes. There is also a special trainee division for 12-15 participants selected from the summer session. This program, under the direct supervision of the chair with support from the senior faculty, provides classes and performances designed to prepare the dancer for a professional career. Both apprentice dancers and trainees from the school perform with the professional company.

Shenandoah University

🏠☀️ *For ballet, jazz, modern, tap dancers, choreographers* Shenandoah Valley of northern Virginia — Dance Division, 1460 University Dr., Winchester, VA 22601 **Voice:** 540-665-4647; 800-432-2266 **Fax:** 540-665-5402 **E-mail:** admit@su.edu **Web Site:** www.su.edu/dance/index.htm **Contact:** Elizabeth Bergmann, Dance Div. Chair **Founded:** 1877 **Open:** Year-round **Admission:** Resume, audition, interview, SAT or ACT scores, high-school transcripts, writing sample, GRE (graduate students only) **Deadlines:** Rolling **Cost:** $18,700 tuition, room, board per year **Financial Aid:** Loans; Scholarship; Fellowship; Stipend; Work/Study **Size-Attendees:** 43 **Size-Class:** 15 **Degree or Certification:** BA in Dance; BFAs in Dance, Dance Education; BS in Arts Management with Concentration in Dance; MFA in Dance Choreography and Performance **Job Placement:** Yes

T HIS PRIVATE university seems to leave no stone unturned. It offers a practical program that provides its students with a wide range of opportunities in dance and dance-related fields.

The university also offers a BA, a BFA, a BFA in dance education and a BS in arts management, with a concentration in dance. Technique classes are offered in ballet, modern, jazz and tap. Classes are small, masterclasses and workshops with visiting guest artists are frequent, and opportunities to work with nationally recognized choreographers are also available. The conservatory has 32 ensembles and more than 300 performing-arts events on campus each year. The dance department itself boasts 3 performing ensembles: the Shenandoah Dance Ensemble, the Shenandoah Chamber Dance Company, and Mind Over Matter. These ensembles travel throughout the area performing in such cities as Greensboro, Richmond and Washington.

The BFA program has an equal emphasis on ballet and modern dance, with additional training in jazz, tap and musical theater. The general philosophy is to train a versatile dancer, so that employment opportunities are increased. The BS in arts management is offered to meet the growing needs of arts organizations in this ever-expanding field. The course work includes an overview of career opportunities and the development of publicity skills. There are 4 specialized courses focusing on arts management in the profit sector, the nonprofit sector, the electronic media and the entertainment industry. For the MFA in choreography and performance, the curriculum addresses the needs of both dancers who are returning to the academic setting following a professional career in dance, and those who have recently completed their undergraduate degree. One area of focus is the 4-semester course in choreography and dance-company direction, which calls for students to develop a personal repertoire and to schedule, program and produce the university dance concerts. The MMus, a pioneer program in the field of dance, is designed to provide a depth of training in studio accompaniment for ballet and modern-dance technique classes, supplemented with skills training in recording techniques, sound operations and computer proficiency.

ALAN LEHMAN

Dancers of the Shenandoah Dance Ensemble, Winchester.

Virginia School of the Arts

🏠 **For ballet, jazz, modern dancers, choreographers** *Foothills of the Blue Ridge Mountains — 2240 Rivermont Ave., Lynchburg, VA 24503* **Voice:** 804-847-8688 **Fax:** 804-847-4380 **E-mail:** vasarts@ aol.com **Web Site:** members.alo.com/vasarts **Contact:** Nataly North, Dir. Adm. **Founded:** 1985 **Open:** Year-round **Admission:** Written application, audition **Deadlines:** Rolling **Cost:** $5,500 per year, $900 for summer **Financial Aid:** Scholarship; Work/Study **Size-Attendees:** 250 **Size-Class:** 10-25

OFFERING TO VIRGINIA what the Harid Conservatory, Walnut Hill and Interlochen offer to Florida, Massachusetts and Michigan, respectively, VSA solves the dilemma for arts-minded youth who want to train for a professional career while still completing their high-school requirements. It can be done, as this school will attest, but the schedule is intense. Students are up at 6:45 A.M. and do not stop until 12 hours later, packing in academics, technique classes and rehearsals with a 45-minute break for food.

The success rate for graduates is quite high, with a large percentage of students receiving offers from at least one dance company upon graduation or being offered scholarships to continue their dance training at the college level. Students also gain exposure to professionals working in the business during the annual Evening of Elegance gala, one of Lynchburg's most popular events, drawing guest dancers from such companies as the Joffrey, Boston Ballet, Royal Winnipeg and Ballet West. The school is run by Petrus Bosman, who had an 18-year career as a soloist and principal dancer with the Royal Ballet. He is joined by dance department chair David Keener, who has also been on the faculty at Interlochen. Completing the school's faculty list are 18 additional teachers, all of them well known for outstanding performing careers and for their teaching credits and abilities. Studio work includes ballet, pointe, men's technique, pas de deux,

repertoire, variations, jazz and modern. Classwork includes dance history, music for dancers, theater for dancers, body alignment, Pilates and nutrition. Importance is also given to performing, with 3 public events produced each year.

Washington

Cornish College of the Arts

🏠 ☀ **For ballet, modern dancers, choreographers** *Pacific Northwest — 710 East Roy St., Seattle, WA 98102* **Voice:** 206-726-5016; 800-726-ARTS **Fax:** 206-720-1011 **E-mail:** admissions@cornish.edu **Web Site:** www.cornish.edu **Contact:** Kathryn Daniels, Dept. Chair **Founded:** 1914 **Open:** Year round **Admission:** Written application, high-school transcript, ACT or SAT scores, college transcript (if applicable), 2 essays **Deadlines:** Aug. 15 **Cost:** $11,540 per year **Financial Aid:** Loans; Scholarship; Fellowship; Stipend; Work/Study **Size-Attendees:** 80 **Size-Class:** 10 **Degree or Certification:** BFA in Dance **Job Placement:** Yes

THE DANCE DEPARTMENT at this small liberal-arts college gets much of its inspiration from the lively Seattle arts scene, which boasts a surprising number of vibrant companies. A significant and rich choreographic and dance community exists in Seattle, the best example being renowned choreographer Mark Morris, who made his start in the city. Cornish combines a solid curriculum in dance with the local cultural resources of the city and the surrounding Pacific Northwest. While absorbing much of the cultural atmosphere, Cornish also offers its students a number of practical outlets to further their dance aspirations. Students are encouraged to audition and perform with professional companies in the area, so that they can experience the realities of a performing career outside the classroom, and other, less conventional options are available to students who need a more flexible schedule during their academic tenure.

The program is definitely geared to the Seattle dance scene, with opportunities and courses designed around meeting the needs of the community and helping to expand the already substantial and flourishing dance movement. Visiting artists have included Mark Morris, David Dorfman, Ralph Lemon, Dwight Rhoden and Lynn Simonson. The curriculum is on the heavy side, with a minimum of 6-8 hours a day divided between technique classes and study in the classroom. Composition and improvisation are also emphasized, with a 3-year sequence of courses required. Those with professional experience can apply to the professional dancers program, which awards up to 2 years of prior learning credit; talented high-school-level students interested in dance can enroll at the college while completing their high-school degree.

Pacific Northwest Ballet School

For ballet dancers, choreographers — 301 Mercer St., Seattle, WA 98109 **Voice:** 206-441-9411 **Fax:** 206-441-2440 **E-mail:** school@pnb.org **Web Site:** www.pnb.org **Contact:** Francia Russell, Artistic Dir. **Founded:** 1972 **Open:** Year-round **Admission:** Written application, audition **Deadlines:** Apply each semester **Cost:** From $233 per semester, $9 per class **Financial Aid:** Scholarship; Fellowship; Work/Study **Size-Attendees:** 600 **Size-Class:** 15-25 **Job Placement:** Yes

ONE OF THE PREMIER regional ballet companies in this country, Pacific Northwest Ballet has an affiliated school that does its parent company proud. Providing superior training for the serious student of ballet, the school operates year-round. The curriculum includes everything from ballet technique to character dance. Students at the school are given the opportunity to perform in company productions, such as that seasonal favorite, *The Nutcracker.*

The Pacific Northwest Ballet School is recognized as the major center of professional ballet training in the Northwest. Under the direction of Francia Russell, the school offers a complete, professional curriculum to more than 600 students. In addition, the school's open program attracts more teens and adults who wish to take class for their own enjoyment. The student division offers 6 levels of instruction. Auditions are required for admission, and placement is based on age, strength and physical development. The professional division offers intermediate and advanced instruction for students planning a professional career. These classes include ballet technique, modern, jazz, classic flamenco and character dance. In the manner of a dance conservatory, classes are also offered in dance history, music, choreography, kinesiology and other related subjects, such as a summer teacher's seminar. The school can boast that half of the members of the company were trained at the school. Advanced students often perform with the company, and apprentices are often drawn from the school's professional division.

The school has 2 locations, in Seattle and in Bellevue. The full-time faculty of 12 includes such dance luminaries as Stephanie Saland, former principal with New York City Ballet; Bruce Wells; Phillip Otto; Lisa Peterson; Marjorie Thompson; and artistic directors Kent Stowell and Francia Russell, who both enjoyed successful careers. The syllabus is based on the classical Russian tradition and is enhanced by contemporary dance forms and ideas, in an effort to produce a versatile dancer in tune with the choreography of today. The Phelps Center location in Seattle has 8 studios, shared equally by the company and the school. The facility in Bellevue was constructed in 1986 for the convenience of Eastside parents of younger students.

University of Washington–Seattle

For ballet, modern dancers
About 3 mi. N of downtown — Box 351150, Seattle, WA 98195 **Voice:** 206-543-0550 **Fax:** 206-543-8610 **E-mail:** recordon@ u.washington.edu **Web Site:** depts. washington.edu/uwdance **Contact:** Susanne Recordon, Prog. Advisor **Founded:** 1892 **Open:** Fall, winter, spring **Admission:** Letter of interest, resume, videotape, 3 letters of reference verifying professional accomplish- ment **Deadlines:** Jan. 15 **Cost:** $11,430 tuition, room, board per year for state resi- dents; $19,455 for nonresidents **Financial Aid:** Loans; Scholarship; Fellowship; Stipend; Work/Study **Size-Attendees:** 45 **Size-Class:** 10-20 **Degree or Certification:** MFA in Dance, BA in Dance **Job Placement:** Yes

MFA student Pamela Geber at the University of Washington Dance Program, Seattle.

THE UNIVERSITY OF WASHINGTON Dance Program is probably one of the most practical MFA dance programs in the country. Taking into consideration the peculiar mix of dance and academia, the program is a specialized training ground for dance professionals who want to make the transition to teaching at the college level once their performing career has ended, which is probably the chief rea- son why most dancers look to an acad- emic program in the first place.

Not for everyone, the program re- quires that an applicant have experience as a professional dancer, preferably a minimum of 8 years. The program is geared toward mature artists who have more life experience than academic credits under their belts. For example, the usual foreign language or GRE re- quirements for most MFA programs are waived here. The 2 or 3 MFA candidates accepted each year receive a tuition

waiver and earn a monthly stipend for working as teaching assistants; dancing with Chamber Dance, the resident pro- fessional modern-dance company; and teaching undergraduate courses. The UW faculty work with MFA candidates both as colleagues and as students. The program is quite intensive, incorporat- ing not only a full workload of classes and thesis preparation, which includes an undergraduate seminar taught by the MFA candidate, but also additional responsibilities performing in the en- semble, and teaching academic and technique classes. But the workload is a taste of reality to come, which is what this program is about. And the school's reputation is second to none.

UW also offers a BA with a major in dance, including courses in dance composition, technique, history and aesthics. Students participate in dance performances and complete a senior seminar.

Wisconsin

Milwaukee Ballet School

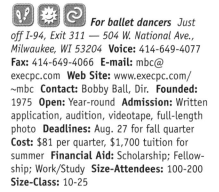

For ballet dancers Just off I-94, Exit 311 — 504 W. National Ave., Milwaukee, WI 53204 **Voice:** 414-649-4077 **Fax:** 414-649-4066 **E-mail:** mbc@ execpc.com **Web Site:** www.execpc.com/ ~mbc **Contact:** Bobby Ball, Dir. **Founded:** 1975 **Open:** Year-round **Admission:** Written application, audition, videotape, full-length photo **Deadlines:** Aug. 27 for fall quarter **Cost:** $81 per quarter, $1,700 tuition for summer **Financial Aid:** Scholarship; Fellowship; Work/Study **Size-Attendees:** 100-200 **Size-Class:** 10-25

I T IS PERHAPS NOT a universally known fact that the Milwaukee Ballet ranks as one of this country's top 10 regional companies, producing and offering employment to some of our most accomplished dancers. A grand operation, the school can also boast that it is the fourth largest professional school in the country, with 3 locations. The school is an excellent training ground for tomorrow's professionals, offering the basic ingredients of quality training, professional exposure and performance opportunities.

Programs here range from a children's division to a trainee/scholarship program. The summer intensive can serve as an informal audition for the regular trainee program offered during the academic year. Once accepted, students maintain a schedule that includes daily ballet technique with the addition of modern, pointe, variations, partnering, floor barre, drama, Dalcroze eurhythmics, history and jazz. Of course, the opportunity exists for students to perform in Milwaukee Ballet productions. An open division is also available for students at all levels who want to take class with no commitment. The company's artistic director, Basil Thompson, is also the school's leading advisor. A longtime Joffrey

Ballet instructor and ballet master, Thompson enjoyed a career with the Royal Ballet and the American Ballet Theatre. Milwaukee Ballet company members along with 22 other former dancers complete the faculty roster. Recent guest teachers include the Trinity Irish Dancers, Kathryn Posin and the Ko-Thi Dance Company.

University of Wisconsin–Madison

For ballet, ethnic, modern dancers, choreographers Southern Wisconsin — Dance Program, Lathrop Hall, 1050 University Ave., Madison, WI 53706 **Voice:** 608-262-1691 **Fax:** 608-265-3841 **E-mail:** dance@education.wisc.edu **Web Site:** www.education.wisc.edu/dance **Contact:** Mary Alice Brennan, Dance Prog. Chair **Founded:** 1926 **Open:** Year-round **Admission:** Written application, statement of purpose, interview, resume, transcripts **Deadlines:** Feb. 1 for fall semester, Nov. 1 for spring semester **Cost:** $1,700 per year for state residents, $7,595 for nonresidents **Financial Aid:** Loans; Scholarship; Fellowship; Stipend; Work/Study **Size-Attendees:** 100-150 **Size-Class:** 10-25 **Degree or Certification:** BS in Dance, Dance Education, BFA in Dance **Job Placement:** Yes

I F YOU'RE LOOKING FOR the hub of dance activity in the Midwest, this school is for you. Leading scholars and innovators in the field have congregated here since its beginnings in 1926. The school has the distinction of being the first university to offer a degree program in dance. Not satisfied to rest on its proverbial laurels, the university continues to push the envelope and attract leaders in the field to its campus, presenting programs of national interest. In 1997–1998 an African/African-American Dance Festival was presented throughout the academic year, featuring dancers, choreographers, drummers, authors and critics, all of whom celebrated the contributions of Africans and African-Americans to dance in this country. This is just one example of the kind of programming offered to students at UW–Madison.

JAY DANIEL

Choreographer Li Chiao-Ping at the University of Wisconsin Dance Program, Madison.

University of Wisconsin–Stevens Point

For ballet, jazz, modern, tap dancers, choreographers Central Wisconsin — Dept. of Theatre and Dance, 2100 Main St., Stevens Point, WI 54481 **Voice:** 715-346-3980 **E-mail:** j2moore@uwsp.edu **Web Site:** www.uwsp.edu **Contact:** James Moore. Prof. of Dance **Founded:** 1894 **Open:** Year-round **Admission:** Written application, interview, transcripts, test scores, writing sample **Deadlines:** Open admissions **Cost:** $1,464 per semester for state residents, $4,605 per semester for nonresidents **Financial Aid:** Loans; Scholarship; Fellowship; Stipend; Work/Study **Size-Attendees:** 125 **Size-Class:** 10-25 **Degree or Certification:** BA in Dance, BS in Dance, BFA in Dance **Job Placement:** Yes

In 1990 the dance program established the Interarts and Technology (IATECH) option, integrating computer technologies with movement, sound and the visual arts. The IATECH curriculum, open to all interested students, is currently a leader in this exciting new field, expanding the frontiers of media and the arts in both practice and performance. The 4-year program provides interdisciplinary experience using computer animation, digital video and sound technologies. Basically, it's for those interested in the arts as well as in the world of technology. The dance program regularly sponsors special masterclasses and workshops by prominent dancers and choreographers, including Bill T. Jones, Meredith Monk and Sean Curran. Madison also attracts such well-known dance companies as Alvin Ailey American Dance Theater, Merce Cunningham, Feld and Martha Graham Dance Company, giving students exposure to these dance giants.

THIS MIDSIZED PROGRAM, accredited by the National Association of Schools of Dance, offers a core curriculum of ballet, jazz, tap, theater dance and dance composition. Theater and dance, with 125 dance and theater majors, is 1 of 4 departments in the College of Fine Arts and Communications. The University has a separate dance center, with 2 spacious studios and an excellent theater in the Fine Arts Center.

For a modest program, there are some great faculty members at this school. Foremost is James Moore, who danced with American Ballet Theatre and Jerome Robbins' Ballets USA. He was artistic director of the Royal Swedish Ballet for 3 years and worked with Robbins and others on a number of Broadway shows. Other faculty members have performance and choreographic experience with some of the leading modern-dance companies. Student choreography is encouraged, and students design and choreograph a full evening each fall called *Afterimages*.

Wyoming

University of Wyoming

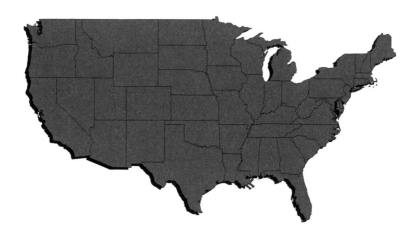 **For ballet, jazz, modern, tap dancers, choreographers** *Southeastern Wyoming — Dept. of Theatre and Dance, Box 3951, University Sta., Laramie, WY 82071* **Voice:** 307-766-2198 **Fax:** 307-766-2197 **Web Site:** www.uwyo.edu **Contact:** Rebecca Hilliker, Chair **Founded:** 1886 **Open:** Year-round **Admission:** Written application, audition, transcripts, test scores, writing sample **Deadlines:** Aug. 10 for fall semester, Dec. 10 for spring semester **Cost:** $4,832 per year for residents, $15,368 per year for nonresidents **Financial Aid:** Loans; Scholarship; Fellowship; Stipend; Work/Study **Size-Attendees:** 15 **Size-Class:** 5-10 **Degree or Certification:** BA in Dance, BFA in Dance **Job Placement:** Yes

THERE MIGHT BE big skies in Wyoming, but not large dance programs. Total enrollment is about 15 students, but this is the program's great strength, since small class size leads to lavish individual attention. As one faculty member puts it, "We can look at each student as an individual." Most graduates go on to teaching or to graduate school.

An interesting university event is the annual Snowy Range Summer Dance Festival, presented with the Colorado Ballet. This summer intensive includes ballet, a resident modern-dance company, tap classes with Tony Coppola and jazz dance with General Hambrick. Good performing facilities and opportunities to choreograph abound. Student work is featured in the various main-stage musicals produced by the department of theater and dance and in operas produced at the university. Faculty members include Chair Rebecca Hilliker, Marsha Fay Knight, Patricia Tate and Margaret Stalder. Professional choreographers are brought in each year, and generally a major dance company as well, to present masterclasses.

PART THREE

The Business of Dance

Finances

Financial Aid — The Inside Scoop

Dancers often don't concern themselves with the important subject of grants, awards and financial aid that might be available to them. In addition to the service organizations listed in Part Two, there are a great number of other avenues to pursue. You should consult the Foundation Center's publications on grants to individuals (keep in mind that most of these are for graduate and undergraduate study), and you should inquire about local grants and scholarships from service organizations in your community.

By your reading this section, we hope to make you a little more savvy about what to expect if you need financial aid to attend one of the programs listed in this book. Those programs described as offering financial aid are indexed as such. Many dance programs are not-for-profit and are, therefore, in need of financial aid themselves to keep operating. If you are able to pay full freight, we urge you to do so, particularly if scholarships are need-based. You might even want to consider a donation to an excellent program you have attended, so that others less economically fortunate might be able to attend in the future. You should realistically calculate how much it will cost you to attend a program, figure out how much you can earn toward this amount, and apply only for that portion of aid you really need.

At dance festivals and summer residency workshops you should expect everything from no financial support at all to free tuition. Seldom, if ever, will the festival or workshop pay for your housing and travel to and from the residency site. A few of the programs have work/study programs through which you can earn all or part of your room and board. Bottom line: most financial aid in this category is in the form of free or reduced tuition.

Masterclasses are usually quite affordable, and they offer opportunities to study with some of the very best teachers. In particular, you should try to take masterclasses taught by company artistic directors. You will have a chance to study first-hand with artistic visionaries and discover if their work or approach to dance works for you. And, significantly, these leaders will have a chance to see you dancing. Many artistic directors I know have "discovered" members of their companies through masterclasses or guest teaching assignments at colleges and universities. Financial aid is uncommon for masterclass situations, but I suppose there is no harm in asking the chair of a department or other person in charge for financial aid or free masterclasses if you really can't afford them.

The subject of financial aid for academic programs is complex and would require its own book. Most universities have both federal and private money to assist qualified students. We suggest that you read the university catalog to see what kinds of scholarships are provided for any ethnic, geographical or gender groups to which you belong. If the University offers extensive financial-aid options, you might want to ask for an annotated list of all scholarships offered. It would also be wise to speak with the financial-aid officer to obtain advice about how to apply for scholarships, and to find out what is available in terms of Pell grants (U.S. government) and students loans.

Are student loans worth the risk? Looked at as an investment in your future, they are. You should be aware that loans are generally not available for workshops and other summer-study programs. By contrast, few people get through college or graduate school without taking on some debt for living expenses and/or tuition. If you believe in yourself, this is one of the best investments you will ever make. That's the rationalization; then there are the feelings. Some people simply hate to carry any debt or hate the fact that banks or the government are charging them usurious interest (though federally insured student loans have relatively low rates). Before you conclude that a loan is the right choice for you, take stock not only of your dollar resources, but also of your attitude toward borrowing in general. Recent graduates of medical school at least have a chance of earning back the investment they made to get their degree. But people with an MFA in dance performance might be climbing a steeper slope to get out of debt. If the loan you are considering is substantial, be sure to take a good look at both your overall financial needs now and those expected in the years immediately following the award of your degree. Put the loan in the context of your other expenses, such as housing, food and medical expenses, and also consider what your earnings will be. If you believe you can handle the financial obligations and really want that degree, by all means step up to the plate and swing away.

It's a scandal that paying back student loans has become, in the words of Shakespeare's moody student, Hamlet, "a custom more honored in the breach than in the observance." No matter how unfair you might think the cold, cruel world out there might be to you and your fellow dancers, not paying back your federally or state-insured loan(s) is hardly good citizenship, and what does it say to the even younger dancers coming along behind you? New legislation empowers the government to prosecute student-loan deadbeats aggressively. So take into your planning the fact that you *will* have to pay back your loan(s).

Finally, we recommend that you "keep your day job," to borrow a phrase from the theater world. The best financial aid you can give to your dancing habit is a paycheck. I dismiss the argument that a life in dance and a paid working life are incompatible. My research assistant on this book finds time to help me, work as an arts administrator and dance at the Metropolitan Opera! It's all about planning and having an understanding boss who can be flexible about hours. A non-dancing job creates benefits that go beyond the value of the paycheck. It gets you up in the morning into a structured day. It takes you out into the world and out of yourself. It makes you appreciate (and put to better use) the time you do assign to your dancing. Remember the old saying: "If you have all morning to write a letter, it will take you until 11 o'clock to find a pencil."

In sum, I'd say the best financial-aid plan for a determined dancer is to balance your financial and artistic needs in the early years, until you become "established" by having a good freelance network or are asked to join a company. This requires real determination and fortitude, especially if you are in New York City, but you can do it!

Getting Your Career Started

So you have completed your degree and are seeking work as a professional. In my opinion, your success in finding work will be in direct proportion to the amount of stage experience you have had. If you came from a university that offered many rich opportunities to perform, you will be at an advantage as you enter the fiercely competitive environment in New York or the increasingly competitive environment outside New York. Doris Humphrey observes in *The Art of Making Dances* that the dancer's focus on stage is outward to the audience, rather than inward as it is in a class. Keep this in mind, and aggressively pursue those performing opportunities, even if they don't pay well. You might consider coming to New York City to audition or for further study.

I strongly suggest some exposure or experience in New York City at some point before you attempt to launch your career. The reason is simple. New York City is incomparable for the variety, quality and quantity of its dance experiences. It has the largest dance collection in the world at the New York Public Library, almost all the important modern-dance companies and two of the world's great ballet companies. To be sure, the dog-eat-dog competition in New York is certainly not for everyone. But you should sample the dance environment there. While you might obtain a first-rate education and pursue a professional career by never going to New York, study or professional experience in the Big Apple is unlike anything available anywhere else in world.

Admittedly, you will have to put up with the noise, the pushy people and expensive housing and food, but there is also an incredible excitement and pulse there. My advice is to try to first find an affordable and safe living situation before you venture out to investigate various dance offerings. Many of the universities in New York offer dormitory space for visiting students, and most of these are well located, clean and safe. Once that is secured, you can begin to sample the delicious smorgasbord of dance. If time and your situation permit, you should try a little of everything. Just be prepared for the fact that the standards of quality here are higher than anywhere else in the U.S. If you were at the top of your class in Des Moines, I can pretty much guarantee that you will not be in New York City.

Still, if you have the right attitude and approach to the New York dance environment, you will be just fine. Classes are generally crowded but surprisingly affordable. Many of the leading companies have official schools, and you definitely want to take advantage of this. My suggestion here is that you get on the mailing list for classes and workshops of those choreographers and companies you find exciting and try to fit in an "intensive" study period with them.

An important thing to realize about the dance world, whether in New York or anywhere else, is that it is very small, and word of mouth and referrals are crucial to your success. You don't need a manager or a press agent; you need diligence and intelligence about networking for yourself. You will meet people in class who know about an upcoming program someone is putting together; your teacher will recommend you to a particular choreographer or artistic director. Keep in touch with your teachers, other people with whom you have performed or gone to school, and the regional theaters and university program(s) with which you have been connected. Let your friends, acquaintances in dance, former teachers, directors and anyone else who might be interested know that you are looking for work. If you have talent and a passion for dance, you *will* work.

Although the economics of the dance world dictate that you will not be able to attract any agents to help you get work (15 percent of a small fee or salary isn't worth their while), there are things you can do for yourself. Be imaginative in marketing yourself. Develop and maintain a personal mailing list. Send a personal letter, note or flyer to everyone on this list when you are either performing or choreographing. Ask your friends about opportunities to dance or work in Europe. My experience is that Europeans love American dancers. If you are a solo artist and experience some success, invite some booking agents and dance managers to your next performance. These people will recognize talent in a performer or choreographer, and you might even get some work through them.

Special Advice for Choreographers

Just about every dancer has an opportunity to choreograph at some point. Perhaps it will be during your teens for your high school or for the dance school where you study. It is difficult to get an undergraduate degree in dance without creating some work, and virtually impossible for the terminal degree of an MFA. Choreographers do not just create for dance companies; theater companies and opera companies often provide fledgling choreographers with their first chance to create a dance.

If you enjoy choreography, and people that you respect tell you that you have talent, pursue it. I think that there is a scarcity of truly gifted and original choreographers, and people of talent will always find opportunities. American dance has always depended on bold new talents to make it vibrant. Also, companies are always looking for new work to interest their audiences, and perhaps some day you will have a chance to become the next Jerome Robbins!

If things go well for you as a choreographer, you might want to consider having an agent or manager. Also, when your dances are fixed, that is to say complete and performed, you should videotape them. Obtain a copyright form from the U.S. Copyright Office, then send $20 and a copy of your tape. There are too many sad instances in which others steal choreography for monetary gain, and the original creator can do nothing about it. By copyrighting your material, you will be protected. If you are not at the stage of your career where you can hire a manager, you should develop on your own a letter of agreement for your engagements that not only covers compensation, travel and housing, but also includes the number of hours of rehearsal you will be given, casting prerogatives and production elements. To find appropriate language for this agreement, ask the Society of Stage Directors and Choreographers for a copy of its standard contract (see Part Two, "Unions & Other Labor Organizations").

The Price Tag on Your Work

When working as a dancer or as a choreographer you will need to determine what your work is worth. Should you estimate its value on the basis of the amount of time you spent studying and practicing, and if so, what hourly rate makes sense? Should you surrender to your sense of the absurd and accept whatever the market tells you your work is worth? Is there any way to be reasonable about all this? The answer is yes—and no.

Companies, dancers, choreographers and presenters everywhere work from precedents, the "going rate." Nobody claims that this is reasonable, but what else is there to do? There is no official pay scale for freelance dancers or choreographers. Unions like SSDC and AGMA (see Part Two) do have official rates if you join a *union* company, and these rates offer some guidance. But realistically, you must bear in mind that oftentimes your first work will be in a small pickup company with a struggling young choreographer who will be lucky to scrounge up enough money to rent a space, do some publicity and pay you a small fee. My advice: If you are determined to be a freelancer, accept these gigs because of the valuable performing experience they offer when you are first starting out. Each one enhances your performance resume.

You should, of course, try to negotiate for the highest possible payment when doing freelance work. Try to find out as much as you can from other dancers. Ask for real numbers, not rough estimates, to determine what you should ask. Sometimes negotiating is like a poker game. Whoever bids first is at a disadvantage. The next guy is bound to make a move to his advantage based on the first bid. ("Sorry, you're too high, or too low.") Get to know other successful freelancers in your market, and set some pay limits for yourself. Sometimes saying "No" will serve you (or your reputation) well later on.

As you career progresses, you will discover that working for unreasonably low pay helps no one. Usually, the program will be underrehearsed, and you might not be shown to good advantage. Remember, the dance world is small and has a very active grapevine. Learn to use some discretion about the jobs you accept. Sadly, in dance, it is usually a buyers' market, unless you are working in the commercial theater. But you can still maintain certain standards, even though the pressure will be on you to work for low rates of pay.

Running Your Business as a Freelance Artist

If things go well for you as a choreographer or even as a solo dancer, you might want to consider incorporating. You will probably not need to incorporate, but incorporation has certain advantages. It gives a group a certain legal status. If you are forming an ensemble or company, your group, once incorporated, can employ its members. It can pay salaries and expenses; and if not-for-profit, it can apply for grants and awards. While there are some bookkeeping and management tasks, they are really not that much more complex than properly keeping records for a sole proprietorship, and they are worth the benefits in my opinion. Don't make guesses about whether you should incorporate. Speak to your accountant and an attorney about it. You should also look around for conferences or seminars that deal with legal and business issues affecting artists. Some of the organizations described in this book offer such seminars; see Part Two, under both "Signing Up: Organizations for Dancers" and "Dance Programs."

Taxes

I don't know of any more tedious subject. However, if you are serious about your career as a freelance artist and your income from this source becomes substantial, you will have to set up a bookkeeping system, keep meticulous records on your expenses and start paying a quarterly estimated tax. Remember, if you do freelance work and your earnings amount to $600 or more per year from any source or sources, you will receive an earnings statement. These earnings are reported to the IRS.

Think of the costs of setting up a bookkeeping system and laying out a plan to minimize your taxes as a basic business expense. Find a book-keeper or accountant who is savvy about self-employment; consider using a software program like Quicken (from Intuit) to put your check-book register on the computer, and save/record all your receipts as only a tax-hating maniac would. (Expenses allowable for an dance artist include unreimbursed travel and meal expenses, stage clothing, dance classes, coaching, and purchase of tickets to see other performers.) An accountant with only general experience, rather than with some taste of the dance world, might miss tax deductions. It's worth paying these number-crunching folks a few hundred dollars to set you up with easy-to-follow systems that will repeat year after year. If you work with appropriate professionals (whose fees are themselves deductible busi-ness expenses), you'll most likely cut your tax bill more effectively than if you muddle through on your own.

You might hear at a conference or seminar that you should contact the IRS to request various tax booklets. These publications are easy to obtain, but reading and understanding them can be another matter. You will certainly have questions about your particular situation. With the IRS it might be difficult to get anyone on the phone and harder still to get help. Start with your accountant.

Investing for Your Future

As a full-time, non-salaried artist, in any genre, you'll need a plan for the long-term just as any salaried employee in a corporation would. Health insurance is one issue. A retirement plan is another. Systematic savings (for a rainy day or for an emergency) should be a third.

Unfortunately, sources for health insurance are few and far between. Various unions offer plans to their members. Some service organizations, like Dance USA, are exploring affordable health-insurance alternatives, but probably only member companies could join such plans. When you obtain health insurance, remember that there is always strength in numbers, so look for service groups that support artists and might already have a plan that you can join. Also research Medical Savings Accounts, a tax-deferred way to help pay for health-care costs.

The IRS allows various retirement-plan payments (into specific accounts, such as IRAs, SEP-IRAs and Keogh plans) for non-salaried workers, providing tax deductions in the years when the contributions are made. See your accountant to discuss which plan is best for you.

For young people the news is good: even a small monthly investment will accumulate nicely by the time you hit 65 or so. Those who are older must invest more aggressively, and an investment advisor is likely to be a key player on your professional-service team. For non-salaried artists the key in all of these decisions is discipline. From every check received, you'll have to set aside tax dollars (for estimated quarterly tax payments), and you should set aside savings/investment dollars, too. If you establish a plan, set up the accounts, keep the paperwork simple and adhere to the discipline, the system will flourish.

Now all you have to do is dance!

PART FOUR

Bibliography & Resources

Bibliography & Resources

General

American Dance Portfolio, by Jack Mitchell. Dodd Mead, New York, 1964.

Ballet and Modern Dance: A Concise History, by Jack Anderson. Dance Horizons, New York, 1992.

Breaking Bounds: The Dance Photography of Lois Greenfield, by Lois Greenfield. Chronicle Books, New York, 1992.

Dance and Photography, by William A. Ewing. Henry Holt & Company, New York, 1987.

The Dance Directory, edited by Jane M. Bonbright. National Dance Association, Reston, VA, 1998.

The Dance Encyclopedia, by Anatole Chujoy and P.W. Manchester. Simon & Schuster, New York, 1978.

The Dance in America, by Walter Terry. Harper & Row, New York, 1956.

The Dancer's Heritage, by Ivon Guest. Dancing Times, London, 1960.

Dancers on Dancing, by Cynthia Lyle. Drake Publishers, New York, 1977.

Dances as Theater Art, by Selma Jeanne Cohen. Dodd, Mead, New York, 1974.

Dancing, by Ellen Jacob. Variety Arts, New York, 1993.

The Encyclopedia of Dance and Ballet, by Mary Clarke and David Vaughan. G.P. Putnam's Sons, East Rutherford, NJ, 1977.

Feeling and Form, by Suzanne Langer. Charles Scribner's Sons, New York, 1953.

Introduction to the Dance, by John Martin. Dance Horizons, New York, 1965.

The Language of Dance, by Mary Wigman. Wesleyan University Press, Middletown, CT, 1966.

Looking at the Dance, by Edwin Denby. Horizon Press, New York, 1968.

Men Dancing: Performers and Performances, by Alexander Bland and John Percival. Macmillan Publishing, New York, 1984.

Movement and Metaphor, by Lincoln Kirstein. Praeger, New York, 1971.

The New York Book of Dance, by Terry Trucco. City & Co., New York, 1996.

Peterson's Professional Degree Programs in the Visual and Performing Arts. Peterson's, Princeton, NJ, 1999.

Striking a Balance; Dancers Talk About Dancing, by Barbara Newman, Houghton Mifflin, Boston, 1982.

Time and the Dancing Image, by Deborah Jowitt. William Morrow & Company, New York, 1988.

To a Young Dancer, by Selma Jeanne Cohen. Little Brown and Company, Boston, 1962.

Ballet

A Very Young Dancer, by Jill Krementz. Alfred A. Knopf, New York, 1977.

The Ballerinas: From the Court of Louis XIV to Pavlova, by Parmenia Migel. Macmillan Publishing, New York, 1972.

Ballet: An Illustrated History, by Mary Clarke and Clement Crisp. Penguin Books, New York, 1992.

The Ballet Companion, by Walter Terry. Dodd, Mead, New York, 1968.

Baryshnikov at Work, by Mikhail Baryshnikov, edited by Charles France. Alfred A. Knopf, New York, 1977.

Basic Principles of Russian Ballet Technique, by Agrippina Vaganova. Dover Press, New York, 1969.

The Classic Ballet, by Lincoln Kirstein. University Press of Florida, Gainesville, 1998.

Classical Ballet Technique, by Gretchen Ward Warren, with photos by Susan Cook. University of South Florida Press, Tampa, FL, 1989.

Dance to the Piper & Promenade Home, by Agnes de Mille. Da Capo, New York, 1980.

Dancing Women: Female Bodies on Stage, by Sally Banes. Routledge, New York, 1998.

I Remember Balanchine: Recollections of the Ballet Master by Those Who Knew Him, by Francis Macon. Doubleday, New York, 1991.

Nijinsky Dancing, by Lincoln Kirstein. Alfred A. Knopf, New York, 1975.

101 Stories of the Great Ballets, by George Balanchine and Francis Macon. Anchor/Doubleday, Garden City, NY, 1989.

Modern Dance

The Art of Making Dances, by Doris Humphrey. Grove Press, New York, 1959.

The Art of the Dance, by Isadora Duncan. Theater Arts, New York, 1977.

Blood Memory, by Martha Graham. Doubleday, New York, 1992.

Don McDonagh's Complete Guide to Modern Dance, by Don McDonagh, Popular Library, New York, 1977.

Martha: The Life and Work of Martha Graham, by Agnes de Mille. Random House, New York, 1956, 1991.

The Modern Dance: Seven Statements of Belief, by Selma Jeanne Cohen. Wesleyan University Press, Middletown, CT, 1966.

Private Domain, by Paul Taylor. Alfred A. Knopf, New York, 1987.

Terpsichore in Sneakers: Post-Modern Dance, by Sally Barnes. Houghton Mifflin, New York, 1980.

Index

Index

General Index

A.C., 122

Academic education, importance to dancers, 134-35

Academic programs, 10. See also Academic Programs Index; financial aid, 180-81; special advice on, 35-36

Accost, Carlos Jr., 92

Actor's Equity Association, 32

Adams, Carolyn, 36, 125

Adams, Diana, 111

Adventures In Movement for the Handicapped, 25

Affruntti, Frank, 89

African American Dance Ensemble, 74

African Heritage Center for African Dance, 25

African/African-American Dance Festival, 175

Afterimages, 176

Alabama Repertory Dance Theatre, 39

Alegado, Joe, 164

Alexander Institute, 61

Alexander technique, 68, 99, 153

Aliev, Eldar, 87

Allan, David, 45, 55

Alonso, Alicia, 17

Amateur performers, 21

American ballet style, 18

American Ballet Theatre, 39

American College Dance Festival, 148, 164

American College Dance Festival Association, 25

American Dance Festival, 63, 138

American Dance Guild, 25

American Dance Legacy Institute, 25, 145

American Dance Therapy Association, 25-26, 82, 113-14

American Federation of Musicians, 32

American Federation of Television and Radio Artists, 32

American Guild of Musical Artists, 32

American Guild of Variety Artists, 32

American Repertory Ballet, 117

American Society of Russian Style Ballet, 26

American Spirit Dance Company, 148

Amherst College, 99-100

Anastos, Peter, 74

Andersen, Bambi, 72

Anderson, Charles, 48

Anderson, Christopher, 48

Anderson, Melanie, 106

Andrew W. Mellon Foundation, 145

Andrian, Ruth, 157

Angelini, Marcello, 149

Ann Arbor Dance Works, 107

Apprentice programs, 10, 114. *See also* Internships and Apprentice Programs Index

Arey, Dana, 154

Arias, Alberto, 84

Arnold, Rebecca, 97

Arova, Dame Sonia, 39, 51

Artist-in-residence programs, 10. *See also* Residential and Artist-in-Residence Programs Index

Asakawa, Takako, 150

Attaway, Larry, 88

Auditioning, 163

Bahr, Jill Eathorne, 158

Balanchine, George, 16, 18, 19, 70, 124, 133, 162

Balanchine Trust, 85, 152

Ballet, 18-19

Ballet Arizona, 43

Ballet Chicago, 85

Ballet dancers, programs for, 39-81, 84-127, 132-33, 135-36, 139-68, 170-77

Ballet Florida, 69

Ballet Hispanico, 19

Ballet Internationale, 87

Ballet New England, 115

Ballet Oklahoma, 149

Ballet South, 39

Ballet West Conservatory, 167-68

Ballet Yuma, 44

Barnes, Clive, 102, 162

Barnett, Robert, 75

Baroque dance, 20

Bartenieff, Irmgard, 127

Bartenieff technique, 68

Baryshnikov, Mikhail, 58, 91, 116, 122, 169

Baton Rouge Ballet Theatre, 92

Beaufort, Zanne, 76

Beck, William, 123

Bedford, John, 148

Benichou, Pascual, 79
Benjamin, Fred, 137
Bennett, Michael, 19
Beppu, Romi, 80
Berman, Joanna, 49
Berry, April, 142
Bertini, Peter, 157
Bessy, Mme. Claude, 62
Bickmore, Rex, 68
Black Dance Conference, 55
Black, Phil, 122
Blair, Patricia, 85
Blunden, Jeraldyne, 143
Boft, George, 142
Bolender, Todd, 111
Bolshoi Ballet Academy, 61
Bonnefoux, Jean-Pierre, 116, 122
Borak, Andrea, 104
Borealis Dancers, 41
Boross, Bob, 92
Bosman, Petrus, 172
Boston Ballet Company, 105
Boston Ballet II, 98
Boston Summer Dance Festival, 103
Brandt, Kristen, 154
Brendel, Janie, 119
Brown, Trisha, 130
Bruce, Billy, 142
Buchmann, Molly, 92
Bujones, Fernando, 98, 166
Buraczeski, Danny, 94
Burke, Dermot, 143
Burman, Julie, 85
Burmann, Wilhelm, 137
Burn, Malcolm, 170
Business of dance, 163, 179-86
Buson, Daniela, 149
Butler Ballet, 87

Cafarella, Doreen, 114
Cammack, Richard and Zola, 47-48
Campaneria, Miguel, 151
Cantwell, Donald and Patricia, 158
Capoeira, 83
Carboneau, Suzanne, 170
Career development: becoming a
    dancer, 16-22; becoming a profes-
    sional, 20-21; freelancing, 184;
    getting started, 182-83; marketing
    yourself, 183; networking, 183;
    pricing your work, 184; remaining
    an amateur, 21
Career Transitions for Dancers, 26
Carnegie Museums, 153
Carpenter, Larry, 87
Carreno, Jose Manuel, 88

Caton, Edward, 95
Cecchetti, Enrico, 104
Cecchetti method, 73, 104
Celestin, Denise, 91
Cesbron, Jacques, 88
Chamber Dance, 174
Chaplin, Tarin, 136
Chapman, Marcia, 108
Chapman, Wes, 39
Chatfield, Steven, 152
Chen, Yan, 48
Chernova, Alla, 73
Chiao-Ping, Li, 176
Chicago City Ballet, 85
Chicago Dance Coalition, 26
Chicago Festival Ballet, 86-87
Choreographers, programs for, 39-40,
    42-57, 59-128, 130-60, 164-67, 169-
    73, 175-77; software programs for,
    145, special advice for, 183-84
Choreography, 20
Chouinard Art Institute, 46
Chouteau, Yvonne, 150
Christensen, William F., 168
Cincinnati Ballet, 146, 147
Cisneros, Evelyn, 48
Citydance, 98
Clark, Carolyn, 116
Classical technique, 18
Cleveland Ballet, 145
Cloudgate, 112
Clouser, James, 60
Cochran, Mary, 50
Cohan, Muriel, 90
The College at Lincoln Center, 121
Colorado Ballet, 57, 177
Colton, Ron, 76
Condon, Karl, 160
Congress on Research in Dance, 26
Conover, Warren, 139
Conte, Lou, 84
Coppola, Tony, 177
Cordell, Fanchon, 139
Corey, Winthrop, 78
Corpus Christi Ballet, 164
Craig, Jennifer, 151
Craske, Margaret, 104
Cravey, Claudia, 69
Creach, Terry, 169
Crockett, Leslie, 49
Cropley, Eileen, 82
Crosby, Jill Flanders, 41
Culpo, Madeline Cantarella, 104
Cunningham, Merce, 16, 17, 130
Cunningham technique, 107, 115
Curran, Sean, 153, 158

Curtis, Paul E. Jr., 53

Da Costa, Mohamed, 74
D'Adarrio, Edith, 106
Dakin, Christine, 60, 107, 128
Dalis, Irene, 54
Dallas Dance Council, 26
Dance Alabama!, 39
Dance Archives: a practical manual for documenting and preserving the ephemeral art, 145
Dance Connecticut, 67
Dance crazes, 83
Dance educators, programs for, 80, 81, 137-38, 156-57, 159
The Dance Ensemble, 46
Dance Forum, 129
Dance Heritage Coalition, 27, 145
Dance history scholars, programs for, 57
Dance Machine, 47
Dance marketplace, 163
Dance in Medicine, 74
Dance Notation Bureau, 27
Dance preservation, 144-45
Dance Professionals Associates, Ltd., 27
Dance Research Journal, 156
Dance schools, special advice on, 34
Dance Space, 123, 127
Dance Theater of Harlem, 76, 124
Dance Theatre Workshop, 27, 129
Dance therapy: programs for, 25-26, 81-82, 103-4, 113-14
Dance-Makers in the Schools, 131
Dance/USA, 27-28, 186
DANCEASPEN, 57
Dancers Responding to AIDS, 28
Danielson, Alan, 127
Danscore, 135
Danseur Development Project, 77
Danspace, 28, 129
Dante, Sharon, 64
D'Antuono, Eleanor, 116
Darvash, Madame Gabriela, 122
Davis, Chuck, 74
Davis, Kelli Wicke, 157
Day, Mary, 68
Dayton Contemporary Dance Company, 143, 147
de la Pena, George, 63
De Mille, Agnes, 107-8
de Ribere, Lisa, 116
de Saa, Margarita, 153
de Warren, Robert, 73
Dean, Laura, 68

Dean Lesher Regional Center for the Arts, 48
Delanghe, Gay, 107
Delaware Ballet, 67
Delta Festival Ballet, 93
DeYoung, Bill, 107
Dickinson College, 152
Disabled individuals, classes for, 111-12, 117
Dishong, Zola, 48
Disney, Walt, 46
Diversity Artists Project, 74
Dobson-Kage, Deborah, 167
Documenting dance, 144-45
Dokoudovsky, Ludmila, 110
Dolid, Laura Gurdus, 95
Donald W. Reynolds Foundation, 113
Donnellan, Eimir, 166
Dorathi Bock Pierre Program for Ballet Studies, 55
Dow, Simon, 137
Dowell, Heather, 48
Drulis, Diane, 67
DuBoulay, Christine, 85
Duell, Daniel, 85
Duke University, 138
Duncan, Isadora, 18
Dunham technique, 120
Dunn, Douglas, 165
Dunning, Jennifer, 77, 152

Ebitz, Gerard, 72
Edwards, Donn, 150
Elam, Lyn, 167
Elkins, Doug, 68, 94
Emergency Fund for Student Dancers, 28
Erlon, Suzanne, 96
Estey, Audree, 117
Esther Boyer College of Music, Temple University, 156
Ethnic dance, 19
Ethnic dancers, programs for, 50-51, 54-56, 59, 62-64, 67-68, 72-73, 74, 76-77, 82, 84-85, 96-97, 99-102, 104, 117, 119, 120-22, 124, 133-35, 142, 161
Evans, Bill, 119
Everett Center for the Performing Arts, 124
Evolving Arts, 123
Expressive Therapies Program, 103
Eylar, Patti, 85

Fagan, Garth, 133-34
Farber, Viola, 130
Farley, Ginger, 84

Fatouros, Sophia, 116
Feldenkrais technique, 68
Fenley, Molissa, 50
Festivals, 11. *See also* Workshops and Festivals Index
Fields, Allen, 109
Financial aid, 12, 180-83
Fischbach, Erika, 79
Flagg, Laura, 149
Flamenco, 115
Florida Dance Association, 28
Floyd, Dorothy, 159-60
Fokine, Michel, 68
Folk dance, 20
Fonteyn, Margot, 17
Fordham University, 121
Fosse, Bob, 19
Foster, Rory, 81
Foundation Center, 180
Franklin, Frederic, 124
Freelancing, 184-85
Frei, Susan, 149
Funk dancers, programs for, 103
Fusillo, Lisa, 112

Gamble, John, 141
Gammage Center for the Arts, 42
Gardner, Robert, 109
Gary Palmer Dance Company, 54
Geber, Pamela, 151-52, 174
Gentle Movement/Release, 131
George Balanchine Foundation, 145
Giacobbe, Leona and Lawrence, 93
Gilbert, Alicia, 104
Gilreath, Nena, 76
Giordano, Gus, 84, 106
Giordano, Nan, 84
Girshov, Natasha, 116
Gitelman, Claudia, 118
Glazer, Susan, 156-57
Goddertz, Charles, 137
Goh, Choo San, 68
Gold, Stuart, 50
Golovine, Serge, 62
Goodheart, Ami, 119
Gordon, David, 130
Gotheiner, Zvi, 119
Grace, Jasmine, 170
Graham, Martha, 17, 70, 128
Graham technique, 60, 65, 107, 115, 143
Gray, Acia, 165
Gregory, Cynthia, 98
Guerard, Leo, 97
Guidi, Ronn, 50
Gulyaeva, Luba, 116

Gutierrez, Haydee, 150-51

Hale, Marie, 69
Hambrick, General, 177
Hamburg, Janet, 90
Hampshire College, 99-100
Han, Kee-Juan, 43
Hancock, Jeff, 84
Harkarvy, Benjamin, 125-26
Harkness Dance Center, 120
Harlem Dance Foundation, 28
Harley, Martine, 164
Harnack, Curtis, 134-35
Harris, Rennie, 94
Hartford Ballet, 43, 64
Hartt School, University of Hartford, 65
Harvey, Cynthia, 49
Hatchett, Frank, 122
Haubert, Alaine, 78, 79
Hawaii State Ballet, 79-80
Hawk, Heather, 85
Hawkins, Erick, 17
Hay, Deborah, 167
Hayden, Melissa, 139
Hayes, Elizabeth R., 168
Herklotz, John, 55
Hilding, Jerel, 90
Hill, Martha, 125, 169
Hilliker, Rebecca, 177
Hip-hop, 83; programs for, 48
Hirabayshi, Kazuko, 136
Ho, Michael, 62
Holcombe, Kelly, 112
Holladay, David, 154
Holm, Hanya, 70
Holmes, Anna-Marie, 98, 105
Holmes, Lester, 95
Hoover, Darla, 152
Horton technique, 122, 143
Houk, Benjamin, 162
How to Dance Forever, 17
Howard, David, 85, 95, 122
Hubbard, Karen, 140
Hubbard Street Dance Chicago, 84
Huh, In-Jung, 136
Humphrey, Doris, 34, 69, 182
Humphrey-Weidman technique, 60, 127
Huskey, Sybil, 140

Ichino, Yoko, 142
Icons, 11
Images of American Dance: Preserving a Cultural Heritage, 145
Incorporation, 185

Information display format, 11-12
Ingram, Kenny, 85
Injury prevention, 124
Interarts and Technology (IATECH), 176
Interlochen Arts Academy, 105
Internships, 10
Irish step dancing, 19, 83, 166
Isadora-Duncan technique, 120
Ives, Charles, 21

Jacob, Judy, 170
Jacob's Pillow, 102
James Sewell Ballet, 109
Jasinski, Roman, 149
Jazz Dance Festival, 43-44
Jazz dancers, programs for, 39-44, 48, 52-56, 59-60, 62-64, 67- 69, 72-74, 76-82, 84, 88-93, 96-108, 114-15, 117-23, 128, 142-44, 156-57, 159, 161, 164-66, 171-73
Jazz dancing, 19
Jefferson, Denise, 150
Jhung, Finis, 78, 122
Joffrey, Robert, 106
Johnson, C. Nicolas, 91
Johnson, Pamela, 161
Johnson, Patrick, 106
Johnson, Virginia, 68
Jones, Alun, 91
Jones, Betty, 79, 127
Jones, Bill T., 44
Jones, Mark, 58
Jones, Susan, 88
Jonson, Nina, 140
Jowitt, Deborah, 120
Joyce Theater, 129
Judson Church, 131
The Juilliard School, 105, 126

Kage, Jonas, 167
Kahlich, Dr. Luke, 156
Kaiser, Daniel, 67
Kane, Julie, 112
Kaufmann, Karen, 111
Keating, Jill, 123
Keener, David, 172
Kelley, Chuck, 122
Kellman, Joy, 63
Kennedy, Linda, 118
Kent, Julie, 88
King, Alonzo, 53
Kinzie, Allan, 150, 164
Kirstein, Lincoln, 17, 18, 124, 133
Kisselgoff, Anna, 18, 102
Kitchen, 129

Klooke, Gretchen, 85
Klopp, Ellie, 50
Knapp, Debra, 87
Knight, Marsha Fay, 177
Koff, Susan, 137
Kopp, Leslie Hansen, 145
Krassovska, Nathalie, 73
Kriegsman, Alan, 94

Laban/Bartenieff Institute of Movement Studies, 28-29, 127, 151
Labanotation, 125, 127, 165
Laeger, Theresa, 39
Landovsky, John, 79-80
Lane, Sharee, 167
Langer, Susanne K., 17
Lanteri, Joe, 137
Larkin, Moscelyne, 149
Laurent, Stephan, 87
Lavender, Larry, 119
Lawson, Cristyne, 46
Leeth, Arthur, 158
LeGere, Mary, 140
Lerman, Liz, 63, 94
Leroy, Pascale, 48
Levy, Monica, 65
Lewis, Daniel, 72, 92
Lewitsky, Bella, 49, 106, 107
Lewtchenko, Natalya, 63
Lexington Ballet, 91-92
Limón Dance Company, 127
Limón, José, 70, 72, 83
Limón technique, 79, 107, 115, 119, 127
Linn, Irene, 160
Lionel Hampton School of Music, 81
Loew, Cornelius, 107
Lomax, Sondra, 167
London, Peter, 72
Long, Larry, 85
Los Angeles Conservatory of Music, 46
Lubovitch, Lar, 70
Lucas, Cynthia, 49
Lucas, Waverly, 76-77
Ludin, Fritz, 79
Lugnasin, Alden, 63
Luigi, 128
Lynch, Molly, 45

McCullogh, Susan, 139
McCullough, Rick, 141
MacDonald, Annette, 54
McDonald, Bradon, 66
MacDougal, Lorn, 117-18
McFall, John, 75

McKayle, Donald, 55, 69
McKenzie, Kevin, 68, 120
McKerrow, Amanda, 68
McLaughlin, John J., 164
McWilliams, Teresa Wylie, 91
Mader, Arnott, 170
Malaty, Jean-Philippe, 59
Marceau, Marcel, 91
Marine Corps Troupers, 84
Markham, Diane, 139
Marks, Bruce, 98, 105
Marks, Victoria, 56
Marriott Center for Dance, 168
Marta, Cecilia, 122
Martha Knoebel Dance Theatre, 47
Martin, John, 16
Martins, Peter, 120, 133, 134
Maryland Arts Festival, 97
Mason Gross School of the Arts, 117
Massine, Leonide, 112
Masson, Gabe, 157
Masterclasses, 180
Mateo, José, 97
Mathews, Fred, 54
Mathews, Sharon, 92
Mathis, Bonnie, 108
Mauzy, Perry, 158
Maxwell, Liz, 46
Maynard, Parrish, 115
Maynor, Dorothy, 124
Mazzarelli, Victoria, 64
Mazzo, Kay, 133
Meehan, John, 88
Meglin, Dr. Joellen, 156
Mertz, Elizabeth, 80
Middle Eastern Culture and Dance
    Association, 29
Miller, Bebe, 94
Miller, Linda Garner, 169
Mind Over Matter, 171
Minnesota Ballet, 109
Minnesota Dance Alliance, 29
Mitchell, Arthur, 124
Mitchell, Ruth, 78
Mitoma, Judy, 56
MMus, 171
Modern dance, 17-18
Modern Dance in a Post Modern World,
    141
Modern dancers, programs for, 39-44,
    46-47, 49-57, 59-61, 63-70, 72-82, 84-
    112, 114-15, 117-23, 125-27, 132-36,
    139-44, 147-48, 150-52, 154-59, 164-
    77
Modern Repertory Dance Theatre,
    150

Monk, Meredith, 68
Moore, James, 176
Moore, Rachel, 97
Morales, Hilda, 111
Morgan, Clyde, 134
Morgan, Robin Sherertz, 51
Morgan, Victoria, 146
Moritel, Fred, 166
Morris, Mark, 172
Mossbrucker, Tom, 59
Movement therapy, programs for, 111-
    12, 113-14
Mt. Holyoke College, 99-100
Muirhead, Juliana, 97
Multimedia Prototype, 144
Munoz, Roberto, 154
Munro, Cristina, 164
Musical theater, 19
Myers, Martha, 63, 138
Myers, Milton, 60, 137

Nagrin, Daniel, 17
Nahat, Dennis, 145
Nash, Matthew, 40
Nat Horne Style, 143
National Association of Schools of
    Dance, 29, 140, 162, 176
National Dance Association, 29
National Dance Council of America,
    29-30
National Endowment for the Arts, 16;
    Dance Program, 145
National Museum of Dance, 30
National Performance Network, 129
Neal, Philip, 115
Neighborhood Performance Center,
    153
Neil, Delia, 140-41
Neill, Jeannette, 103
Nevada Ballet Theatre, Youth Com-
    pany, 113
New Orleans Youth Ballet, 93
New Performing Theater, 118
New World School of the Arts, 72-74
New York City Ballet, 18-19, 133
Nicholas Music Center, 118
Nicolay, Dana Eugene, 164
Nikolais, Alwin, 70, 89
Nissenen, Mikko, 49
Nixon, David, 142
Noble, Duncan, 139
Norman, Leona, 49
Nureyev, Rudolf, 51, 58
Nutmeg Ballet, 64

O'Day, Kevin, 84

Ohman, Frank, 115
Okada, Kimi, 50
Oklahoma Festival Ballet, 150
Open Performances, 131
Oregon Ballet, 150-51
Organizations for dancers, 24-33
Orr, Terrence S., 154
Otto, Phillip, 173
Owen, Norton, 102
Owens, Michael, 137

Page, Ruth, 85
Palmer, Gary, 54
Pap, Andrew, 157
Parker, Stephanie Rae, 124
Patrick, Josef, 84
Peck, Leslie, 88
Pell grants, 181
Penn, Jane, 52-53
Pennsylvania Ballet, 155
Pentacle, 30
Pepper, Cynthia, 49
Pereyaslavec, Valentina, 95
Perra, Lenette, 160
Perry, Igal, 132
Perry, Sue, 41
Pestov, Pytor, 62
Peterson, Lisa, 173
Petipa, Marius, 18, 68
Petrutiu, Vasile, 73
Philadelphia Dance Alliance, 30
Phipps, Sarah, 80
Physical therapy, 52-53
Piece, Nancy Ropelewski, 104
Pilates Center, 61
Pilates instruction, 43, 88, 89-90, 123,
    124, 152, 160, 172
"PillowTalks," 101
Pimble, Toni, 81
Pitts, Bryan, 149
Pittsburgh Ballet Theatre, 153
Pittsburgh Dance Council, 30
Pizzuto, William, 115
Plastino, Janice, 45
Pliesetskaya, Maya, 17
Pons, Denise, 99
Poole, Dennis, 146
Preobajenska, Olga, 110
Preserve, Inc., 30-31, 144-45
Preventive therapy, 52-53
Princess Grace Foundation, 66
Private teachers, 10-11. See also Studio
    Schools and Private Teachers
    Programs Index
Professional Dance Teachers Associa-
    tion, 31

Pugh, Dorothy Gunther, 160
Purchase Dance Corps, 136

Quigley, Colin, 56

Rae Dance, 124
Ragsdale, Amy, 111-12
Rainer, Yvonne, 130
Raleigh Dance Theatre, 140
Ramirez, Tina, 121
Raphael, Brett, 62
Rapp, Richard, 133
Rein, Richard A., 115
Reinhart, Charles, 102
Reiss, Noel, 141
Reiter, Liz, 148
Reitz, Dana, 169
Renaissance II, 125
Repertory Dance Theatre, 168
Residential and artist-in-residence
    programs, 10. See also Residential
    and Artist-in-Residence Programs
Retirement plans, 186
Richardson, Desmond, 21
Ririe-Woodbury Dance Company, 168
Riverdance, 19, 86
Robards, Kim, 60
Robbins, Jerome, 19
Robinson, Cleo Parker, 59
Robinson, Gregory, 143
Robinson, LaVaughn, 157
Rodey Theatre, 118-19
Rodriguez, Jon, 147-48
Romantic style, 18
Rommett, Zena, 137
Rousseve, David, 56
Rowan, Jo, 148
Rudner, Sara, 169
Russell, Francia, 173
Russo, Karen, 143

Sage Cowles Land Grant Chair, 110
Saland, Stephanie, 173
Saleem, Khalid, 134
San Francisco Ballet School, 47
San Jose Cleveland Ballet, 145
Sandel, Kay, 148
Sandonato, Barbara, 157
Sanford, Lathan, 167
Sankofa, 134, 135
Sapienza, Robb, 122
Sappington, Margo, 84
Sarazin, Anamarie, 99
Sawyer, Elizabeth, 136
Scanlon, Jennifer, 99
Schaffenburg, Nancy, 154

School of American Dance and Arts Management, 148
Schorer, Suki, 48, 85
Schultze, Denise, 62
Schuman, William, 125
Scottsdale Center for the Arts, 42
Screen Actors Guild, 32-33
Second Avenue Dance, 131
Seravalli, Rosanna, 136
The Shapes of Change, 144
Shapiro and Smith, 70
Sharir Dance Company, 167
Sharir, Yacov, 167
Shawn, Ted, 70, 100, 102
Shelburne, Norman, 41
Shenandoah Chamber Dance Company, 171
Shenandoah Dance Ensemble, 171
Shields, Susan, 170
Shook, Karel, 124
Siegal, Marcia B., 86, 144
Sills, Bettijane, 136
Silva, Donna, 99
Simonson, Lynn, 123
Simonson technique, 123
Singleton, Trinette, 78
Skinner, Randy, 137
Smith, Amanda, 106
Smith College, 99-100
Smith, Frank, 139
Smuin, Michael, 48
Snider, Susan, 89
Snowy Range Summer Dance Festival, 177
Society of Dance History Scholars, 31, 156
Society of Stage Directors and Choreographers, 33, 184
Sofras, Pamela, 141
Sokolow, Anna, 69
South of SoHo, 159
Spanish dance, programs for, 117
Sparling, Peter, 107
Splinters & Shards, 40
Spriggs, Linda, 82
Stalder, Margaret, 177
Starr, Helen, 91
Steinberg, Risa, 127
Steivel, Bruce, 113
Steps on Broadway, 121, 136-37
Stevens Arts Center, 139
Stevens, Kristen, 142
Stevenson, Ben, 162
Stinson, Sue, 141
Stoddart, Amy, 152
Stolet, Jeffrey, 152

Story, Sharon, 76
Stowell, Kent, 173
Strand, Deirdre, 165
Student Dance Coalition, 110
Student loans, 181
Studies Project, 131
Studio Maestro, 128
Studio schools and private teachers, 10-11. *See also* Studio Schools and Private Teachers Index
Sulich, Vassili, 112-13
Sultzbach, Russell, 85
Summer programs, special advice on, 33-34
Sund, Robert, 45
Sutherland, Paul, 116
Sutowski, Thor, 51
Suzeau, Patrick, 90
Swiadon, Lynda, 69
Swindlehurst, Deirdre Duffin, 104

Tallchief, Maria, 85
Tap dancers, programs for, 40, 41, 48, 52-53, 56, 59-60, 62-64, 67-69, 74-76, 78, 80-81, 84, 89-90, 92-93, 103, 109-11, 114, 119-21, 142, 147-49, 161, 164-66, 171, 176-77
Tap dancing, 19
Tassone, Ron, 155
Tate, Patricia, 177
Tatum, Milton, 161
Taxes, 185
Taylor, David, 60
Taylor, Mark, 153
Taylor, Paul, 132, 165
Tcherkassky, Marianna, 154
Ted Shawn Theatre, 101
Tennessee Children's Dance Ensemble, 159-60
Terekov, Miguel, 150
Terricciano, Alan, 55
Texas Clogging Council, 31
Texas Education Association, 166
Tharp, Twyla, 17, 58, 68, 84
Theater dancers, programs for, 103
Thomas, Nasha, 165
Thomas, Pat, 157
Thompson, Basil, 175
Thompson, Liz, 7, 101, 102
Thompson, Marjorie, 173
Thompson, Mary, 97
Time-release programs, 68-69
Tokunaga, Yatsuko, 99
Tomal, George, 116
Tomasson, Helgi, 51
Tomlinson, Mel, 158

Toole, Renee William, 76
Training styles: American, 97, 146; Danish, 146; English, 43; French, 146; Italian, 93, 146; Russian, 26, 93, 95, 118, 146, 173
Tremaine, Joe, 48
Trump, Chrystelle, 95
Tudor, Antony, 69
Tyler School of Art, Temple University, 156

United Scenic Artists, 33
United States Amateur Ballroom Dancers Association, 31
University Dance Company, 97
University Dance Theatre, 110
University of Hartford, Hartt School, 65
University of Massachusetts, Amherst, 99-100
University Research Park, 141
Utah Ballet, 168
Uthoff, Michael, 43

Vaganova method, 18, 43, 73, 98, 115, 153
Van Dyke, Jan, 141
Van Swoll, Janet, 54
Vandestienne, Nicole, 132
Verdy, Violette, 48, 70, 88, 106
Vickery, Robert, 153
Villella, Edward, 71, 116
Vinton, Deborah, 73
Vivona, Diane, 116
von Heidecke, Kenneth, 86-87
Vorus, Ann, 140

Wagoner, Dan, 63
Walker Arts Center, 109-10
Walker, Carol, 136
Walker, Chet, 122
Walker, Suzanne, 148
Walton, Fred, 123
Wang, Jian, 48
Watanabe, June, 50
Weary, Marcia Dale, 152
Weber, Septima, 68
Weidman, Charles, 70
Wellesley College, 104
Wells, Bruce, 173
West Side Story, 19
Western Psychiatric Institute and Clinic, 154
White, David, 129
White, John, 153
White, Pamela, 148

Wigman, Mary, 16
Wildberger, Kathy, 123
Williams, Ann, 161
Williams, Anthony, 114
Williams, Stanley, 133
Wilson, Robin Marie, 107
Wingert, Deborah, 111
Winslett, Stoner, 170
Wishinski, Melissa, 65, 66
Wood, Reagan, 118
Woodson, Amanda Thom, 95
Workshops and festivals, 11. *See also* Workshops and Festivals Index
Wright, Mathew, 79
Wynn, Kevin, 94, 136

Yagudin, Shamil, 78
Yoshimura, Catherine, 142
Young Dancer's Summer Workshop, 98
Young, Gayle, 136
Youskevitch, Igor, 95
Youskevitch, Maria, 65, 170
Yuan, Tina, 46
Yukihiro, Ko, 150

Zalewski, Antoni, 110
Zane, Gred, 80
Zide-Booth, Rochelle, 87-88
Ziemann-DeVos, Michele, 77
Zollar, Jawole Willa Jo, 69, 74

Dance Programs

550 Broadway Dance, 119
92nd Street Y–Harkness Dance Center, 120
Academy of Ballet Florida, 69
Academy of Ballet Internationale, 87
Academy of Ballet Theatre of New Mexico, 118
Academy of Colorado Ballet, 57
Academy of Dallas Black Dance Theatre, 161
The Ailey School, 120-121
Alabama School of Fine Arts, 39
Alaska Dance Theatre, 40
American Dance Festival, 138
American University, 67-68
Antioch New England, Graduate School, 113-14
Arizona State University, 42-43
Aspen Ballet, 59
Atlanta Ballet Centre for Dance Education, 75-76
Augusta Ballet School, 76
Ballet Academy East, 121

Ballet Arts Minnesota, 108-9
Ballet Center of St. Louis, 110-11
Ballet Hawaii, 78
Ballet Hispanico School of Dance, 121-22
Ballet Idaho Adademy of Dance, 80-81
Ballet Pacifica, 45
Ballet Theatre of Annapolis, 95
Ballet Theatre of Boston, 97-98
Ballet West Conservatory, 167-68
Ballethnic, 76-77
BalletMet Dance Academy, 142
Barat College, 81-82
Bates Dance Festival, 93-94
Bennington College, 169
Boston Ballet Center for Dance Education, 98
Boston Conservatory, 99
Broadway Dance Center, 122
Butler University, 87-88
California Ballet School, 45
California Institute of the Arts, 46
California State University–Long Beach, 47
Central Delaware Dance Academy, 67
Central Pennsylvania Youth Ballet, 152
Charleston Ballet School, 158
Chautauqua Institution, 122-23
Cleo Parker Robinson Dance Ensemble, 59
Columbia College, 159
Columbia College of Chicago, 82
Connecticut Ballet Center, 62
Connecticut College, 63
Contra Costa Ballet Centre, 47-48
Cornish College of the Arts, 172-73
Dance Alloy School, 153
Dance Center, 48
Dance Space, 123
Dance Theatre of Harlem, 124
Dancer's Workshop, 92-93
Dancers Studio, 159-60
Dances We Dance, 79
David Taylor Dance Theatre, 60
Dayton Ballet School, 142-43
Five College Dance Department, 99-100
Florida State University-Tallahassee, 69-70
Fort Worth School of Ballet, 162
George Mason University, 169-70
Georgia Ballet, 77-78
Giacobbe Academy of Dance, 93
Giordano Dance Center, 84
Goucher College, 95-96

Granite State Ballet, 114
Harid Conservatory, 70-71
Harlem School of the Arts, 124-25
Hartford Conservatory, 63-64
Honolulu Dance Theatre, 79
Houston Ballet Academy, 162-63
Indiana University, 88
Interlochen Center for the Arts, 105-6
Jacob's Pillow, 100-102
Jeannette Neill Dance Studio, 103
Jeraldyne's School of the Dance, 143
Juilliard School, 125-26
Juneau Dance Unlimited, 40
Kim Robards Dance, 60
Laban/Bartenieff Institute of Movement Studies, 127
Lesley College, 103-4
Limón Institute, 127
Lou Conte Dance Studio, 84
Louisville School of Ballet, 91
Luigi's Jazz Center, 128
Marin Ballet Center for Dance, 49
Martha Graham School of Contemporary Dance, 128
Memphis Concert Ballet School, 160
Merce Cunningham Studio, 130
Metropolitan Ballet Theatre and Academy, 96
Miami City Ballet School, 71
Mills College, 49-50
Milwaukee Ballet School, 175
Movement Research, 130-31
Munro Ballet Studios, 164
Nevada Ballet Theatre, 112-13
New Jersey Ballet School, 116
New World School of the Arts, 72-73
New York University–Tisch School of the Arts, 131-32
North Carolina School of the Arts, 139
North Star Ballet School, 41
Nutmeg Conservatory for the Arts, 64
Oakland Ballet Academy, 50
ODC Performance Gallery School, 50-51
Ohio State University, 143-44
Oklahoma City University, 148-49
Pacific Northwest Ballet School, 173
Paul Taylor School, 132
Pennsylvania Academy of Ballet, 153
Peridance Center, 132
Pittsburgh Ballet Theatre School, 154
Point Park College, 154-55
Portland School of Ballet, 94
Princeton Ballet School, 117
Raleigh School of Ballet, 140

Richmond Ballet Center for Dance, 170

Rock School of Pennsylvania Ballet, 155

Roger Williams University, 157-58

Rutgers University, 117-18

Ruth Mitchell Dance Studio, 78

Ruth Page Foundation School of Dance, 85

Sam Houston State University, 164-65

San Diego School of Ballet, 51

San Francisco Ballet School, 51-52

San Francisco Dance Center, 52-53

San Jose Dance Theatre, 53-54

San Jose State University, 54

School of Albany Berkshire Ballet, 104

School of American Ballet, 133

School of Ballet Arizona, 43

School of Ballet Chicago, 85

School of Ballet New England, 115

School of Ballet Oklahoma, 149

School of Cleveland San Jose Ballet, 145-46

School of Dance Connecticut, 65

School of Grand Rapids Ballet, 106

School of Hawaii State Ballet, 79-80

School of Nashville Ballet, 160-61

School of Oregon Ballet Theatre, 150-51

School of Sarasota Ballet, 73

School of Southern Ballet Theatre, 73-74

School of the Cincinnati Ballet, 146

School of the Lexington Ballet, 91-92

School of the Minnesota Ballet, 109

Shenandoah University, 171

Southern Methodist University, Meadows School of the Arts, 165

St. Paul's School, 115-16

Stanford University, 54-55

State Ballet School, 111

State University of New York–Brockport, 133-35

State University of New York-Purchase, 135-36

Steps on Broadway, 136-37

Tapestry Dance Company Academy, 165-66

Teachers College-Columbia University, 137

Temple University, 156

Tennessee Association of Dance, 161

Texas Christian University, 166

Towson University, 96-97

Trinity College, 65-67

Tulsa Ballet, 149

University of Alabama, 39-40

University of Alaska–Anchorage, 41

University of Arizona–Tucson, 43-44

University of Arkansas–Fayetteville, 44

University of California–Irvine, 55

University of California–Los Angeles, 56

University of California–Riverside, 57

University of Cincinnati, 146-47

University of Colorado-Boulder, 61

University of Florida College of Fine Arts, 74

University of Hawaii–Manoa, 80

University of Idaho, 81

University of Illinois, Urbana–Champaign, 86

University of Iowa, 88-89

University of Kansas, 90

University of Michigan, 107

University of Minnesota, 109-10

University of Montana, 111-12

University of Nebraska–Lincoln, 112

University of New Mexico, 118-19

University of North Carolina–Charlotte, 140-41

University of North Carolina–Greensboro, 141

University of Oklahoma, 150

University of Oregon, 151-52

University of South Florida, 74-75

University of Texas-Austin, 166-67

University of the Arts, 156-57

University of Utah, 168

University of Washington–Seattle, 174

University of Wisconsin–Madison, 175-76

University of Wisconsin–Stevens Point, 176

University of Wyoming, 177

Vail International Dance Festival, 61-62

Vine Street Ballet, 89-90

Virginia School of the Arts, 172

Von Heidecke's School of the Chicago Festival Ballet, 86-87

Walnut Hill School, 104-5

Washington School of Ballet, 68

Western Kentucky University, 92

Western Michigan University, 107-8

Wichita State University, 90-91

Wright State University, 147-48

Yuma Ballet Academy, 44

🏠 Academic Programs

Academy of Colorado Ballet, 57
The Ailey School, 120-121
Alabama School of Fine Arts, 39
American University, 67-68
Antioch New England, Graduate School, 113-14
Arizona State University, 42-43
Ballet West Conservatory, 167-68
Barat College, 81-82
Bennington College, 169
Boston Conservatory, 99
Butler University, 87-88
California Institute of the Arts, 46
California State University-Long Beach, 47
Chautauqua Institution, 122-23
Cleo Parker Robinson Dance Ensemble, 59
Columbia College, 159
Columbia College of Chicago, 82
Connecticut College, 63
Cornish College of the Arts, 172-73
Dance Theatre of Harlem, 124
Five College Dance Department, 99-100
Florida State University-Tallahassee, 69-70
George Mason University, 169-70
Goucher College, 95-96
Harid Conservatory, 70-71
Harlem School of the Arts, 124-25
Indiana University, 88
Interlochen Center for the Arts, 105-6
Juilliard School, 125-26
Laban/Bartenieff Institute of Movement Studies, 127
Lesley College, 103-4
Mills College, 49-50
Nevada Ballet Theatre, 112-13
New World School of the Arts, 72-73
New York University-Tisch School of the Arts, 131-32
North Carolina School of the Arts, 139
Ohio State University, 143-44
Oklahoma City University, 148-49
Point Park College, 154-55
Rock School of Pennsylvania Ballet, 155
Roger Williams University, 157-58
Rutgers University, 117-18
Sam Houston State University, 164-65
San Francisco Ballet School, 51-52
San Jose State University, 54
School of American Ballet, 133
School of Dance Connecticut, 65
Shenandoah University, 171
Southern Methodist University, Meadows School of the Arts, 165
St. Paul's School, 115-16
Stanford University, 54-55
State University of New York-Brockport, 133-34
State University of New York-Purchase, 135-36
Teachers College-Columbia University, 137-38
Temple University, 156
Texas Christian University, 168
Towson University, 96-97
Trinity College, 65-67
University of Alabama, 39-40
University of Alaska-Anchorage, 41
University of Arizona-Tucson, 43-44
University of Arkansas-Fayetteville, 44
University of California-Irvine, 55
University of California-Los Angeles, 56
University of California-Riverside, 57
University of Cincinnati, 146-47
University of Colorado-Boulder, 61
University of Florida College of Fine Arts, 74
University of Hawaii-Manoa, 80
University of Idaho, 81
University of Illinois-Urbana/Champaign, 86
University of Iowa, 88-89
University of Kansas, 90
University of Michigan, 107
University of Minnesota, 109-10
University of Montana, 111-12
University of Nebraska-Lincoln, 112
University of New Mexico, 118-19
University of North Carolina-Charlotte, 140-41
University of North Carolina-Greensboro, 141
University of Oklahoma, 150
University of Oregon, 151-52
University of South Florida, 74-75
University of Texas-Austin, 166-67
University of the Arts, 156-57
University of Utah, 168
University of Washington-Seattle, 174
University of Wisconsin-Madison, 175-76
University of Wisconsin-Stevens Point, 176
University of Wyoming, 177

Virginia School of the Arts, 172
Walnut Hill School, 104-5
Western Kentucky University, 92
Western Michigan University, 107-8
Wichita State University, 90-91
Wright State University, 147-48

 Internships and Apprentice Programs

Academy of Ballet Internationale, 87
Alaska Dance Theatre, 40
American Dance Festival
American University, 67-68
Arizona State University, 42-43
Ballet Arts Minnesota, 108-9
Ballet Theatre of Boston, 97-98
BalletMet Dance Academy, 142
Boston Ballet Center for Dance
    Education, 98
California Ballet School, 45
California State University–Long
    Beach, 47
Central Pennsylvania Youth Ballet,
    152
Charleston Ballet School, 158
Columbia College, 159
Contra Costa Ballet Centre, 47-48
Cornish College of the Arts, 172-73
Dance Theatre of Harlem, 124
Dancer's Workshop, 92-93
Dayton Ballet School, 142-43
Fort Worth School of Ballet, 162
George Mason University, 169-70
Georgia Ballet, 77-78
Giacobbe Academy of Dance, 93
Granite State Ballet, 114
Harlem School of the Arts, 124-25
Houston Ballet Academy, 162-63
Indiana University, 88
Interlochen Center for the Arts, 105-6
Jacob's Pillow, 100-102
Jeraldyne's School of the Dance, 143
Juneau Dance Unlimited, 40
Kim Robards Dance, 60
Lesley College, 103-4
Louisville School of Ballet, 91
Marin Ballet Center for Dance, 49
Memphis Concert Ballet School, 160
Merce Cunningham Studio, 130
Metropolitan Ballet Theatre and
    Academy, 96
Miami City Ballet School, 71
Mills College, 49-50
Milwaukee Ballet School, 175
Munro Ballet Studios, 164

Nevada Ballet Theatre, 112-13
New Jersey Ballet School, 116
New York University–Tisch School of
    the Arts, 131-32
North Carolina School of the Arts, 139
North Star Ballet School, 41
Nutmeg Conservatory for the Arts, 64
Ohio State University, 143-44
Oklahoma City University, 148
Pacific Northwest Ballet School, 173-
    74
Peridance Center, 132
Pittsburgh Ballet Theatre School, 154
Princeton Ballet School, 117
Raleigh School of Ballet, 140
Richmond Ballet Center for Dance,
    170
Rock School of Pennsylvania Ballet,
    155
Roger Williams University, 157
Rutgers University, 117
San Francisco Ballet School, 51-52
San Jose Dance Theatre, 53-54
School of Albany Berkshire Ballet, 104
School of American Ballet, 133
School of Ballet Chicago, 85
School of Ballet Oklahoma, 149
School of Dance Connecticut, 65
School of Hawaii State Ballet, 79-80
School of Oregon Ballet Theatre, 150-
    51
School of Southern Ballet Theatre, 73-
    74
School of the Cincinnati Ballet, 146
School of the Lexington Ballet, 91-92
Shenandoah University, 171
State Ballet School, 111
State University of New York–Pur-
    chase, 135
Trinity College, 65-67
University of Arizona–Tucson, 43-44
University of California–Irvine, 55
University of California–Los Angeles,
    56
University of Cincinnati, 146-47
University of Florida College of Fine
    Arts, 74
University of Idaho, 81
University of Iowa, 88-89
University of Kansas, 90
University of Michigan, 107
University of Minnesota, 109-10
University of North Carolina–Char-
    lotte, 140-41
University of North Carolina–Greens-
    boro, 141

University of Oklahoma, 150
University of Texas–Austin, 166-67
University of Utah, 168
University of Washington–Seattle, 174
Vine Street Ballet, 89-90
Western Michigan University, 107-8
Wright State University, 147-48
Yuma Ballet Academy, 44

⌂ Residential and Artist-in-Residence Programs

92nd Street Y–Harkness Dance
   Center, 120
Arizona State University, 42-43
Chautauqua Institution, 122-23
Jacob's Pillow, 100-102
Movement Research, 130-31
Towson University, 96

👣 Studio Schools and Private Teachers

550 Broadway Dance, 119
92nd Street Y–Harkness Dance
   Center, 120
Academy of Ballet Florida, 69
Academy of Ballet Internationale, 87
Academy of Ballet Theatre of New
   Mexico, 118
Academy of Dallas Black Dance
   Theatre, 161
Alaska Dance Theatre, 40
Aspen Ballet, 59
Atlanta Ballet Centre for Dance
   Education, 75-76
Augusta Ballet School, 76
Ballet Academy East, 121
Ballet Arts Minnesota, 108-9
Ballet Center of St. Louis, 110-11
Ballet Hawaii, 78
Ballet Hispanico School of Dance, 121-
   22
Ballet Idaho Adademy of Dance, 80-81
Ballet Pacifica, 45
Ballet Theatre of Annapolis, 95
Ballet Theatre of Boston, 97-98
Ballethnic, 76-77
BalletMet Dance Academy, 142
Boston Ballet Center for Dance
   Education, 98
Broadway Dance Center, 122
California Ballet School, 45
Central Delaware Dance Academy,
   67

Central Pennsylvania Youth Ballet,
   152
Charleston Ballet School, 158
Cleo Parker Robinson Dance Ensem-
   ble, 59
Connecticut Ballet Center, 62
Contra Costa Ballet Centre, 47-48
Dance Alloy School, 153
Dance Center, 48
Dance Space, 123
Dancer's Workshop, 92-93
Dancers Studio, 159-60
Dances We Dance, 79
David Taylor Dance Theatre, 60
Dayton Ballet School, 142-43
Fort Worth School of Ballet, 162
Georgia Ballet, 77-78
Giacobbe Academy of Dance, 93
Giordano Dance Center, 84
Granite State Ballet, 114
Hartford Conservatory, 63
Honolulu Dance Theatre, 79
Houston Ballet Academy, 162-63
Jeannette Neill Dance Studio, 103
Jeraldyne's School of the Dance, 143
Juneau Dance Unlimited, 40
Kim Robards Dance, 60
Laban/Bartenieff Institute of Move-
   ment Studies, 127
Limón Institute, 127
Lou Conte Dance Studio, 84
Louisville School of Ballet, 91
Luigi's Jazz Center, 128
Marin Ballet Center for Dance, 49
Martha Graham School of Contempo-
   rary Dance, 128
Memphis Concert Ballet School, 160
Merce Cunningham Studio, 130
Metropolitan Ballet Theatre and
   Academy, 96
Miami City Ballet School, 71
Milwaukee Ballet School, 175
Munro Ballet Studios, 164
New Jersey Ballet School, 116
New World School of the Arts, 72-73
North Star Ballet School, 41
Nutmeg Conservatory for the Arts, 64
Oakland Ballet Academy, 50
ODC Performance Gallery School, 50-
   51
Pacific Northwest Ballet School, 173
Paul Taylor School, 132
Pennsylvania Academy of Ballet, 153
Peridance Center, 132
Pittsburgh Ballet Theatre School, 154

Portland School of Ballet, 94
Princeton Ballet School, 117
Raleigh School of Ballet, 140
Richmond Ballet Center for Dance, 170
Ruth Mitchell Dance Studio, 78
Ruth Page Foundation School of Dance, 85
San Diego School of Ballet, 51
San Francisco Dance Center, 52-53
San Jose Dance Theatre, 53-54
School of Albany Berkshire Ballet, 104
School of Ballet Arizona, 43
School of Ballet Chicago, 85
School of Ballet New England, 115
School of Ballet Oklahoma, 149
School of Cleveland San Jose Ballet, 145-46
School of Grand Rapids Ballet, 106
School of Hawaii State Ballet, 79-80
School of Nashville Ballet, 160-61
School of Oregon Ballet Theatre, 150-51
School of Sarasota Ballet, 73
School of Southern Ballet Theatre, 73-74
School of the Cincinnati Ballet, 146
School of the Lexington Ballet, 91-92
School of the Minnesota Ballet, 109
State Ballet School, 111
Steps on Broadway, 136-37
Tapestry Dance Company Academy, 165-66
Vine Street Ballet, 89-90
Von Heidecke's School of the Chicago Festival Ballet, 86-87
Washington School of Ballet, 68
Yuma Ballet Academy, 44

 Workshops and Festivals

Academy of Dallas Black Dance Theatre, 161
Alaska Dance Theatre, 40
American Dance Festival, 138
Antioch New England, Graduate School, 113-14

Ballet Arts Minnesota, 108-9
Ballet Hispanico School of Dance, 121
Bates Dance Festival, 93-94
Boston Ballet Center for Dance Education, 98
Charleston Ballet School, 158
Chautauqua Institution, 122-23
Connecticut College, 63
Dance Space, 123
Dance Theatre of Harlem, 124
David Taylor Dance Theatre, 60
Indiana University, 88
Interlochen Center for the Arts, 105-6
Jacob's Pillow, 100-102
Jeannette Neill Dance Studio, 103
Kim Robards Dance, 60
Laban/Bartenieff Institute of Movement Studies, 127
Limón Institute, 127
Milwaukee Ballet School, 175
Movement Research, 130-31
ODC Performance Gallery School, 50-51
Paul Taylor School, 132
Rock School of Pennsylvania Ballet, 155
Rutgers University, 117-18
Ruth Mitchell Dance Studio, 78
School of Ballet New England, 115
School of Dance Connecticut, 65
School of Nashville Ballet, 160-61
Tapestry Dance Company Academy, 165-66
Tennessee Association of Dance, 161
Tulsa Ballet, 149-50
University of Alabama, 39-40
University of Arizona–Tucson, 43-44
University of Florida College of Fine Arts, 74
University of Kansas, 90
University of South Florida, 74-75
University of Texas–Austin, 166-67
University of Wyoming, 177
Vail International Dance Festival, 61-62
Western Michigan University, 107-8

About the Author

ARK W. JONES'S CAREER encompasses work with a wide variety of dance and arts organizations. He is currently the executive director and producer of the Limón Dance Company, America's oldest repertory company. After joining Limón in 1992, he restructured its operations to include commissioning new dances, preserving dance masterworks, international touring and developing two homes for the company in New York and Silicon Valley.

Jones began his dance management career at the Pennsylvania Ballet and American Ballet Theatre—where he welcomed Baryishnikov to his first performances in America—and then co-founded the Cleveland Ballet. He was a consultant to the Institute of International Education, developing cultural programs in Eastern Europe and is an adjunct professor at Columbia University's Graduate Program in Arts Administration.

In 1996 Jones was elected co-chair of the Manager's Council of Dance USA. In 1998 he was the first dance manager to receive the Arts & Business Council's "Arts Management Excellence Award." He has been a panelist for the National Endowment for the Arts, and serves on boards of directors and as a consultant to several arts organizations.

About Getting Your Act Together™

The Watson-Guptill Resource Guides to
• **Workshops**   • **Conferences**   • **Artists' Colonies**   • **Academic Programs**

ith attendance soaring at workshops, seminars, conferences and other opportunities for continuing education, this particularly timely series presents dependable, candid resource guides tailored to meet the needs of adult artists in several specific categories.

Taking the frustration and guesswork out of the process of finding the right venue for further training, each guide offers a comprehensive and critical review of arts programs, organized alphabetically by state, covering workshops, conferences, artists' colonies and academic programs.

Each program entry provides such key information as contact name and address (plus phone and fax numbers, e-mail and Web site addresses), application requirements, financial aid opportunities and size of program. The books also cover general information on relevant associations, organizations and unions, as well as the business side of each discipline.